TURNER PUBLISHING COMPANY

TURNER PUBLISHING
COMPANY
The Front Line of Military History Books

Turner Publishing Company's Staff:
Douglas W. Sikes: Publishing Consultant
Trevor W. Grantham: Project Coordinator
David Polk: Author
Luke A. Henry: Designer

This publication was compiled using available information. The publisher regrets it cannot assume liability for errors or ommissions.

Library of Congress
Catalog Card No. 93-060962
ISBN: 978-1-68162-312-2

Limited Edition

TABLE OF CONTENTS

OVER THE TOP
VETERANS OF THE FIRST WORLD WAR

INTRODUCTION

As we approach the end of the 20th century and glance back, two world wars tower above the rest like bloody beacons. On the seventy-fifth anniversary ending World War I, we might well pause, look back, and recall our involvement in that great war. Its great cost demands we consider and reconsider our expense. The more than 117,000 American lives lost are the most obvious loss, but the final cost is incalculable. Such a price compels our reflection over and over again as each generation inherits the grave legacy of this conflict.

The horror, sacrifice and heroism of World War I live not only in the history books, but in the memory of some 50,000 American veterans — most in their ninth decade of life now. What was the experience of that era like for them? It is the purpose of this book to suggest some answers — in pictures and words — to that question. You will find this book to be, for the most part, and overview — a bird's eye view including commentary and evaluation of key aspects of the war.

It will begin with some brief background — the war's causes, the erosion of American neutrality, our military and home front build up. After that, rather than recount our achievement battle by battle, we will look more closely at our soldier's unique experience in trench warfare and the kind of offensive warfare it dictated. We will then reflect on the special contribution made by our Navy, Air Corps, and Marines. We will describe innovations in weaponry such as the tank, describe the medical service, and the plight of our prisoners of war. And finally, we will see how those who fought this great war moved to perpetuate their bonds in the American Legion.

PRELUDE TO WAR

In July and August of 1914, a dark cloud began to grow over Europe which would eventually engulf much of the whole world. War had broken out—tension created by a web of alliances and old festering animosities had finally upset the delicate balance between the Central Powers (Austria-Hungary, Germany, and Italy) and the Allies (Russia, France, and Britain). Americans watched with bated breath.

Then on August 4, 1914, President Woodrow Wilson made his proclamation of US neutrality. We must remain neutral, he said, "not only in act but in word and thought." Not the least reason for doing so was the nature of the war's immediate causes. Legitimate grounds were difficult to find. Seldom had human frailty so clearly been responsible for a major conflict; everywhere the clear-eyed could see overweening pride, fanatical nationalism, uncompromising belligerence, corruption, and indecisiveness in the leadership of Europe.

In addition, President Wilson and his government knew quite well that America consisted of nearly one third European immigrants, and any stance but neutrality might touch off, if not a civil war, at least an unpredictable conflict among citizens whose old country ties were strong. There were especially large segments of German and English peoples. There were Irish people whose antipathy toward England was hot. There were Russian-American Jews who deeply resented their relatives treatment in Czarist Russia, and so on.

And there were many other good reasons for not entering this war. Obviously, internal security was not yet seriously threatened. Also, American banks were successfully loaning money to both sides, and the economic recession of 1914 was ending with the boom in the war material business. England and France were especially dependent on US supplies and credit. Besides, the European leaders made no bones about it—both sides said it would be over quickly, and both, of course, predicted they would win handily. A German General Staff officer said it would only take four months to cut down "those dreaming sheep."

Of course, it would not end quite so fast. How long could Woodrow Wilson— could the United States abstain? How long could the country remain uninvolved in the war of all wars? A photograph of a 1916 Democratic National Committee publicity truck was plastered with signs asking the voter to re-elect President Wilson because it is he "Who Keeps Us Out of War?" "Vote for Wilson—Peace with Honor." Five months later, after his successful re-election, the President declared war on Germany. Let us look closer at this gradual drift toward the war that Wilson and many Americans fervently hoped to avoid.

NEUTRALITY ENDS

In spite of announced neutrality, from the beginning the President, his close associates, and much of America was sympathetic to the Allies. A number of other factors drew the country gradually from her neutral stand, for instance, bold headlines beckoned to the prospective young Americans, resulting in unprecedented volunteerism. In their very first move, the Germans offended many Americans by violating Belgian neutrality. They shelled the neutral city of Antwerp. These acts and many to follow were characterized by Prussian militaristic arrogance which did not go down well with the average American. Even before August 1914, the Kaiser (Wilhelm II) was not only encouraging Mexico to go war against the US but was actually shipping arms to Mexico.

Britain, on the other hand, was a long-time friend and trading partner with whom the U.S. shared a common heritage. The US media was biased in favor of the British and the French. In the eyes of the average man of military age the English were to win the propaganda battle against the Germans. Horror stories about the "Hun" and his brutality as a soldier abounded in the American press. Closer to home, the German naval attache in Washington was exposed in espionage activities.

Thus, as the grim war wore on, our neutrality eroded. Another major factor was certainly Germany's unrestricted submarine warfare. The sinking of the British luxury liner Lusitania—whose passengers included 114 Americans—was an incendiary act by a German U-boat. Not least important, US trade was being interrupted—America couldn't do worldwide "business as usual" since merchant vessels were never safe from German torpedoes. Now and then, the Kaiser

A submarine prepares to dock at Pearl Harbor. The pictured submarine may be the SS35 Kentucky (ex Walrus). She was built at the Moran Co., Seattle, WA. Her keel was laid Jan. 27, 1912, commissioned Oct. 24, 1914, Lt. J.P Olding, commanding. (Brandis)

restricted his submarines to placate one or another neutral nation, but then the lawlessness would begin again. German strategy called for a U-boat offensive—beginning February 1, 1917—against all nations' shipping; and as a result, more Americans were to die. Clearly, the Germans did not think the US much of a threat should she enter the war. They assumed it would simply take too long to get troops to Europe should it be decided to act.

One of the final precipitating causes was, of course, the notorious Zimmerman note which emerged in February of 1917. A telegram from German Foreign Minister Arthur Zimmerman to the German minister in Mexico proposed that if Mexico were to join the German cause and declare war on the US, she could

McKees Rocks, Pennsylvania. These three young men went into the service together.

expect—after the victory—to reclaim "the lost territory of Texas, New Mexico, and Arizona." The British intercepted and decoded this message and made a great noise with it. Needless to say, the American public was incensed.

Shortly after his election, the President knew he had to find a way to facilitate peace in Europe—or go to war. His efforts in this regard failed, of course; and so it was that his agonized deliberations over our involvement drew to a close. In his defense, one need only look at the casualty lists for just one battle of this war—such as Verdun—to see why he hated to commit to this foreign cause. Nonetheless, in early 1917 he broke off diplomatic relations with Germany, and on April 2 he asked Congress for the declaration of war. April 6, 1917, the die was cast. The President who had restrained now called for "force, force to the utmost, force without stint or limit."

April 6, 1917...and our vaunted isolation from far-reaching foreign involvement came to an end. Historians agree that there is only one way to imagine us staying clear and neutral—if we had broken off all ties with Europe. But in the second decade of the 20th century, that was simply impossible. Historian John H. Moore writes that "For better or worse, the United States was an integral part of the Atlantic world, and thus had a share in its promises, problems, and profits, whatever the cost might be."

THIS WAS THE GREAT WAR

The committment made to the European community at the declaration of war was enormous. In his statement accompanying his military draft proclamation in May, 1917, the President stated that "In the sense in which we have been wont to think of armies, these are no armies in this struggle. There are entire nations armed.... It is not an army that we must shape and train for war; it is a nation." It was, in short, a world war—the first.

The soldier who fought in this war took part in a unique moment in world history. There had been wars where annihilation of whole armies had taken place; there had been "scorched earth" policies before; there had been nationwide conscription in Napoleon's time; there had been some trench warfare in the Russo-Japanese War which signaled the greater firepower of modern weapons; even so, World War I was a departure from all previous conflicts.

In his World War I, military historian Hanson Baldwin sums it up this way: "never before 1914-18 had a war absorbed so much of the total resources of so many combatants and covered so large a part of the earth. Never had so many nations been involved. Never had the slaughter been so comprehensive and indiscriminate." Furthermore, Mr. Baldwin echoes President Wilson when he sounds the keynote of totality of means and ends and effort in this war. And finally, he points out that there was the weaponry to achieve such totality and "make possible promiscuous, wholesale slaughter and revolutionize tactics. The submarine, the plane, the machine gun, the tank, and poison gas wrote new and forboding chapters in the history of war."

It was a war like humankind had never seen before. It was into this situation that optimistic, untrained and willing young men were plunged — into the very middle of this holocaust. Soldiers were expected to tip the balance in a stalemate that had already cost far too much. On the western front in 1916 alone, there were a million casualties at Verdun, a million more in Flanders, and yet another million on the eastern front in Brusilov's break-through. The American doughboys believed they could help stop this kind of insanity, and they did.

Two million American soldiers were to arrive in Europe before the armistice was signed in November of 1918. They came from Brooklyn and Louisville and Kansas City and San Francisco—from every-where within our borders. They came from every religion and race and background—including German and Austrian and Hungarian. And they spilled their blood from north Russia to North Italy, and, of course, on the Western Front from the North Sea to the Swiss border. If the average doughboy was, in the beginning, untrained and green, he and his leaders evolved to superior fighters in the end.

If it was a war with new and modern weapons and attitudes, it was also a war of crown princes and Kaisers, of cavalry and Czars into which the democratic

Three men from the U.S. 42nd Infantry "Rainbow" Division in France. Note sword.

youth of America were flung. Photographs show us the plumes and sashes and swords of leaders on both sides. It was the end of the old Europe—the old regime of the aristocracy was playing its last act, and the star of the United States as a world power was ascendant. The American soldier at the battles of the Marne and Soissons and Meuse-Argonne—and many more—helped hoist that star into place.

DRAWING THE BATTLE LINES

At the war's beginning, six to seven million men altogether took up arms against each other. They represented seven countries—to be joined later by 23 others world-wide. Germany's two million strong army would swell to four after full mobilization which gave her superiority to France and Russia. She was inferior only to the English at sea. Then add to the German ranks the nearly half a million of the Austro-Hungarian army, and you have a formidable, well-trained foe.

The French alone were sizeable competition to the Germans. Their initial 1,650,000 troops would swell to three and a half million. At the start, the British on land fielded a tiny group in comparison—125,000. But later, when she added by conscription the Indian and African troops with its finest at home, she would total 5,900,000 worldwide.

Italy had quickly backed out of her treaty with the Central Powers, but Bulgaria and Turkey were to take her place. Italy hung back until May, 1915, when she would side with the Allies which included—beside the original three and the US—many British dominions and colonies, Greece, Japan, China, and many Latin American countries. Many of these Allies contributed little more than lip service, but the total of men at arms would eventually reach 65 million.

The major battle lines were, of course, drawn before American troops began arriving on the shores of France in 1917. The lines were drawn, the adversaries had dug into their trenches and a murderous war of attrition had set in.

In the five months of battle in 1914, the Allies suffered somewhere near a million and a half casualties. The Central Powers probably suffered just as much, and, contrary to the expectations of most, the end was nowhere in sight. In 1915, the war only widened. After the initial German drives, the Western Front had

Newport News, Virginia. (Clayton)

been established along a line from Nieuport in Belgium on the English Channel—then due south to near Compiegne on the French river Oise—then west to near Verdun—then southwest from Saint Mihiel along the German border to where it terminates at the Swiss border.

Troops in France. C.Q. Grunder holding his dog. (Grunder)

The Central Powers' Generals—primarily the Germans—were divided; some were convinced only a victory along the Western Front would win the war, and others favored the East and an offensive against the Russians. The Kaiser decided the latter were right, and in 1915 the Russian casualties were somewhere near 2 million killed and wounded. 1,300,000 more Russian troops were captured and in German prison camps.

The Western Front at the end of 1915 was still a stalemate after a total of 2 million casualties. On the high seas, the German U-Boats were wreaking havoc along the international shipping lanes.

More bitter killing on a monstrous scale followed in 1916 on the Western Front, where the stalemate continued. One side or the other might take a few miles of salient ground only to lose it six months later. "Back home," the great machines of industry and manufacturing had by now turned to the production of war material. This was increasingly true of American business and industry as well.

In January of 1917 the German army—straining to cover several fronts—found itself outnumbered on the Western side; its two and a half millions troops faced nearly four million Allied. Therefore, her plan for 1917 was defensive, just as the Allied powers' strategy was offensive. Still, it was a surprise when the Germans staged a withdrawal from the "Noyon bulge" and took up a series of carefully prepared positions to be called the Hindenburg Line.

The fiasco of 1917 preceded the arrival of the doughboy and was perpetrated by the infamous French General Robert Nivelle. His much touted offensive ended in May with around 120,000 French troops slaughtered by the Germans. At that point the French army was at its lowest ebb—mutiny was spreading among the ranks. Then General Henri Petain—the "saviour of Verdun"—took charge and began to refurbish and motivate an exhausted and divided army, but it would take time.

The Allied armies obviously needed some reinforcement and not least important a new attitude. Gen. Petain told the British that they must take the main share of the work on the Western Front while the French rested and regrouped. Meanwhile, the Russian Revolution which began in March helped free-up German troops to shift to the Western Front. Italy was doing poorly in her mountain fighting with the Austro-Hungarians. What had begun as a year for Allied offensives had turned out far differently.

Thus, the stage was set for the entrance of the American doughboy.

Motor truck train enroute at Camp Travis, San Antonio, TX. (Marston)

THE AMERICAN MILITARY, 1917

The American Military Giant, slumbering peacefully since its last conflict, was unprepared for the Great War. Organization would take time.

If you took the Federalized National Guard which had recently been mobilized to track down Pancho Villa in Mexico—and add it to the regular US Army, there were not much more than 200,000 troops. It is true there were slightly more than 100,000 Guardsmen in state service, but they were not combat ready by any measure. In fact, there was—in the whole lot—not one single complete division.

The Air Force? There was none — little more than a decade had passed since the Wright brothers first flight at Kitty Hawk. There were eight aero squadrons in the Army Air Corps, and they were primarily for observation and reconnaissance. Altogether, there were 130 pilots and 50 planes.

The Navy was better prepared, perhaps, than any other branch since it had started a major construction program in 1916.

Front row (l to r): Lieutenants Charles G. Fleet , 'A' Flight Commander; Charles M. Clark, Armament Officer; Edward C. Landon, Commanding Officer, 135th Aero Squadron; Charles D. Stoner, Supply Officer; and Percival G. Hart, Operations Officer, Chief Observer.

Gen. John J. "Black Jack" Pershing in front of Sergeant's Club, Coblinz, Germany, 1921.

The Marines were consisted of a small band of 13,000.

What the new soldier did have going for him was his morale and behind him a country which had come alive with a spirit some compared to the medieval crusades. A nation-wide hit song like "The Yanks are Coming" summed it up. In addition, there was a solid, well-trained core of military officers who had earned their stripes at West Point and Annapolis. Moreover, "Citizen officers" had been recently trained at Plattsburgh, New York.

Major General John J. "Black Jack" Pershing was moved up to head the American Expeditionary Force (AEF). Gen. Pershing was no doubt chosen for his performance as leader of the force which sought Pancho Villa. He was ordered to have a division in France soon as a symbol of our forthcoming support, and he did—piecing it together from various Regular Army Units and a Marine regiment. Regardless of its lack of training, he had to have his division in France by June!

"THE YANKS ARE COMING!"

As the President's words made clear, the first problem before the nation after declaring war was mobilization—not only of men, but of industry and the whole country as well. Victory, he knew, would depend as much on nationwide commitment and industrial superiority as on manpower in the trenches.

Congress passed the first Selective Service bill on May 18, 1917, but only after bitter debate. The Speaker of the House, Champ Clark, declared that a conscript was the next thing to a convict. The constitutional legality of a national draft was questioned again and again. As it first passed, only men aged 21 to 31 had to register; later in August 1918 the draft expanded to take in all men from 18 to 45.

Registration day was June 5, and it passed quietly. According to Census Bureau figures, around 10 million were of draft age—and 9,600,000 registered without significant protest. Those who did not show up would be soon enough rounded up, said the Department of Justice. They would be charged with a misdemeanor which was punishable by a year in jail, then compulsory registration. Needless to say, the bloody riots which followed Lincoln's conscription of troops during the Civil War did not occur. The high turn-out was taken to indicate overwhelming approval of the citizenry regarding the warpath the government had chosen. Then, after registration, the spirit of war permeated the air.

The predominant mood of the nation regarding the draft is clearly revealed in the following numbers. More than 24 million men were ultimately registered during this war; 2.8 million were inducted. However, by the time the war ended in November, 1918, 4.8 million were wearing the uniform. In other words, volunteering was very high.

When the President stated that each man registering for the draft "shall be classified for service in the place to which it shall best serve the general good to call him," he was readying the nation to accept the exemption of farmers, railroad men, seamen, and the essential workers in the war industries.

There were precedents to follow for this draft or for economic and industrial mobilization either. No inventory of weapons or other war material existed to accommodate the new troops and there was no system for producing and distributing them either. Clearly, an enormous task lay ahead for the government and the people. The War Industry Board under New Yorker Bernard Baruch was created which had authority over production, labor relations, and to act as a liaison between the army and industry. Unionization of industry increased.

In addition, a food control program under Herbert Hoover was initiated. A Food Administration had the power to control prices of such items as wheat and meat. This brought the war home to every American supper table; for example, Tuesdays were "meatless." And thus, by the end of the war America produced three times as much meat, wheat, and sugar as before. In the end, and for better or worse, such programs as these helped create a much more authoritative and centralized administrative government for our country.

When the young man proudly volunteered as a marine, army infantryman, naval seaman, or an aviation mechanic, he could clearly see himself as part of a nation-wide effort which included his mother, as she shopped for groceries, or his father, who might work in a plant which was retooling to manufacture weapons or equipment for the Allies.

College men of Co. E, 1st Delaware Inf. Deming, NM. **Top row - (l to r):** *J.W. O'Daniels, Loomis, Marshall, Smart, Fugerson and Kalmy.* **Front row - (l to r):** *Bowers, Allison O'Daniels, Ramsey, Melvin Wood and John Hall. Not Pictured: Alex Crothers, Harvey Bounds. Allison O'Daniels was later killed in France.*

"LAFAYETTE, WE ARE HERE."

Heavily escorted against German submarines as they crossed the channel from England, the first American soldiers stepped onto French soil at Boulogne-sur-Mer—a seaside resort—on June 13, 1917. Major General Pershing was in charge of this group of 177 which included mostly officers and sergeants—and a few riflemen. They briefly toured the sunny town, had lunch, and boarded a train for Paris 175 miles away. In Paris they were wined and dined, cheered and revered. Seventy miles northeast beyond Paris was the German Western Front—behind the Aisne River above Soissons. The Germans would be there waiting when these Americans were ready.

Fourteen thousand more US troops arrived on June 28 and came ashore at Saint-Nazaire—the 1st Infantry Division to be. Two thirds of them were "raw recruits." General Pershing pronounced, "They are sturdy rookies." Lawrence Stallings, a WWI veteran and author of The Doughboys, described their uniforms this way: "The Regulars stood at attention in campaign hats, neck-choking collars that permitted no rolls of fat, breeches tailored for a gymnast's knees, leggings pipe-clayed and fitted to the calf, blouses with patch pockets that would hardly hold a pack of cigarettes."

Typical of so many thousands who would come after them, they were, Mr. Stallings writes, "boys from all over America who had volunteered, enlisting the instant war was declared." And thankfully, among them there was "a slight leavening of seasoned troops."

Who, by the way, was this General Pershing who met and greeted them on the docks that day—this stern, ramrod-straight prototype of an officer? Briefly, John Joseph Pershing was a West Point career officer who was born near LaClede, Missouri, a year before the Civil War began. He came up the hard way and worked for every inch he gained. After West Point, Lt. Pershing served against the Sioux and the Apaches. He had a scholarly side also and took military science at the University of Nebraska and a West Point, and earned a law degree.

He served in Cuba in the Spanish-American War as an officer with the Negro 10th Cavalry and was made Captain for gallantry at Santiago. Hence his nickname "Black Jack."

Then he led troops who put down uprisings in the Philippines where he became the military governor of Moro Province. As an attache, he observed the Russo-Japanese War. Next, when he was commanding officer during the Mexican border disputes, tragedy struck. Back home, he lost his wife and children in a San Francisco fire.

Although he never caught up with Pancho Villa after chasing him 250 miles into Mexico, he marched his 10,000 troops enough to make a real army of them; and he—and the War Department—learned lessons about supply procurement and logistics they would apply when throwing together the first infantry divisions in France.

So that is the man those first doughboys looked to for leadership. The Army was small enough then that many felt they knew him—although, given his inflexibility and detachment, he was always more admired than liked.

He marched those 14,000 "sturdy rookies" past the cheering French crowds. The regimental chaplain of the 16th Infantry saw many women in black weeping among the thousands of Parisian well wishers. France was already full of war widows—did the young Americans understand that? It was no doubt best not to think of such things. At the American Revolutionary War General Lafayette's tomb, Captain Charles Stanton coined the phrase which 35 million Frenchmen were repeating by the end of the week, "Lafayette, we are here." The date was July 4, 1917.

In the summer of 1917, it was assumed by the Allies that they could not win the war for at least two years. This is because the French could not be counted on for another major offensive until the end of the year. The British Expeditionary Force was alive and well, but they were not strong enough at this time to lead an offensive either. Therefore, a break-through could not be expected before 1918. There was indeed time for Pershing to train a fighting force that could make a decisive difference.

On July 10, he sent a request to Washington for 30 divisions to ship to Europe in the next 18 months. The general staff cringed, gritted their teeth and went to work. The Germans, of course, knew they must defeat the Allies before the doughboys began coming on strong. The doughboy got his chance to tip the

Artillery Support in the field. The cannon was a breech-loader, pre-cursor to the Howitzer.

"The first American Troops to set foot on German soil," The striped pole near the center of the picture is a marker of the 1914 boundary between France and Germany, Setheim, Alsace.

scales in the Allies' favor. And with true grit, he did not let his chance go by.

Of course, by now—75 years after the war—the reasons for American Troops being in Europe are clear, and historians agree they were legitimate. To begin with, there had been the German submarine destruction of American life and property, and their secret conspiracies to provoke others such as Mexico to war against the U.S. Then, looming large before the doughboy in Europe there was the illegitimacy of the Germans's current position—and ambitions. They forcibly occupied Belgium, Serbia, and Montenegro. Moreover, they occupied parts of France, Russia, and Roumania. As to their eventual aims in this war, they were evasive, but their intentions were clearly to take as

Soldiers in France. (Grunder)

much as they could get until they were stopped. Among other things, they would love to rule the seas worldwide, and as a major economic power with interests abroad the U.S.A. simply could not afford that possibility.

TURNING THE TIDE

American soldiers began pouring into France by the thousands. New Year's Day, 1918, however, there were still only 100,000 in France, and they have been described as often "half-trained."

These troops were to figure importantly in turning back the German offensive which was to begin in March in the French Somme Valley. The Germans were planning to finally decide the war in this advance, but the added force the Americans contributed insured the Germans would be turned back. The Germans were able to push within 50 miles of Paris in May, but the Allies, in concert, held firm. Americans recaptured Belleau Wood in June, and in July played a key role in repulsing the Germans at Reims. At this point, General Pershing had his million troops in Europe, and by August the German offensive had been squelched.

Beginning in mid-summer of 1918, American troops in huge numbers were landing in Europe—somewhere near 250,000 a month. By November, there were 2 million in all. Their first major offensive took place at St. Mihiel and bitter fighting drug on for six weeks before they were able to start advancing on a 200 mile wide push in the Argonne Forest. By October, there were more than a million doughboys giving the enemy hell in the infamous Verdun and Sedan regions. In November, the Allies were overrunning the German positions and crossed the Meuse River and took out the vital German rail lines. Victory was in sight.

St. Mihiel Front — German machine gun nest. Overrunning the Germans would be no easy task. German positions were almost always heavily fortified and well defended. (Dexter)

The doughboy, although a fighter, was also a catalyst. It was he who accelerated the pace of the war. His tenacity and courage was vital in securing the promise of victory. Therefore, the type and duration of his preparation and training was a prerequisite to Allied victory.

TRAINING AND DEPLOYMENT

By July 31, 1917, all the elements that were to fit into the 1st Division were in place in France, and had began training around the small villages of Gondrecourt and Langres in the Marne River valley. Training lasted a hurried three months. If anything, it was more intense than the camps back home. The Blue Devils (the French 47th Alpine Division) rushed them through; the specialists went to train with grenades, gas, bayonet, and demolition. The majority in the companies worked hard in dummy trench systems, learning about Mills bombs, Livens projectors, and Strokes mortars — all new at the time. They would be the first doughboys to see combat.

Circa 1918. Joseph T. Byrne of the left. Others unidentified. (Byrne)

In October 1917, three more divisions arrived in France and the additional division pushed the American Expeditionary Forces' total close to 100,000 men. In addition to the 1st Division, there was the 2nd, the 26th (National Guardsmen from New England); and the 42nd, or Rainbow, so named for its cross-section-of-America composition. Totaling 28,000 men, each division included four infantry regiments, one artillery brigade, one engineer regiment, and various attachments. This made them twice as large as the other Allied divisions.

The French and British Generals eagerly eyed these fresh troops; "couldn't we brigade some of them to other Allied armies which had been so decimated?" Pershing gave an adamant NO; this would be an American army under American command. (Of course, there would be exceptions — such the 4th Division which — by Brigade and Regiment — was often detached to serve with British and French Divisions).

Soon after the draft began, training back in the States was also picking up steam. By mid September 1917, the draftees began to pour into the new frame cantonments in camps spread across the country; the National Guard divisions were mainly tent camps. NCOs from the Regular Army were chosen to train the draftees where discipline problems were expected, but the reverse proved to be true. The draftees attitude and morale was so good that the training process went smoothly even though it was often very harsh and exhausting.

Six days a week were filled with drill, field work, inspection, and reviews. Hikes of 20 miles were common. First call was heard at 5:30 am — and the men were pushed until retreat at 5:30 pm. All Uncle Sam supplied for the trainee was clothing, bedding, razor, and tooth brush. Yet protestors and slackers were few. For a trainee, leave was unheard of except for emergencies.

The training of the 4th Infantry Division which began in the winter of 1917-18 was typical. They cut green firewood and slept in smokey barracks at Camp Greene, North Carolina, where the flivver-typed vehicles and horse-drawn artillery bogged down in the mud just as they would in France. Shipping out through New Jersey and New York camps, 29,180 strong they boarded several troop ships and embarked for Europe. One day out of Liverpool, England, a U boat torpedo hit the <u>Moldavia</u> and sank it. 56 doughboys of Company B, 58th Infantry died before they ever set foot on French soil.

In Europe, the Ivy Division was attached to the seasoned 16th British Division for more training and supply. Later, some Brigades were attached to the French Divisions as well. According to an account by Col. Christian Bach, with the French in the Marne Valley training proceeded in spite of German aeroplane attacks at night. "It was here that the infantry handled live grenades for the first time and received their Chauchats, facetiously termed Hot Cats, otherwise automatic rifles." They learned the French method of attack, and "how best to pass through barrages with minimum of loss; as well as... digging trenches and stringing barbed wire. While ranges were still being constructed, they practiced rifle firing. The nearness of the front line gave to all this a reality impossible to find in the training camps in the States."

Barracks at Punta Mala, January 1, 1918. (Brandis)

Camp Lee, Virginia during WWI. Ca. 1918. (Grunder)

The troops were composed of a mixture of men; those who received minimal training and those who receive thorough training. Rowe B. Myers, who was inducted into service in March of 1918 at Frankfort, Indiana was typical. "Our group had little training at Camp Taylor, Kentucky," he wrote, "before we were sent to Camp Upton, N.Y. to ship overseas. At Upton we were scattered amongst various companies of the 112th Infantry, 28th Division of the Pennsylvania National Guard which had been training for six months at Camp Hancock in Georgia."

Eventually arriving in France and boarding 40 to a boxcar with his buddies, Myers ended up at a little village in the north called Seningham. "Since about six of the recruits had no gas mask drill and no bayonet drill," he reported sarcastically, "we were given a demonstration to perfect our technique." Meanwhile in the distance, "We could see the flashes of guns and hear the roar of explosions."

In the end, of course, no matter how thorough the training there would be no preparation for the fire and brimstone combat which lay ahead for the naive doughboy arriving fresh from the farm or the factory.

THE WAR EXPERIENCE

The Trenches. Trench warfare is, of course, one of the hallmarks of this war. Gen. Pershing's <u>Combat Instructions</u> included the following: "Trench warfare is marked by uniform formations, the regulation of space and time by higher commands down to the smallest detail... fixed distances between units and individuals... and little initiative." It was, then, a type of warfare suited to the stereotypical German personality. The stereotypical American temperament was very much the opposite, and Pershing made sure his soldiers were trained whenever possible in "open warfare" as well.

After years of stalemate, many trenches on the Western front were likened to gutted snakes weaving through blackened and charred fields. No living thing survived because of the endless shelling. The shell holes within shell holes often filled with water and were an enemy in the "no man's land" between the two armies. Blasted craters might be as small as an automobile or as large as a baseball diamond. Rotting wood and heaps of stones remained where houses had stood.

Miles and miles of barbed wire obstacles followed the lines in front of the trenches as a defensive measure. It was common to see decaying bodies lodged in this wire, often it was cold enough to freeze the corpses and preserve them for another day. Dead horses and livestock might litter the ground as well. Only rats could thrive in such circumstances, and they too became the enemy when they invaded the trenches looking for food.

Before a battle of any consequence, the artillery and/or mortar attacks begin before dawn. A "rolling artillery attack" would target the troops in position in the front trenches or the rear, and then gradually work in the opposite direction. Thus, the doughboy had time to hear and feel the barrage growing nearer and nearer.

Here is a more detailed description of the kind of barrage the doughboy experienced in his trenches: On July 15, 1918, around 6,400 pieces of German artillery began to shell the Allied positions across the Marne River. This, according to Joseph Gies, is what the doughboys heard and saw and felt: "For about ten minutes along the entire front of 60 miles, the German field artillery and heavy artillery rained down on all depths of the Allied line." For an hour or more, the shells rained down on first "the rear or battery positions, exclusively. Next came a period of concentration on rear infantry positions. Finally the climax: the 2,200 mortars joined in for two solid hours of deluging the forward infantry positions...."

After the artillery pounding, the infantrymen would be ordered "over the top," and they hoisted themselves out of their holes and into the line of enemy fire. In one scenario, only one side would be attacking — and this could be the most dangerous tactic. With fixed bayonets, they flung themselves forward toward the enemy trench line and tossed grenades ahead to neutralize the defenders. Dodging machine gun fire, mortars and sharp-shooter riflemen, they pushed on. At this point, survival might well depend on how well they could judge the origin of the enemy fire. If the doughboys were successful thus far, the end might come in hand-to-hand combat with the Boche down in his heavily defended trench. When push came to shove, there was the trench knife to do the job.

On the other hand, of course, the attack might come from the other side. The first American deaths in combat came about during such an attack by a elite German Assault Group on November 2, 1917. Following is the vivid account of Lawrence Stallings, who describes how the 1st Division was first sent into the trenches around the long quiet region of Lorraine. Stallings tells us how the doughboys had moved "through deep communication trenches to the fire steps of the first line. The trenches were deep, with muddied bottoms from the constant fall rains; they were ...wickered and sandbagged, with bays cut in long traverses to localize shell burst and mortar fire."

As noted above, the attack first began with the softening up by the artillery barrages. This November morning they began at 3:00 a.m. — "tons of metal descended heavily along the Yank front" and "communicating trenches were plastered with mortar fire" and "machine guns sent their whispering streams of steel over the heads of the doughboys in the line." For the first time, they — as so many after them — knew the "bone-shaking, head-rocking effect of eight inch mortar shells breaking nearby." This hell fire barrage was soon concentrated on F Company, 2nd Battalion, 16th Infantry.

The German Assault Company troops blasted their way through the barbed-wire walls with Bangalore torpedoes, but the Americans did not even know the enemy was on them until potato-masher grenades began to burst in the trench among them. The German trench knives were sharp as razors.

"It was over in three dark minutes — pistols, bayonets, knives. The pla-

Battle scene, 2nd Division, WWI. The artificial tree was used for observation. (Cummings)

Cecil M. Stanley, Sgt. Burgess and Clyde W. Baker. (Baker)

toon did not move,' Stallings reports. "There was no mad rush for the communication trench or a deep dugout." And when it was over, the highly trained Germans had what they wanted — a sampling of this new American soldier which included a Sergeant and ten enlisted men. The three Americans who lay dead in the trench mud were Cpl. James Gresham, Pvt. Thomas Enright, and Pvt. Merle Hay. A French General of Division came to their funeral the next day. It was America's war now.

A typical pattern for duty in the trenches was common in the 42nd Division — six days fighting, then six days in the rest billets near the rear of the line. Resupply and replacement and any other such movement would take place only at night for safety's sake, but constant shelling might make this impossible for days. The German "star shells" that illumined the night skies also hampered movement. Who could sleep in such a situation?

The unusual lulls in the fighting and shelling gave the sanitation and burial units a chance to retrieve the bodies of their fallen comrades which were removed and sometimes transported to the hospital units for burial later.

The heavy rains in northern France often meant one lived in mud as a matter of course, but never got used to it. A bath was a luxury doughboys only dreamed of. Body lice were a problem. Once a month a portable boiler was transported to the doughs to delouse the uniforms.

In his book Goodbye to All That, Lt. Robert Graves, Second Royal Welsh Infantry, vividly describes some trenches among the brick-stacks at Cuinchy. "The Germans were very close; they have half the brick-stacks, we have the other half. Each side snipes down from on top into the others trenches. This is also a great place for German rifle-grenades and trench mortars." He then describes the kind of reflexes every doughboy had to develop to survive: "We can sort out all the different explosions and disregard whichever don't concern us — such as the artillery duel, machine-gun fire at the company next to us, desultory rifle fire. But we pick out at once the faint plop! of the mortar that sends off a sausage (mortar bomb), or the muffled rifle noise when a grenade is fired."

He goes on to report on the psychological stress that was the daily fare of the doughboy in the trenches. "We were now under rifle-fire. I always found rifle-fire more trying than shell-fire. The gunner was usually, I knew, firing not at people but at map references — cross-roads, likely artillery positions, houses that suggested billets for troops, and so on. Even when an observation officer in an aeroplane or captive balloon or on a church spire was directing the gun-fire, it seemed unaimed, somehow. But a rifle bullet, even when fired blindly always had the effect of seeming aimed. And we could hear a shell coming and take some sort of cover, but the rifle bullet gave no warning. So, though we learned not to duck to a rifle bullet, because once it was heard it must have missed, it gave a worse feeling of danger."

"Rifle bullets in the open went hissing into the grass without much noise, but when we were in a trench the bullets, going over the hollow, made a tremendous crack. Bullets often struck the barbed wire in front of the trenches, which turned them and sent them spinning in a head-over-heels motion-ping! rockety-ockety-ockety-rockety into the woods behind." In the sometimes endless waiting and

listening which characterized war in the trenches, the emotional toll of such sounds could be enormous.

The stalemate of the earlier years of trench warfare was broken when the doughboy began to arrive in large numbers. In short, the Americans were not going to sit quietly in the trenches and wait for the war to happen to them. In the beginning, they were often deployed in the quiet sectors, but they would not stay quiet for long. The American soldiers were charged with such energy and freshness that the Germans were to eventually be exhausted and driven back. Good examples are abundant.

In May, 1918, the Germans had crashed through the exhausted French defense and reached the Marne River only 37 miles from Paris. General Pershing responded to Gen. Petain's request and sent two divisions to support the French — our Second

John M. Caylor, HQ Co., 150th F.A., 42nd Division.

German guns captured by the 4th Inf. Div., Sept. 26, 1918.

and Third Divisions. Thus the Marne crossings were held against the German onslaught; the Chateau-Thierry road which led to Paris was secured. Then the Marines — a brigade in the Second Division — retook Belleau Woods. Meanwhile, the First Division in the Somme salient had won a key victory at Cautigny. In sum, the doughboy had saved Paris — and France.

Out of the trenches and in open warfare, the Americans had fought with aggressiveness at the Marne. American infantry had "showed itself skilled in maneuvering," a French communique read. "The courage of officers and men approached recklessness..." It was equalled "only by the superb coolness of some of their medical corpswho, in a perfect hail of bullets, gave aid tothe wounded."

Then, on July 15, 1918, the Second Battle of the Marne began as the Germans under Gen. Ludendorff again attacked. Elements of the US Third Division were involved here too, and they were aggressive in taking the battle to the enemy, especially the 38th Infantry. In addition, the Twenty Eighth and Forty Second Divisions were praised as calm, tenacious, and demonstrating great endurance. 300,000 American troops in all were involved in this bitter fighting, and their rifle accuracy was described as "phenomenal." The German drive was once again halted.

Afterwards, the Americans were criticized by the French and British press for being too "prone to forward rushes," but Gen. Pershing had taken the war out of the trenches. Consequently, the loss of American life was high. The assaults upon the Hindenburg line would of necessity produce high casualty rates, but there was no alternative to win and end the war.

August 8, 1918, Gen. Ludendorff said, "Was the black day of the German

Army in the history of the war.... It put the decline of our fighting power beyond doubt.... The war must be ended.'

The evolution of military defense had accelerated greatly in World War One. Treatment, such as barbed wire, improved weaponry, such as the machine gun, made conquering impregnable positions possible. In fact, the ultimate tragedy of trench warfare may have lain in one simple fact: the trenches were so well fortified and defended, that few "over the top" charges were ever to gain much ground. Until 1917, the dead simply piled up between the trenches. The doughboy's arrival — and his aggressive bravery — changed that.

Open Warfare. Gen. Pershing, in spite of criticism by the British and French commanders, had insisted on as much training in the open warfare as possible. In his combat book, "Open warfare is marked by... irregularity of formations... comparatively little regulation in space and time by higher commanders... that greatest possible use of the infantry's fire power to enable it to get forward, variable distances and intervals between units and individuals... brief orders and the greatest possible use of individual initiative by all troops engaged in the action.' In short, it was the opposite of trench warfare, and this, of course, was more to the liking of many doughboys and their officers.

The great victory at the Second Battle of the Marne in July 1918 and another Allied victory in September at the Saint-Mihiel salient were prelude to major counter offensives — the Aisne-Marne and the Meuse-Argonne. Gen. Pershing's victory at Saint-Mihiel was the first achievement of the American army

Second Balloon Co., operating throught the center of the Aisne-Marne Salient, helped wipe out the German bulge that spearheaded for Paris in WWI. The German drive was finally stopped by the Second and Third Divisions at the Marne River. American observers made 135 [balloon] parachute jumps on the front, 61 of these from burning balloons. (Herbert)

as an independent force. For this encounter, in August he had put together 550,000 doughboys from across France into the First US Army. By the end of September, American troops had taken and then secured about one fourth of the front line.

The Meuse-Argonne offensive would involve mainly American troops. Here was an opportunity for more open warfare, and there would be plenty more until the war's end.

Throughout the war, the railroads were a key element in the German strategy; they used the rails to great effect in quick movement of troops and supplies. Hence, the final battles of 1918 were to focus on the German rail lines. In the Meuse-Argonne offensive the Allied plan was for two pincer attacks to converge from west of Verdun (the Americans and French) and from Lens to La Fere (the British and French). Rail junctions of Mezieres and Sedan, and Aulnoye and Maubeuge were the objectives.

On September 26, then, the final drives of the war began.

The First US Army — along with the FrenchFourth — commenced a three corps offensive. It was to be the greatest battle for the American troops up to that time. There were many green divisions of doughboys who would lose their innocence and their lives. For the first time in four years, from Verdun to the sea, the whole Allied line would be moving forward.

The first day out, the doughboys encountered light opposition and took three miles. In the Argonne forest, however, the fighting seemed sometimes to be more in a maze rather than the "open warfare" they had trained for. With heavy casualties, they had fought halfway through the forest by October 1. The Germans were retreating slowly, and their rear guard actions were fierce. One machine gun nest would be wiped out only to give way to another. Pershing replaced one General with another who failed to push open the gate.

Finally, by November 1, the heights above the Meuse were secured; Granpre was in Pershing's possession. A wide hole had been smashed in the Hindenberg Line, and the Americans poured forward until November 11. The First US Army was joined by a French corps and the US Second Army.

General Pershing summed up the Meuse-Argonne offensive in these words: "Between September 26 and November 11, 22 American and 4 French divisions — on a front extending from southeast of Verdun to the Argonne forest — engaged and decisively defeated 46 different German divisions representing 25% of the enemy's entire division strength on the Western Front." He went on to point out that 1,200,000 men were engaged in the 47 days of fighting — the greatest battle in American history until World War II.

"The First Army suffered a loss of about 117,000 killed and wounded. It captured 26,000 prisoners, 847 cannon, 3000 machine guns, and large quantities of material." The fighting ended almost a year to the day after the American Expeditionary Force suffered its first casualties in the trenches at Bathelemont.

The following divisions fought in this offensive: 1st, 2nd, 3rd, 4th, 6th, 26th,

28th, 29th, 32nd, 33rd, 35th, 36th 42nd, 77th, 78th, 80th, 81st, 82nd, 89th, 90th, 91st, and 92nd.

By November 11, the lateral rail line so valued by the Germans — the Montmedy-Sedan-Mezieres — was cut apart by our artillery. Brigadier General Douglas MacArthur and his 42nd Division stood poised before Sedan, and the French secured Mezieres. In open warfare, the doughboys had proven themselves as brave and skillful as they were in the trenches.

On November 11, 1918, the killing stopped.

The Meuse-Argonne offensive resulted in some of the bloodiest combat of the war. Here is another passage from the pages of Lawrence Stalling's excellent account. (He was with the Marine Brigade of the 2nd Division and seriously wounded in the final charge which captured Belleau Wood). We take up the fighting on September 27; the 35th Division of Kansas and Missouri National Guardsmen and draftees are on the right wing of Gen. Hunter Liggett's I Corps, and they are flanking Maj. Gen. George Cameron's V Corps which is assaulting Montfaucon.

Stallings speculates if perhaps the 35th didn't have "the roughest road of any as it moved at dawn up the Aire River valley.... Every feature there had been zoned for four years for defensive fire; no army was to be permitted to reach the Varennes on the Aire — where the 35th was expected to go with all possible haste."

"No US division had faced more pestiferous terrain," he goes on. "Green troops made three shocking attacks among the jackstraws in the ten hours of daylight that first day." Their bravery was uncanny as they drove against the Vauquois Heights and pushed toward the town of Cheppy. "The Heights had repulsed all attacks by the French in 1915; the ground was tunneled and cratered

Direct hit at Chateau-Thiery. (Cummings)

by mines and countermining operations." There was artillery in a three fourths circle around them.

"In the noon attack, Capt. Alexander Skinker carried ammunition for his last Chauchat gunner until he was killed at the gun port of a barbed wire concrete pillbox. Pvt. Nels Wold, a Chauchat gunner, with a lone carrier, got four machine guns that afternoon; when his buddy was wounded, he fetched him back to shelter, then proceeded alone against the fifth gun of a cluster until his luck ran out. The state of Missouri erected a monument there to such Medal of Honor winners as these and the hundreds of other doughboys left there and long since forgotten."

"When the division was momentarily checked, light tanks came up and it proceeded to reorganize, attack again, and carry its first objective, the left of the division engaging in house-to-house fighting in Varennes, a specialty in which none of them had been schooled. Hundreds of thousands of other doughboys would pass through (the bottleneck the 35th created in this heroic drive)." By September 30, the 35th would have suffered 6,000 casualties.

The greenest of doughboys had helped create the American reputation for crack open warfare.

U BOATS AND CONVOYS

In the early years of the war, the struggle on the seas was wide spread, but as time wore on it narrowed to the areas around the Central Powers and the British Isles. By that time, just as the Allied ground troops badly needed support in the summer of 1917, so did its naval forces. It was the British Royal Navy, of course, which was the Allied mainstay on the seas.

The Germans offered conditional peace terms to the Allies at the end of 1916, and when they were refused it seems likely the Germans knew that they must destroy the Allies' sea power if they were to win the war. Thus, in February the Germans unleashed their submarines for unrestricted warfare. By this time, they had 111 U boats in service and many more under construction. It was this activity — the preying on neutral shipping — as much as anything triggered America's entry to the war.

Soon after war was declared, the Commander-in-Chief of Naval Forces, Admiral William Sims, conferred with British Admiral John Jellicoe and found that in the first three months of 1917 the Germans had sunk 1,300,000 tons of Allied and neutral shipping. Admiral Jellicoe stated simply that the Allies could not go on this way and hope to win the war. If German success had continued at its April rate, the British population would starve and the country would no longer be capable of supporting and maintaining her army. Thus, the Germans were justified in their grandiose confidence in the submarine.

"Cup Fight" on board the USS <u>Susquehanna</u> (ID No. 316). She was the ex-<u>Rhein</u>, a passenger steamship operated by the North German Lloyd Lines. Seized in port at Baltimore by the U.S. Subsequently overhauled, reconditioned and fitted out as a transport, recommissioned at Norfolk Sept. 5, 1917. Placed out of commission on Aug. 27, 1919. (Felty)

Looking aft aboard the USS Leviathan. Leviathan (SP-1326), ex-SS Vaterland, was built as Germany's largest passenger liner. Captured at Hoboken, NJ in 1917, she was re-named Leviathan Sept. 6, 1917. Part of the cruiser and transport force, she carried more than 119,000 men into combat. She made nine trips to return soldiers to the U.S.

The German U boats were ordered to sink all Allied merchant ships on sight without warning.

Admiral Sims helped convince the British that a convoy system was the best hope. So it was that in March, the Allied convoy system was begun. But where were the escort vessels — mainly destroyers — to come from? Admiral Sims sent word to Washington requesting destroyers and the other smaller ships needed for convoy duty. The USN flotilla which sailed for England from Queenstown was much needed.

Rear Admiral Albert Gleaves was put in charge of the Atlantic convoy system which included many US naval escorts. Convoy protection involved naval ships, aircraft to locate and target submarines, and a system of bases. By the end of May, the system was fully engaged and the results were immediately evident. Not only were a million American servicemen safely transported to Europe in the next several months, but merchant vessel losses dropped to 30 ships in the second quarter of 1917, then 20 in the third quarter. Then from May through June of 1918, 600,000 American troops were carried safely across and landed in France. The U boats no longer held their advantage.

When the war was over, 88,000 ships had sailed under convoy, and only one half of one percent were lost. Experts disagree on whether this was the US Navy's most important contribution or not, but it is certain that the Navy played a major role in this system.

What was it like aboard one of the destroyers on convoy duty? Here is vivid description by John Dos Passos from Mr. Wilson's War: "Destroyer service in the Irish Sea and the adjacent Atlantic was a punishing business. Fine weather was rare. Often the wind blew half a gale lashing up steep and spiteful seas. The rain never seemed to stop."

"Repairs were endless. Steering engines jammed. Generators died. Guns and torpedo tubes needed continual attention. Every operation was made twice as difficult by the vibration of the hull slamming through the great weight of the seas."

"Action when it came was short. Something that might be a submarine periscope seen through the heavy rain would broach ahead. Battle stations would sound, and the destroyer would bound at full speed over the waves. Over would go the 'ashcans' (depth charges) at the place where the periscope figured to have been. While the ship cruised in a circle, every eye would search for an oil slick or bits of wooden deck that might indicate a hit." (The American invention called the "Y gun" made dropping the ashcans more effective; the gun enabled the destroyer men to shoot the depth charges overboard in pairs at either side of the ship's wake).

Meanwhile, US financial aid came to the rescue when the British budget was strained beyond capacity because of the build up of its antisubmarine capability. By the end of 1917, the submarine menace had been largely neutralized, and after a few months in 1918 it was all but terminated. Besides the aid with convoy defense, the US Navy's greatest contribution toward this end was its mine laying effort. The navy laid down mines across a 250 mile wide passage between Norway and Scotland. More specifically, they closed the northern entrance to the North Sea from the Orkney Islands to the Norwegian coast.

The Royal Navy had considered such a mining

The USS Arkansas (BB-33). She patrolled the Eastern Seaboard in WWI. Ordered to Europe, she served with the 6th Battle Squadron of the Grand Fleet. During WWII, she saw action at Normandy, Cherbourg, the invasion of Southern France, Iwo Jima and Okinawa.

project, but had rejected it as too formidable a task. To make the job easier to handle, the US Navy's Bureau of Ordnance developed a much improved mine and antenna system. The mines were made in the US. In June 1918, the minelaying began. Before the Armistice was over 70,000 mines were set. The US and British vessels which dropped them were escorted by the British Grand Fleet which included a USN battle squadron.

These mines posed a major threat and deterrent to the most important German submarine operations against the British ocean supply lines. German subs were sunk and damaged; although exact figures are not available, it is estimated that at least eight went down and many more were damaged. And after the war it was determined that the mine barrage was instrumental as a cause in the mutiny of the German navy near the end of the war. (It is noteworthy that during the war, Thomas Edison was a USN consultant and contributed much toward the development of submarine, antisubmarine and mine technology).

Lewis Ross, a US Navy seaman, served in the Communications office of the battleship USS Texas which was attached to the Royal Navy's Grand Fleet (six battleship divisions, two large battle cruisers, and many destroyers). Of his mine laying duty in the North Sea, Lewis reported: "The North Sea was known for drizzle, fog and rain. I don't believe I saw the sun the whole year I was there. Most of our engagements were at night. Sometimes the gun fire was so fierce I thought the ship would capsize."

In the end, casualties at sea did not compare with the astronomical slaughter on land, but sea war never does. Britain's naval casualties were close to 40,000 — including 33,527 dead. Germany had 25,000 killed at sea, 30,000 wounded, and 12,000 taken prisoner. The US lost one cruiser and two destroyers.

But these figures belie the importance of the Allied victory at sea. In 1917, Germany's unrestricted submarine warfare almost defeated the British. If she (Britain) had not be able to counter it, who knows how quickly she would have gone under and the Allies with her. In addition, the Allied naval blockade of the Central Powers — with US Navy participating — was an essential ingredient in winning the war.

Last but not least important in this area, US Naval Aviation had it start in the Great War. What was a small aviation detachment in June 1917 had grown to 16,000 men and 500 aircraft by the end of the war. They operated from 26 different air stations overseas. As mentioned earlier, their primary mission was antisubmarine patrols in the beginning, but they later bombed submarine bases.

In his account of service on the USS Texas Seaman Lewis Ross discussed aviation. "The Texas was the only ship at that time with airplanes on board. They could take off for reconnaissance, but had to land on nearby fields ashore. They were returned to the ship on a smaller boat and hoisted back up on deck by a crane."

"The Texas had three small spotter planes on board. One was set up on turret 2 by the crane. The other two were stored aft ship. The pilot would start the engine while about 6 to 8 men would hold on to it. When the pilot thought he had the engine running fast enough to take off, he would holler at the deck crew to let go, lie flat, and he would take off." Thus, the state of the "air craft carrier" in 1918.

The USS <u>Florida</u> (BB-30). She steamed with Battleship Division Nine to join the British Grand Fleet. Participating in the Grand Fleets maneuvers and evolutions, she then served with the 6th Battle Sqaudron, convoy duty, through the remainder of the war.

"BOX SCORES"

When America entered the war in April of 1917, the Germans had already won superiority in the air. From July 1 to November 1 alone, the Royal Flying Corps lost 867 combat pilots. German zeppelins were bombing London. In the air, as on the land and sea, the Americans were desperately needed to help turn the war around. Aircraft were needed for observation and reconnaissance, fighting and bombardment.

Here is an accounting of an American aviation wing in April: there were 52 officers and 1,300 enlisted men. That was it. And of the 52 officers, only 26 were qualified pilots. There were 55 aircraft, all characterized by Gen. Pershing as obsolete. There was no American aircraft industry, no design, no stockpile of raw material, and no courses in aeronautical engineering offered. And the French were asking for a flying corps of 4,500 aircraft, 5,000 pilots, and 50,000 mechanics to be ready for the 1918 campaigns.

On July 24, the bill authorizing $640 million was signed by President Wilson, and a full fledged Aviation Section was born. Its goal was to build 40,000 aircraft in one year, but it had to practically start from scratch. A new industry was started to supply aviation instruments, but it was to be a year before they were turning out parts. 20,000 troops were set to work in the north-east felling the special trees used for constructing the aircraft.

Unfortunately the kind of high-speed production of aircraft needed wasn't reached until the war was all but over. 697 American built combat planes were on the front lines when the war ended. 3,500 first line aircraft had been built — mostly DH-4s. February 28, 1918, General Pershing complained there was not a single American made plane in Europe, but the first DH-4s (De Havillands) were soon on their way.

As for the pilots, there was no shortage. By June 1918 almost 40,000 young men had volunteered to train. But to give an idea of the art of flying at this time, of the first 210 American volunteers who trained with the Royal Flying Corps,

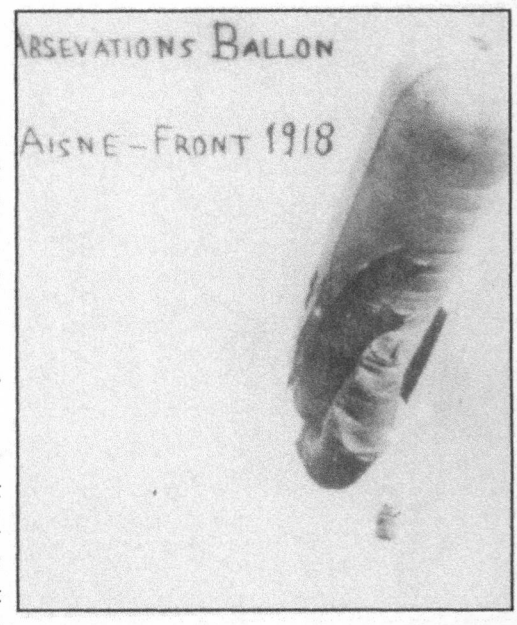

Observation balloon, Aisne-Front, 1918. *(Cummings)*

51 were killed, 30 wounded, 14 were captured, and 20 found unfit — all before the training period was over.

Billy Mitchell, Chief of Air Service, 1st US Army, saw early on that — in terms of strategy — flights and squadrons of dueling fighter pilots was as wasteful and fruitless as the war of attrition on the ground. He favored a massed air power concept. He would simply deny the enemy the air space while Pershing attacked on the ground.

According to Herbert Mason's history of the US Air Force, Gen. Mitchell massed together "nearly 1,500 pursuit, observation, and bombardment aircraft on an eighty mile front along the approaches to the St. Mihiel salient when the infantry went over the top on the morning of September 12, 1918." It was a grey, hardly flyable day, "still, Mitchell's aerial armada took to the skies during the next few days regardless of the weather, regardless of the losses." The victory at St. Mihiel, of course, is still a matter of pride, and the air corps played a key role.

Mr. Mason goes on to describe a mission which followed "on September 14, when 18 DH-4s took off to bomb the German held town of Conflans." The bombers were to rendezvous with an escort of Spads, but poor visibility aloft made this impossible. Soon enough "a dozen Fokker DV-IIs fell on the American formation and shot one down," but the Americans continued their mission and dropped their bombs. On their return, however, more Fokkers were waiting and a 40 minute battle raged in the sky. "Only five out of the 18 bombers reached home. Nearly every pilot and gunner had been wounded at least once, and the planes were flying sieves. Mitchell was moved to comment, 'They had never once

A captured British DH-4 of the RFC/RAF. The twin Lewis machine guns were mounted on a scarf ring for use of the observer while the pilot was armed with a single gun mounted on the crowl and designed to fire through the prop. Note German soldiers, at right.

Curtiss JN-4, the venerable "Jenny." It was in [these types] of aircraft that cadets were trained... The Jenny was one of the best training aircraft developed in the war.

broken formation or failed to obey the orders of their leader. They furnished an example of precision and bravery which is required of all airmen." And so a tradition was established that would inspire American bomber pilots for years to come.

During the bitter fighting in the Argonne Forest, "Mitchell's airmen had no breather from one offensive to the next; they pushed twice a day, seven days a week. St. Mihiel was the beginning of two months of heavy combat relieved only by days of incessant rain which were few." Mitchell's new strategy paid off, and the aviation corps had earned its place as a team player with the ground forces.

Combat pilots such as Edward Rickenbacker from Columbus, Ohio helped set the pace for this new breed of warrior. His first victory came on April 29, 1918 when he shot down an Albatros D.V. over Baussant. Rickenbacker flew a French Nieuport 28 in the days before the American aircraft were available, though he was to be as much at home in the new Spad when his 94th Pursuit Squadron was outfitted with them. He would become the Squadron Commander and end the war with 23 aircraft kills to his credit in addition to three balloons.

Even before April 1917, however, the US Army was flying a squadron in the war under French officers — the Lafayette Escadrille. This may be one of the strangest behind-the-scenes phenomena of the war. Hundreds of missions against the Germans were carried out by these American flyers while we were still officially neutral. The unit was largely financed by wealthy patriotic Americans such as the Vanderbilts, and the young aviators were often well-to-do themselves. They had to first join the French Foreign Legion who asked few questions, then seek transfer to the Aviation corps.

At its peak, this unit included 19 American and two French officers. Thirty eight Americans in all (none of them commissioned officers) and four Frenchmen served in this squadron. They shot down 106 enemy planes. Eight of their number were killed in combat, and several others died of combat wounds.

The colorful style of these aviators made them international attractions — with their lion cub mascots and their American Indian warrior head insignia. Once we had officially joined the war, these airmen became such heroes that "box scores" of their exploits were carried in the <u>New York Times</u>. After the official American troops began arriving in France, the group was disbanded.

Flying in 1916 and 1917 was quite hazardous under ordinary conditions, not to mention in combat, so the early Army pilots had to be good at it. The planes were little more than frames covered in fabric. They were small — a 20 foot body, 25 foot wing span, weight around 1,100 pounds. Their engines were often coughing and sputtering, and the pilots spoke of their two speeds — on and off. In fact, however, they could attain speeds of up to 100 miles per hour.

As for weaponry, the 30 caliber machine gun which the pilot had to fire while navigating called for his pulling a cord which dangled in the cockpit. (The gun and its ammunition drum which held 47 rounds were mounted on the upper wing so the pilot could not shoot off his own propeller.) At some point in a real "dogfight," the pilot would have to stand up in the cockpit and change drums while steering and eye balling the enemy. Synchronized weaponry did come into use before the end of the war.

Although the figures were neglible compared to other means of destruction, the air war had proved itself. The air raids on Britain's home front took lives and were devastating to morale. Fifty nine German airplane attacks killed 857 Britons. Allied attacks killed 720 German civilians. In the end, American combat planes active in the Zone of Advance comprised 10% of the Allied total.

According to Mason, "Americans carried out 150 bombing missions, dropping 138 tons of bombs...." They penetrated 160 miles inside the German borders. "Two hundred thirty seven airmen were killed in combat. Americans claimed 781 enemy aircraft destroyed, while losing 289 planes of their own." These figures, however, belie Allied Aviation's larger contribution, a profound psychological effect on the enemy and the demoralization of Germans near the end of the war.

Army Aeroplanes, Kelly Field, San Antonio, TX. (Marston)

"RETREAT, HELL! WE JUST GOT HERE!"

When war was declared, the total Marine strength was only 13,000, a large number of these were engaged in the West Indies. However, a regiment was quickly gathered, and the 5th Marines were among the first US units to land in France — at St. Nazaire, June 27, 1917.

Back home, the training program geared up and a second regiment, the 6th Marines, and a machine gun battalion soon followed. These units joined the 5th in France to form the 4th Marine Brigade, the largest tactical unit of Marines ever assembled to date. Joining the Third Army Brigade, they became the US 2nd Division.

1st Lt. Alfred A. Cunningham became the Marine Corps' first aviator after making his solo flight on Aug. 1, 1912.

By August 1917, the Marine Corps had grown to 30,000 — and later swelled to an unprecedented 75,000. The recruits trained at boot camps at Parris Island, South Carolina, or Mare Island, California, then at Quantico, Virginia, for advanced and specialized training.

The Marine Brigade was first ordered to the Western Front in March 1918, and, as with most new American troops, they were positioned in a quiet zone — this one being southeast of Verdun. At this stage, both the Allies and the enemy were water-logged in the trenches and little open offensive fighting occurred, except for occasional raids across no man's land.

It was the spring of 1918 that the Germans made an all-out onslaught and broke through in the Somme area. When the British Fifth Army fell back before the Germans, Gen. Pershing ordered the US 2nd Division — which included the 4th Marine Brigade — to help stop the advance. Then the 9,400 Marines got their first taste of blood. It was a Marine captain whose famous words here were spoken to a retreating French officer who suggested the Americans join them. "Retreat, hell! We just got here!"

Squaring off with the Germans in the Belleau Woods, the Marines did what they have since become famous for — close-in combat against a dug-in enemy armed with automatic weapons. Twenty three days later — on June 26 — AEF Headquarters was informed: "Woods now US Marine Corps' entirely." The price was high: 50% casualties, 1,062 killed, 3,615 wounded.

The battle at Soissons followed quickly — and here again the Marines charged across open ground against a well-entrenched enemy. In 30 minutes, the 2nd Battalion, 6th Marines, suffered more than 50% casualties, as did other units. The two American divisions — the 1st and 2nd — were given credit for spearheading this initial attack which began the general retreat of the German army, a retreat which was to continue until the war was over. Such was the role of this small but ready band of Marines. It was perhaps in recognition of their role that on July 28, Brigadier General John A. Lejeune was made the commander of the 2nd Division — the only Marine to ever take charge of an Army Division.

Gen. Lejeune's 2nd Division joined the First Army in late October for the operations in the Argonne Forest. The American's objective was to break through the Hindenburg Line and take two key fortifications: Brunhilde and Freya Stellung.

On All Saints Day, the 4th Brigade drove the Germans back toward the Meuse as one battalion replaced another to keep the pressure constant. The Germans were kept on the run, and the Marines took 1,700 prisoners. An Army General had the highest praise for their aggressiveness at taking mile after mile against stiff resistance: "It was a brilliant advance of more than nine kilometers

"Noisy Nan." 1st Lt. A.A. Cunningham at the prop.

— destroying the last stronghold in the Hindenberg Line, capturing the Freya Stellung, one of the most remarkable achievements of any troops in this war. These results must be attributed to the great speed and dash of the troops, and to the irresistible force with which they struck and overcame the enemy." At this point, the end of the Germans was only days away.

At war's end, the Marines had given in blood: 2,455 dead, 8,894 wounded. They had received 2,468 medals. The enemy at Belleau Wood had nicknamed them forever — "Devil Dogs."

The Marine's traditional role as an amphibious force was — of necessity, of course — largely ignored in this war. However, the Marines first Aeronautical Company was formed, and in the long term this foreshadowed the innovative close-air support role they would play during amphibious invasions in the next war.

Marine aviation grew from no aircraft, five officers, and 30 enlisted men in 1917 — to 2,500 personnel and 340 planes at the end of the war. They flew their first bombing mission on October 1918 in De Havillands borrowed from the French. Their bombs — according to Phillip Pierce in his Compact History of the Marine Corps — were loaves of French bread and canned goods, and their target was a regiment of French infantry trapped by the Germans. Then on October 13, they made their first and last raid on a German submarine base. The following day the enemy began its general withdrawal. The war had ended before Marine aviation could mature, but it would prove itself invaluable in the future.

NEW WEAPONRY

The British .303 Lee Enfield rifle — used by many doughboys if they did not have a Springfield — was so serviceable that it would suit the infantryman through WWI and into WWII; but technological advances have always changed warfare,

"Modern" radio equipment, 1917. (Brandis)

and for the Great War this was particularly true. Side by side with cavalry, horse-drawn artillery, and carrier pigeons, the latest modern innovations such as the tank and the field telephone played their role.

Tanks. Early in the war, the armored car had outlived its usefulness when the stalemate in the trenches was reached. The continuous obstacles of the trenches and stretches of barbed wire called for a new approach, and a British Royal Engineer came up with the first tracked armored fighting vehicle (AFV). It would essentially be a tractor carrying "a steel box armed with guns and machine guns across no man's land and the enemy trenches so that the escorting infantry could reach their objective with minimum casualties," reads the Penguin Encyclopedia of Modern Warfare. "Slow and clumsy as they were, they succeeded beyond all expectations when employed in mass, first at Cambrai in 1917, and then even more successfully at Amiens in 1918."

The small battle at Cambrai in late November 1917 was to revolutionize modern warfare in the long term. The British Tank Corps had been looking for a situation in which to use armor en masse and this situation appeared ideal. The right terrain was picked, and 324 tanks were ready. The target of 12 Allied divisions that day was the Hindenburg Line which had a fortified depth of 4,000 yards. For surprise and protection, the tanks' attack would be screened by a curtain of smoke.

Leading five infantry divisions, the tanks rolled out on November 20 and caught the Germans unaware. The tanks carried fascines on their noses to enable them to cross wide trenches, and fortunately they worked. Two enemy divisions were broken and 8,000 prisoners were taken. More ground —10,000 yards —was taken in six hours than had been won in Third Ypres in four months. Although the true promise of this success was not fully realized by either side, it was to change military operations for the rest of the century.

Inside these monsters which have epitomized the horror of modern warfare, here —according to Alan LLoyd in his <u>The War in the Trenches</u> —is what the crew

A World War One era tank lays at rest in a "Tank Cemetery."

experienced. "Fumes and noise from the big engine were almost unbearable. Tossed from side to side over bumpy ground, sweating beneath goggles and leather anti-bruise helmets, the crews struggled to hold their unwieldy ships on course, praying that the spark plugs would not give up or a leaky exhaust pipe asphyxiate anyone." Amidst the clutter of oil and grease drums, ammunition, and food tins, etc., there might even be a basket of smelly carrier pigeons aboard to fly progress reports back to headquarters.

Early on, $200,000,000 was allocated to the American War Department for tank production. Of the 4,400 put under contract, only 15 ever reached France —and those after the armistice. The Army adopted two types of tanks —a light six and a half ton, and a heavy 35 ton. A three ton for a two man crew was also produced by Ford. As far as success in France, however, this production was not important.

At St. Mihiel, 515 Renault tanks were used, and many were crewed by Americans. It was the greatest effort made by American manned tanks in the war. In his Tank Warfare, Kenneth Macksey reports "that they got into action at all was a miracle of determination, for they had formed their tank corps only the previous November and since then had lived on borrowed tanks and goodwill. The Commander was Brigadier General S.D. Rockenbach; his command was but three battalions, one equipped with British Mark Vs and the rest French Renaults. Indeed, for the 35 companies formed in the USA there were no tanks to be seen...."

"The commander of the tanks committed to the Argonne was Col. George Patton..., but he was wounded and leadership fell to Maj. S. Brett. In short, the Brigade did not fight as such but in scattered groups until, by Ocbober 5, it was exhausted."

In summing up the effect of the Allied tank operations on the enemy, the psychological aspect is important. Mr. Macksey reports that some Germans gave up to tanks without firing a shot in the French attacks near Soissons (after Amiens). A skirmishing line of tanks supported the infantry in all the attacks, and of some German soldiers it was said — "Their sense of duty is sufficient to make them fight against infantry, but when tanks appear many feel that they are justified in surrendering." After one attack south of Albert, "a tank commander claimed the destruction of 30 machine-guns, and a major cause of complaint among the crew — rather than of enemy action — was of exhaustion in the suffocating heat of poorly ventilated vehicles."

Chemical Warfare. Although the 1899 Hague Convention prohibited the use of such a weapon, the British, French, and Germans were experimenting with chemicals before World War I began.

Reluctant at first to invest in it, the Germans were eventually convinced the Allies could not retaliate in kind, so they energetically went ahead. The Germans transported the gas — chlorine at first — by rail, in liquid form, in cylinders, from which they then dispersed in clouds. They were the first to make significant use of poison gas on January 31, 1915, against the Russians in a Polish town called Bolimov, Gen.Hindenburg ordered 18,000 tear gas shells, but lack of practical experience meant only limited effectiveness.

Unfortunately, the Russians failed to properly notify the Allies of the innovation. Consequently the Allies failed to recognize other signs indicating that the Germans would use it on the Western Front. When chemical warfare was used again at Ypres, the Allies were not at all prepared.

In Flanders on April 22, the Germans shelled the Ypres salient all day, then at 5:00 pm, near sundown, a yellowish-green mist began to waft slowly toward the 45th French Reserve Division. It was described as similiar to the mist seen over watery meadows on a frosty night — the mist was chlorine gas emanating from more than 5,700 metal cylinders. The French, mostly Algerians, gasped for breath, vomited and choked, then fled in panic. Here again the Germans failed to effectively follow up. A subequent attack on April 24 established chemical warfare as a tactic both sides were to fear and use.

The Germans used it intermittently during 1915. By July of that year, the British and the French had several companies of their own for gas operations. The British developed a technique using gas-filled shells and special projectors that fired gas bombs instead of dispersing gas from cylinders. Of course, on either side, the wind direction and velocity determined the success or failure of an attack, and a number of times the results were disastrous "backfires."

As time went on, the Allies and the Germans began to favor phosgene which was harder to detect, even after first inhaling it. Allied protective respirators were successfully developed, thus the Germans looked for new, more potent chemicals and came up with "dichlordiethyl sulphide" — called "mustard gas" because of its odor and the yellow cross on its cannister. It blistered the ex- posed skin, and could lie on the ground for days — still potent. The Allies were not to be outdone and produced their own as well.

Here is a brief account of an American soldier who suffered from a gas attack in France — Rowe B. Meyers, 112th Infantry, 28th Division. He reported that "The Germans shelled the main road leading up to Fismes to interrupt supply trucks. Frequently they sent over gas shells, mostly at night. They (our officers) would...warn us to put on our gas masks. On August 12, 1918, they gassed our area. I put on my mask and lay down to go to sleep — we learned to do most everything with our masks on.

"When daylight came, I woke. The sun was shining. I lifted the side of my mask, took a whiff and didn't smell anything. Phosgene gas does not have a strong odor. I lay back down and went to sleep (without the mask). A little later I was awakened by a slight irritation in my nose. Soon my throat started to burn and on down into my lungs. My eyes burned terribly, and pretty soon I was almost unconscious. My head felt like it would burst. The suffering intensified. You felt like you wanted to claw your lungs out....

"They did not send me to a hospital. Oscar Yohn took care of me. In a few days, I got better. Oscar helped me down to the first-aid station. They gave me some white tablets about the size of a dime. That was all the medicine I received."

When the war was over, chemical warfare had been so successful that estimates are 91,198 deaths were caused by gas with far more than one million veterans injured.

Machine Gun. In his Encyclopedia, Kenneth Macksey points out that the machine gun, though not new to warfare in 1914, was in its improved versions much responsible for determining the "positional warfare" so characteristic of World War I. It was, of course, used effectively by both sides in the conflict.

The "Maxim," the first successful automatic machine-gun (MG), was the namesake of Hiram Maxim, an American. Its key innovation was in the operation based on recoil energy. In the late 19th century versions, it could give a sustained rate of fire of up to 500 rounds per minute.

The British used the Maxim effectively in the Russo-Japanese War (1904),

A World War One unit of the 42nd Rainbow Division serving in the Army of Occupation in Germany in 1918.

and soon all European armies had it. Mr. Macksey reports that the British Vickers MMG was rather "heavy and cumbersome with its tripod, ammunition, water supply, and the water-jacketed gun itself. The British, perhaps partly for this reason, originally concentrated their MGs into special MG Corps; only later was it seen as an essential infantry support weapon and integrated into battalion organization. At about the same time, the French introduced a gas-operated Hotchkiss model." It was "air-cooled but with a heavy, finned barrel to dissipate the heat...."

In answer to the need for a light-weight weapon one man could carry and operate, the two models were created. The most popular was the American developed, British 7.69mm Lewis gun; and the American 7.62mm(0-30in) Browning automatic rifle. They could be used with a bipod or fired like a rifle. Many doughboys also used the French Chauchat automatic rifle, the "Hot Cat."

The 114th Machine Gun Battalion served with the 30th Division which was constituted of National Guard troops from North Carolina, South Carolina, and Tennessee and augmented by many draftees from other southern and midwestern states. This is the kind of withering machine gun oppostion the 30th Division faced on the September 29, 1918 offensive against the Hindenburg Line near the Tunnel of St. Quentin. "The Line curving west of the tunnel consisted of three main trench systems, protected by vast fields of barbed wire entanglements.... The dominating ground enabled the Germans to bring devastating machine gun fire on all approaches. The lines had all been strengthened with concrete machine-gun implacements."

In spite of this formidable opposition, the 30th captured the entire Hindenburg System in that sector. In this attack, which covered a front of about 3,000 yards, a count of only some of the machine guns captured totalled 426. On this day and in the week to come, the 30th Division suffered close to 5,000 casualties.

Artillery. In the beginning of the war, the artillery of all combatants was much the same — appropriate to fight a war of movement. Preceding wars had laid this "rule," and the Allies and the Germans were ready for more of the same. To their surprise, of course, the war began to slow down. It eventually became a positional or siege-like stand-off — lighter, mobile weapons were simply no longer ideal. Because of this, guns and ammunition were often ineffective, and the consequent waste grew ridiculous.

So quickly did the French go through these weapons that within two months they were calling on their manufacturers for more — and they had begun the war with 5,556 75mm guns. By the spring of 1915, Mr. Hogg reports, the British had to ration four rounds per gun a day — to be used carefully.

At the beginning of the war, artillery seemed adequate. As the war progressed it was soon realized that bigger, more powerful artillery would be required. Here is a survey by Ian Hogg in his History of Artillery: "field and horse artillery used weapons about three inches in calibre firing shrapnel shell to about 6,000 yards, the principal difference between the two branches lying in the weight of the weapon."

Second Lt. Le Roy Brown stands before a cannon still on a Paris street in 1919, shortly after the end of WWI. (Brown)

"There might also be field howitzers with the forward troops, about 105mm to 120mm calibre, again shrapnel firing but probably with a small proportion of the new high-explosive shells. Siege howitzers of larger calibre existed in small numbers, and between the extremes were a scattering of long-range guns in the 5 inch/ 155mm class."

Soon, however, the British had a 9.2in howitzer in production, and a 15in one in the design stage. But the latter — as was true of the German 42cm — proved to have an effective range of only 10,000 yards, therefore both were sidelined.

Bigger and heavier shells seemed to be the answer to the need to blast through heavy defenses and wipe out barbed wire. To this end, the French designed one of the most innovative artillery pieces of the war — the railway gun. As the name indicates, it was mounted directly to a rail car — guns up to 18in in calibre.

It is generally conceded that the Germans were the winners in long distance shelling. In 1918, their "Paris Gun" or "Kaiser Wilhelm Geshutz" hit the French capital from a range of 68 miles. The basis for this gun was a 38cm barrel in a railway mounting; it had been previously used as a "Max" gun. The Germans laid rail into the Forest of Gobain, and a concrete firing base was put down. In March of 1918, the first shots landed on buildings in Paris.

How would the artillerymen know where the shells were falling? At 68 miles from target, there was no way to determine a hit or miss. The Germans devised a method of communication to relay this vital information to the gunnery commander. Evidently, German agents in Paris contacted agents in Switzerland who then telegraphed Berlin, and four hours after the shells left the barrel the gunnery commander would have his report.

Another innovative weapon came out of British experiments with anti-aircraft guns that resulted in improvements on the Maxim 1lb. Pom-Pom. Even so, it took the British an average of 1,500 shells — and sometimes as many as 8,000 shells — to bring down one aircraft. In contrast, the American record is astounding. Although only in service for four months, American anti-aircraft crews brought down 58 enemy aircraft with an average of 608 shells apiece. All this with only two skeleton battalions and two machine-gun battalions in action.

The Germans, too, sought to perfect anti-aircraft weaponry, and it appears that their anti-aircraft artillery shot down 1,588 Allied planes during the war.

Artilley support was of vital importance to the infantry. Without supporting artillery units, doughboys were in grave peril. In <u>Make the Kaiser Dance</u>, here is what Sgt. Russell Adams, Co. B., 103rd Infantry, 26th Division, reports: "It was the barrage that counted; it meant everything to the infantry. Take Saint Mihiel — I don't think our whole 1st Battalion had more than a handful of casualties in that fight. This was because we plastered those Germans for four hours with artillery before we went over. I can tell you what happened.... I had been out on a patrol the night before; I'd seen all this barbed wire the Germans had set up. I was scared to death when I thought what it would be like to charge through it. Then we had that barrage starting at 1:00 am on September 12. Why, all that barbed wire just disappeared — t'wasn't nothing to it."

Of the 2,251 artillery pieces used by American troops during the war, only 130 were manufactured back home. Of the nearly 9 million rounds of artillery ammunition used, slightly more than 200,000 were made at home. This attests, of course, to the lag time from ordering to delivery; industrial power converted as quickly as possible to war production, but as with tank and aircraft production, industries simply could not gear up as quickly as wished. In contrast, the Germans and French had been gearing up for this war for decades.

World War One tanks in action in France. (Dexter)

"...IN THE POWER OF THE ENEMY"

The first American troops taken prisoner in 1917 were 39 sailors kept at a camp in Brandenburg, Germany. The total number of American prisoners taken by the enemy was 4,120. Some 3,973 were repatriated. An estimated 147 died while in captivity.

Of prisoner of war suffering, Winston Churchill wrote: "You are in the power of the enemy. You owe your life to his humanity, your daily bread to his compassion. You must obey his orders, await his pleasure, possess your soul in patience. The days are very long, hours crawl like paralytic centipedes. Morevover, the whole atmosphere of the prison is odious. Companions quarrel over trifles and get the least pleasure from each others society. You feel a constant humiliation in being fenced in by railing and barbed wire, watched by armed men, and webbed about by a tangle of regulations and restrictions." Even his words fail to convey the suffering and degradation men experienced in the German camps.

After World War II, Korea, and Vietnam, there were extensive studies of the special trauma suffered by prisoners of war, but the World War I POW veteran received little or no attention. The scarcity of any record or other material on their condition in the short or long term is as regretable, perhaps shameful, as is the lack of follow up treatment on what we now can Post Traumatic Stress Disorder. Therefore, according to POW expert Michael Moynihan, "There is no way of gauging how many veterans of the war may have died prematurely or became psychiatric cases as a result of their prison camp experiences."

From modern studies, we do know that all POWs suffer some kind of stress disorder or least a "premature aging" with this arithmetic: one year of exposure to war ages a man two years, while one year as a POW ages a man four years. Stanley G. Sommer, former National MedSearch Chairman of the American Prisoner of War Associ-ation found that the typical loss of 40-60% of body weight a POW suffers for a prolonged period causes irreversible damage to all body systems and organs. In addition, the deficiencies in exercise, nutrition, adequate heating, and medical care often lead to serious medical problems later in life.

In his Prisoners of the Great War, Carl Dennett, an American Red Cross Deputy Commissioner in Switzerland in 1917 and 1918, had this report to make: "From time immemorial, it has been the custom of the captor state to provide food and clothing for its prisoners of war. Germany, however, notoriously failed to even provide them with the necessities of life, and it is a fact...that the ravages of disease due to malnutrition, and even starvation, killed tens of thousands of prisoners in the hands of the Germman military forces. Other thousands have been interned in Switzerland, or repatriated to their homes, human wrecks as a result of the failure of the German Government to treat its prisoners of war as human beings, or make much effort to preserve their lives...."

In addition to the many deprivations and degradations, the POW might also have had to work like a slave. In February 1917, not long before the first American prisoners were taken, a general order from the German government commanded that all prisoners of war who were able must perform useful work. This might include labor for enlisted men in coal mines, stone quarries, and salt mines, as well as agricultural work. At Westerholt Camp in the Ruhr region of coal mines, there was such a dirty, cheerless work site. In addition to permanent work camp sites, POWs might be marched here and yon behind the German lines to do road repair and the like. Work crews could be sent as far away as Russia.

There were well-known camps in Westphalia — one at Minden Lager, Gutersloh, and Dulmen Camp — where inmates worked a 12-hour day felling trees on nothing more than a diet of watery soup and black bread. At Camp Tuchel, Americans were forced to chop fire wood from dawn to dusk. At such camps, potato peelings on the menu were considered a luxury. At Doberitz near Berlin, typical labor would involve menial tasks at German barracks.

For officers, there was camp at Crefeld near Dusseldorf, and Schwarmstedt north of Hanover. An entry from British Captain Douglas Grant's diary gives an idea of the officer's ease: "1917 brought the coldest weather in living memory, and opportunity for the officers to add winter sports to their programme, with ice hockey and skating on rinks improvised on the tennis courts." At such camps, punishment might include cutting off the sale of wine and beer. Although officers were given much better treatment than enlisted men, even amidst their comparitive luxury, many suffered severe depression and other typical psychological effects common to all prisoners.

Prisoner of war mistreatment at the hands of their German captors resulted in several maladies, physical, emotional and psychological. Dennett describes

Some of the wounded, Camp Dodge, 1918.

"barbed wire disease," the typical syndrome he observed among the POWs as they poured into the Swiss camps. This form of neurasthenia was often characterized by fatique, loss of energy and memory, as well as feelings of inadequacy — all due to exhaustion and deprivation, and so on. Mr. Sommer further refines this disorder as KZ Syndrome, and adds these symptoms: "difficulty in concentrating, irritability, restlessness, traumatic dreams, headaches, depression, moodiness, loss of initiative, and shunning large crowds and social activities."

After the war, many POWs experienced hostility and aggressiveness when the joy at being released wore off. After being helpless and constantly regimented and oppressed, they had difficulty in adjusting to freedom. Many found competing on a daily basis with normal people difficult and could not seem to fit in. Ex-POWs had a high divorce rate and higher incidence of alcohol abuse.

The World War I ex-POW had to go on suffering years — even decades — after his release. In effect, many went on serving their country all their lives because recovery was slow and was never final. What's more, the lack of medical and psychological insight at the time meant they and their families had to bear this burden without professional assistance.

HEALTH AND MEDICINE

Medical treatment for the soldier in World War I has been called "tragically inadequate." In spite of the heroic dedication and energy of thousands of caregivers from the battle field corpsman to the surgeon and nurses behind the lines, at times the treatment seemed to be little improved over The American Civil War. Young Americans in numbers enlisted in the Red Cross, the American Field Service, and the Norton-Harjes Ambulance Corps, yet their equipment and supplies were never enough.

An ambulance returning from Chatteau-Theary. (Grunder)

To set the scene for the doughboys arrival in France, here is the commentary of a British surgeon early in the war. "Streams of ambulances a mile long waited to be unloaded. The whole area of the camp, a field of five or six acres, was completely covered with stretchers placed side by side, each with its suffering or dying man. We surgeons were hard at it in the operating theater, a good hut with four operating tables. Occasionally we had a brief look around to select from the thousands of patients those few we had time to save. It was terrible." This improved, of course, but the trauma of crude transportation continued as a problem. Even the ambulance trains were hard on the wounded and sick; they were often cattle cars and trucks.

Unique to this war was the contamination of wounds by the dung-laden soil of northern France. A gas-forming organism found in the mud and muck of the trenches caused a fatal infection known as "gas gangrene" (unrelated to chemical warfare). Antibiotics, of course were unknown, and the treatment of widespread infections was simple and often ineffective.

The crippler "trench foot" as well as "trench fever" also took their toll. Neither responded well to any known treatment. Not until after the war was the cause of the fever related to lice. And there were the high explosive shell and hand grenade wounds of such complexity that most doctors had no necessary training to threat them.

Le Roy Brown, World War One Veteran, sits outside the VA Medical Center as a memorial service begins. (Brown)

During this war a great influenza epidemic struck worldwide. A half million Americans died at home — and millions of others abroad. The doughboy too was hit hard. But by far the most killing disease was pneumonia. More than 23,000 American soldiers died of it. Why? It was so often so cold and wet in the trenches, and the medical system was not up to the job.

In Alan Lloyd's judgment, the most important advance in medical treatment for the doughboy was "the acceptance for the first time of various nervous reactions to battle conditions as clinical problems. Though 'shell shock,' the general label for the mental distress, seems crude in retrospect, it was considerably more enlightened than its earlier designation — 'lack of moral fiber.'"

Its seems clear here that Mr. Lloyd's definition of "shell shock" is more than simply "battle fatigue"; rather he means no doubt the mental breakdown of what was a normal human being under the stress — the horror — of modern warfare. According to Victor Hicken — in his The American Fighting Man — "Many of these never did recover, and still live or relive their terrible visions of combat in Veteran Hospitals."

Dr. Harvey Cushing presented a case history of a soldier who was somewhat a hero at Belleau Wood and at Vaux. He became a stutterer after that combat experience and reported: "The chief trouble I have now is dreams — not exactly dreams, either, but right in the middle of an ordinary conversation the face of a Boche I have bayoneted — with its horrible gurgle and grimace — comes sharply into view. Or I see the man whose head one of our boys took off by a blow on the back of his neck with a bolo knife and the blood spurted high in the air before the body fell."

Today, this type of mental collapse is called post-traumatic stress disorder, and there are sophisticated treatments for it. Not so for the World War I veteran.

"... IT'S OVER — OVER THERE"

Here is one doughboy's account of the day the war ended: "On the afternoon of November 11, our outfit was told that an Armistice had been in effect since 11:00 that morning. There were a few half-hearted cheers, but that was about all. I guess we really didn't believe it until that night when a few of the boys began to gather firewood and build fires. That brought the end of the war home to us — the fact that you could build fires and sit by them and get warm and dry right out in the open. Then we looked around us, and all along the Western Front we saw the lights from other fires, and we began to believe that maybe it was true, the fighting had really stopped."

Here is a summary of what had to happen in the weeks leading up to that moment. Bulgaria had quit the fight in September. President Wilson's appeal for an armistice in early October was returned from Germany with certain conditions specified. But it was clear by then that the enemy had no ground to make demands, and Gen. Ludendorff was forced to resign on October 27. Mutiny in the Central Powers fleet was spreading to the ground troops. Turkey signed an armistice on October 30, then Austria on November 3. The Socialist Friedrich Ebert became German Chancellor on the 9th, and the Kaiser fled to Holland on the 10th. It was over.

At 11:00 on the 11th, in some places soldiers came shouting with joy from the trenches and from behind the remnants of houses and churches. A doughboy approached a Hun and shared a pack of cigarettes. Americans traded with the Germans for Iron Crosses, belt buckles, even Luger pistols.

It seemed the war was over. The Great War of 1914 was over. Some men fell to the ground weeping with exhaustion. The cautious stayed close to their ground cover and kept their rifles at hand. Some knelt in a prayer of thanksgiving.

Associated Press and United Press wire services had flashed the news as early as 3:00 am, and at an hour before sunrise the Statue of Liberty — long darkened — was lit up as ferry and tugboat whistles in the harbor joined the

June 1919, USS Madawaska troop transport ship returning from France. Originally named König Wilhelm II, she operated for the Hambug-American line prior to her capture in Early 1917. Renamed Madawaska on Sept. 1, 1918. As part of the cruiser and transport service, she made 17 trips overseas to both England and France, returning 29,000 troops to the U.S. (Herman)

1915 — Victor F. Kubly in Texas. He was later made eligible for the Purple Heart after being wounded in World War One.

air-raid sirens in celebration. At 6:00 am on our East coast, it was 11:00 in northern France. President Wilson's statement was succinct: "The Armistice was signed this morning. Everything for which America fought has been accomplished."

The refrain of a popular song of the day ended: "And we won't come home til it's over — over there."

This combat description by Alan Lloyd is typical of what our doughboy faced daily: he charged into a no man's land "swept by traversing machine guns, hindered in many places by uncut barbed wire." His unit would be "straddled by German shells." He might have stopped for a moment as a five thousand pound mine exploded "crippling men in several advancing battalions. Wave upon wave was shattered." And he himself might finally be hit. Those behind him would see "those ahead mown down; leading groups, clinging desperately to won positions," would wait "in vain for reinforcements which had, in turn been massacred."

And thus, one man at a time, the grim tally rose. Four million American men and women were inducted into the army alone, and 800,000 in the other branches. Half of those saw overseas service. No reliable figures for the whole war present themselves, but estimates range from 25 to 30 million killed and wounded if you include civilians. Probably 6 million were crippled or made invalid for life. Allied losses are often given at around 5 million dead and 13 million wounded. The Central Powers had around 3 million dead and more than 8 million wounded.

According to the Historical Statistics of the United States, the American battle deaths (53,407) and deaths by other causes totaled over 117,000. There were 204,002 men wounded. Such figures are cold to the eye, but for each there was a mother and father, brothers, sisters, or wives and children to whose door the dreaded message finally came.

Here is one way to measure the value of those deaths; according to Victor Hicken in "January 1918, American doughboys and Marines were holding six miles of Allied trenches in France. Seven months later, they were in possession of 55 miles of trenches, and in October they held 101 miles of the line...."

Pvt. Rowe Meyers took part in a burial detail for three of those thousands who gave their lives. He was a member of the 112th Infantry, 28th Division of the Pennsylvania National Guard). The time he describes here is August 9, 1918; his unit had shortly before been in combat at Chateau Thierry on the Marne and was now east of Fismes.

"I was assigned burying detail. Three bodies were brought to our area in the shade of a large oak. The three bodies had turned black but had no odor. Green scum had formed around the mouth and the eyes. A grave about three feet deep, five feet wide, and six feet long was dug. The bodies were wrapped in army blankets.

"The three bodies were placed in the grave. There was some delay. Probably it was because the chaplain had not yet arrived. In the meantime, one of the fellows who helped dig the grave went down the road to the place where he stayed. A shell came over and killed him. They brought his body back to be buried in the grave he had helped to dig.

"Pvt. Seminitis made crosses from an ammunition box. I began printing the names and army number on the cross piece of the cross. This print was in red. (I have the names of the soldiers in my diary, but the writing was in pencil and is so worn I can't make out the names). Everyone had left. The dog

Raymond M. Rupp, WWI Veteran wounded during the Hindeburg Battle. A 1932 Act of Congress made the Purple Heart retro-active to 1918 in order to include WWI Veterans.

tag was nailed at the center where the small boards were nailed together. As I finished, I sat there alone and thought a long while.

"Then I recalled a verse from the Bible...John 3:16. 'God so loved the world that he gave his only begotten Son so that whosoever believeth in Him should not perish but have everlasting life.' I felt that these soldiers had given their lives so that our nation might live, and those of us might have the privilege to live our lives in a free country."

With those words and the Bible verse he wrote on the makeshift crosses, Pvt. Meyers summed up the patriotism and faith of the doughboy as well as anyone might.

FOUNDING OF
THE AMERICAN LEGION

President Theodore Roosevelt's son, Ted, Jr., was a highly decorated officer in our war — as he was to be in WW II as well. On February 15, 1919, he invited 20 reserve officers and National Guard officers of field rank to the Allied Officers Club in Paris for dinner on February 16. The officers were in Paris on orders from American Expeditionary Forces General Headquarters to discuss "the betterment of conditions and development of contentment in the American Army in France" since the demobilization of the troops was proceeding at a slow pace.

At that dinner, Ted, Jr., was voted the chairman of an ad hoc committee which was to father the American Legion — today the largest organiation of its kind in the world. Further meetings were held, sub-committees were formed, and a caucus was planned for March 15-17 in Paris. Since the organization they were groping their way toward would primarily be for the enlisted men's benefit, the big question was how to get enough men shaken loose from their units and present for the caucus.

The tricks used to bring those men together were marvelous: some officers brought enlisted men as orderlies; one Sergeant came under the guise of delivering important orders — his dispatch case was full of wadded paper; another non-com came under orders to obtain rat poison; some wagoners, farriers, and buck privates suddenly came down with diseases so rare only the Parisian physicians could treat them...and so on. Collections were taken up to send some enlisted men; one man said that his buddies deliberately lost money to him so he could afford to go.

So, one way or another, they made it to Paris and came together. Nearly a thousand were present — both enlisted and officers. Once the meeting was called to order by Eric Fisher Wood, Lemuel Bolles, a high-ranking officer, moved that rank be forgotten inside the conference hall, and once that passed you might see privates arguing with generals, and so forth. Unlike the European armies, there was a democratic tendency waiting beneath the formality of the American ranks. And so together, the men chose the name "American Legion" (proposed by a Kentuckian Maurice Gordon), a tentative constitution was adopted, and another caucus was scheduled to be held in May back in the States.

Ted, Jr., as Mrs. Roosevelt recalled in her book, immediately got busy at home and with the help of patriotic friends had temporary organizations set up in all the states by the time of the caucus in St. Louis in May. At the caucus (which was truly representative of every branch of the service and every state), Lt. Col. Roosevelt had to repeatedly turn down the call to be the new group's chairmen. He did this to quash any speculation that he was active in the group to further his political ambitions. Henry Lindsey was elected National Commander and Eric Wood the Adjutant.

"Ted had a hand in writing the preamble to the constitution adopted at the caucus on May 10, 1919," Mrs. Roosevelt wrote. "I think it expresses well the aims and ideals of the American Legion." In addition to dedication to community and national interests, the preamble contains the following purposes: "to preserve the memories and incidents of our association in the Great War" and "to consecrate our comradeship by our devotion to mutual helpfulness."

On September 16, 1919, the new association was incorporated by an act of the US Congress. At that time, the four major program areas of the association were already delineated: rehabilitation, child welfare, national security, and Americanism. After World War II, Korea, and Vietnam, the national charter would be amended to admit new veterans. The requirement for admission is honorable service and an honorable discharge.

One of the many concerns of the Legion from the beginning has been care of disabled and sick veterans, and to this end it was aggressive in establishing hospitals and other services for WW I veterans — and so on after each subsequent war. It also pushed for compensation and pensions for the disabled, war widows and orphans.

The American Legion's interests and activities are too many to detail here, but let us end by noting that in their work the patriotism of Pvt. Rowe Meyers is alive and well today.

CONCLUSION

Seventy five years have passed since that precious silence in November 1918 — since the first tentative cheers went up, the laughing and the weeping. The horror and the heroism of mankind's first global war was over. Its legacy is immense. It changed the world in every imaginable way, and changed so many millions of individuals one by one.

It clearly changed forever the techniques and the strategy of warfare. At its beginning, "the spade and the bullet ruled the battlefield," as Jack Murphy points out; "traditional offensive tactics were impotent against that combination. This impasse was broken by a new element of technology — the internal combustion engine which made possible the tanks that drove through the trenches and the planes which assaulted them from the air." Add to that the new wireless telegraphy which sped battlefield communications, and, of course, the submarine, which before the war was thought by many to be a German joke. Yes, this new technology made war " a contest of machines as much as men, of numbers of factories as much as numbers of soldiers."

It was, of course, to be "the war to end all wars," and one of its major legacies was the situation in Europe which led to World War II. Let that fact, however, not take away the least credit from the American doughboy. The new technology was important, but it was also true that a fresh young democratic soldier tipped the balance of that war — a young American fighting in a war with and against Europe's last generation of unimpeachable aristocrats. And he — the doughboy — made all the difference. He had the bravery, the energy, and that special American willingness of heart.

THE VETERANS OF
WORLD WAR I OF THE USA, INC.

Among the 4,734,991 America's participants in World War One, 40,000 are still living today; all of them are over 88 years young and their average age is 97.5 years. Present death rate is more than 60 World War I veterans per day.

The purpose for which the non-profit, Federally chartered by the United States Congress, Corporation was formed from it's humble beginning in the Olmstead Hotel, Cleveland, Ohio, October 1949, was to unite in fraternal, civic, and social comradeship, those who have served honorably in the armed forces of the U.S., during the period of World War I as defined by the Congress of the United States; to provide for their welfare in health, sickness, and distress, to give aid to the families and dependents of their deceased comrades, to seek and label for preferential legislation and the enactment of laws, in Federal, State, and local legislative bodies, which laws may be beneficial to the buddies who served honorably in the World War I.

The Veterans of World War I of the USA, Inc. are still making presentations before the House Veterans' Affairs Committee, and the Senate Veterans' Affairs Committee, urging passage of H.R. 1918 (to amend TITLE 38 U.S. Code, to provide a service pension for all veterans of World War I and certain surviving spouses and dependent children, without income limit restrictions), and whatever companion bill on the Senate side.

The Veterans of World War I is the most exclusive veterans organization in existence today as the membership is made up only of veterans who served in World War I. To be a card-carrying member in the Veterans of World War I which includes receipt of our official publication, The Torch, membership is $5.50 the first year and $4.00 each year thereafter.

The Torch publication is printed every six weeks and contains stories, letters, photos, and articles of the era when World War I veterans were young and idealists, and their thoughts today, 70 years later. It also keeps its readers up-to-date on Federal Benefits and tracks the progress of World War I service pension bills.

A subscription to The Torch by a member of the National Ladies Auxiliary to the Veterans of World War I, the yearly rate is $3.50.

Subscriptions for non-World War I members, or non-Auxiliary members, is $5.50 per year.

Membership for wives, daughters, granddaughters, widows, mothers, etc., in the National Ladies Auxiliary to the Veterans of World War I may contact: Mrs. Pauline Charping National Secretary-Treasurer National Ladies Auxiliary to the Veterans of World War I, P.O. Box 2907, Bay St. Louis, MS 39521-2907, telephone (601) 467-9799.

The 1993 National Convention will be August 29-September 1, 1993, at the Oak Brook Marriott Hotel, Oak Brook, IL. This year's National Convention will be the commemoration of the 75th Anniversary of the signing of the Armistice with many events to stir awareness, which includes the awarding of a 75th Commemorative Medal to all surviving World War I veterans.

WAR CASUALTIES

The number of casualties in World War I exceeded by far those of any other war before World War II, in which almost 17 million men of the armed forces perished. Civilian deaths from military action, massacre, starvation, and exposure in the war between 1914 and 1918 are estimated at 12,618,000. These charts include only casualties in the armed forces. The charts on pages 68 - 70 were taken from the Encyclopedia Americana, © 1993

AMERICAN ARMY CASUALTIES IN WORLD WAR I

Cause of death	Overseas	Domestic
Killed in action	36,926	5
Died of wounds received in action	13,628	45
Died of disease	23,853	38,815
Died of accident	2,557	1,946
Drowned	328	399
Committed suicide	296	671
Murdered	159	159
Executed	11	25
Died of other causes	131	190
Total	77,889	42,255
Total wounded	198,059	=
Grand total, dead and wounded	275,948	42,255

ARMIES MOBILIZED AND CASUALTIES
IN WORLD WAR I

Countries:	Total mobilized forces	Killed and died	Wounded casualties	Prisoners and missing	Total casualties	% of mobilized forces
Allied and Associated Powers:						
Russia	12,000,000	1,700,000	4,950,000	2,500,000	9,150,000	76.3
France	8,410,000	1,357,800	4,266,000	537,000	6,160,800	73.3
British Empire	8,904,467	908,371	2,090,212	191,652	3,190,235	35.8
Italy	5,615,000	650,000	947,000	600,000	2,197,000	39.1
United States	4,355,000	126,000	234,300	4,500	364,800	8.2
Japan	800,000	300	907 ·	3	1,210	0.2
Romania	750,000	335,706	120,000	80,000	535,706	71.4
Serbia	707,343	45,000	133,148	152,958	331,106	46.8
Belgium	267,000	13,716	44,686	34,659	93,061	34.9
Greece	230,000	5,000	21,000	1,000	27,000	11.7
Portugal	100,000	7,222	13,751	12,318	33,291	33.3
Montenegro	50,000	3,000	10,000	7,000	20,000	40.0
Total	42,188,810	5,152,115	12,831,004	4,121,090	22,104,209	52.3
Central Powers:						
Germany	11,000,000	1,773,700	4,216,058	1,152,800	7,142,558	64.9
Austria-Hungary	7,800,000	1,200,000	3,620,000	2,200,000	7,020,000	90.0
Turkey	2,850,000	325,000	400,000	250,000	975,000	34.2
Bulgaria	1,200,000	87,500	152,390	27,029	266,919	22.2
Total	22,850,000	3,386,200	8,388,448	3,629,829	15,404,477	67.4
Grand Total	65,038,810	8,538,315	21,219,452	7,750,919	37,508,686	57.6

As reported by the U.S. War Department in February 1924.

AMERICAN WAR CASUALTIES BY STATES AND TERRITORIES

State or territory	Total casualties	Killed or died			
Alabama	5,160	1,251	Montana	3,443	934
Alaska	15	6	Nebraska	3,041	855
Arizona	557	150	Nevada	250	71
Arkansas	2,658	883	New Hampshire	1,535	358
California	6,650	1,747	New Jersey	10,166	2,367
Canal Zone	3	2	New Mexico	860	228
Colorado	1,759	537	New York	40,222	9,196
Connecticut	6,625	1,265	North Carolina	5,799	1,610
Delaware	303	87	North Dakota	2,560	700
District of Columbia	773	202	Ohio	16,007	4,082
Florida	1,171	467	Oklahoma	6,356	1,471
Georgia	4,425	1,530	Oregon	1,577	512
Hawaii	13	4	Pennsylvania	35,042	7,898
Idaho	1,351	409	Philippines	7	3
Illinois	18,264	4,260	Puerto Rico	11	1
Indiana	5,766	1,510	Rhode Island	1,562	355
Iowa	7,311	2,161	South Carolina	3,919	1,138
Kansas	5,182	1,270	South Dakota	1,867	554
Kentucky	5,380	1,436	Tennessee	6,190	1,836
Louisiana	2,160	823	Texas	10,133	2,722
Maine	2,090	518	Utah	1,006	302
Maryland	3,812	975	Vermont	1,170	300
Massachusetts	13,505	2,955	Virginia	6,130	1,635
Michigan	10,369	2,751	Washington	3,070	877
Minnesota	7,323	2,133	West Virginia	4,018	1,063
Mississippi	2,303	904	Wisconsin	9,813	2,649
Missouri	10,385	2,562	Wyoming	676	233

BIBLIOGRAPHY

Baldwin, Hanson. World War I. New York: Harper & Row, 1962.

Berry, Henry. Make the Kaiser Dance. New York: Doubleday, 1978.

Carrison, Capt. Daniel. The U.S. Navy. New York: Praeger, 1968.

Craig, Berry. The 2nd Infantry Division, Paducah, KY: Turner, 1989.

Dollar, Charles, ed. American: Changing Times. New York: John Wiley, 1982.

Dos Passos, John. Mr. Wilson's War. New York: Doubleday, 1962.

Graves, Lt. Robert. Good-bye to All That. New York: Doubleday, 1957.

Hatch, Gardner, ed. American Ex-Prisoners of War. Paducah, KY: Turner, 1988.

Hatch, Gardner, ed. 4th Infantry Division, Paducah, KY: Turner, 1987.

Hatch, Gardner, ed. 42nd Rainbow Division, Paducah, KY: Turner, 1987.

Herr, Col. John. Operations of the 30th Division. A First-hand Account of the War. 1980.

Hicken, Victor. The American Fighting Man. New York: MacMillan, 1969.

Hogg, Ian. A History of Artillery. Hamlyn: London, 1974.

King, Jere, ed. The First World War. New York: Walker & Co., 1972.

Lloyd, Alan. The War in the Trenches. New York: MacKay Co., 1976.

Macksey, Kenneth & Woodhouse, William. The Penquin Encyclopedia of Modern Warfare. New York: Viking, 1991.

Macksey, Kenneth. Tank Warfare. New York: Stein & Day, 1972.

Marshall, S.L.A. The American Heritage History of WWI. New York: American Heritage Publishing, 1964.

Meyers, Rowe. A Veteran's First-hand Account of the War. 1980.

Molloy, Herbert. The United States Air Force. New York: Mason/Charter Publishers, 1976.

Moynihan, Michael, ed. Black Bread and Barbed Wire. London: Cooper, 1978.

Murphy, Jack. History of the U.S. Marines. New York: Exeter Books, 1984.

Pierce, Lt. Col. Phillip. Compact History of the U.S. Marine Corps. New York: Hawthorn, 1964.

Stallings, Lawrence. The Doughboys. New York: Harper & Row, 1963.

Roosevelt, Jr., Mrs. Theodore. Day Before Yesterday. New York: Doubleday, 1959.

Ross, Lewis. A Veteran's First-Hand Account of the War. 1980

DOING ONE'S BIT
PERSONAL WAR STORIES
BY THE VETERANS
OF WORLD WAR ONE

ON THE TRANSPORT...

Submitted by Benjamin Dexter

Our boat was the old White Star liner <u>Caronia</u>, a four stacker English Boat with an English crew. "Blyme," the loading officer said, "She is riding four feet below the load line." The afternoon that we left Port Hoboken, we were a convoy of about two dozen ships, some transports, some liberty ships and cargo boats about two hundred feet long that could only make about eight to ten knots. As we watched the Statue of Liberty fade in the distance, I was the last one to leave the deck. It seems that I carried a vision of that last glimpse of Liberty, until I saw her again nearly a year later.

As we approached the submarine zone, things began to happen. We were instructed to wear life belts night and day. One day, during the voyage, we were assembled on deck for a life boat drill. "Now this is your boat," the instructor said, "any of you fellows know how to row?" I sat down on the deck with some others making a motion like rowing. He said, "If you don't make the boat, there are life rafts on the aft part of the ship." To be prepared for all contingencies, I made my way to investigate. I couldn't believe my eyes, the canvas on these so called life rafts was in tatters. Making way back to my quarters, I happened to look up to the deck where we had our drill, low and behold there was another group being instructed in the use of the same boat we had.

I continued to prowl the ship and came across what appeared to be the kitchen area. As I watched, the workers rolled out a huge chunk of frozen fish, whole with head on, not dressed and weighing about a thousand pounds. With a maul, they broke open the block and the fish was cut up into four or five inch pieces. A big container was rolled up to carry the fish, heads and insides included, to the cooker, which was a big steam vat. Before supper that night, I told my comrades about my earlier kitchen observation. As we sat at our big, long table waiting for our food, someone called out, "Here comes the fish!" The pan was pushed right down the table to the last two men, and someone opened a port hole and out went the fish. We nearly got keel hauled for that.

My next duty, put me on guard in the companion way. I was given a club to maintain order. All of a sudden, there was a thump and a bang, then there was a stampede. I picked myself out of the stairway, discovering that I was all by myself. My orders were to remain on my post until relieved by an officer, but I thought to myself, if the water starts to come in, I am going out! Finally someone showed up to relieve me. I asked him what happened. "Oh," he said, "one of the ships fired a gun." That night, I couldn't find a soul who had paid the least attention to the affair.

Late one afternoon, there was a flurry and a yell, "Gangway, gangway!" Along came a delegation of troupes bearing a makeshift stretcher with a mock up of a monkey. There was a card on the stretcher saying, "Be it resolved, that when and if we get home again after the war is over, we will petition the Congress to enact legislation to the effect that in future wars, soldiers won't have to eat their ancestors." We had been fed so much salmon and corned willy, that we had nick-named the latter as monkey meat. In retrospect, that's exactly what happened in WWII. G.I.'s always seemed to have "K" rations handy.

We arrived at Liverpool to find the harbor blocked. They had two German subs trapped inside. They got one of them, so to lure the other out, it seemed that there had been a false alarm about two o'clock in the morning, stating that an armistice had been signed. There was turmoil in the wards; pillows going out the windows, cheering and dancing (some fellows on one leg). But it turned out to be just a rumor, and on the strength of it, some doctors were quick to note that the end of the war was near. So they packed us off on the Forty-eight train to a seaport, as a forty-seven hospital case.

All of a sudden the train stopped. I was sitting in the doorway alone, contemplating the scene before me. Suddenly, I realized that all the other men had gone and left me by myself, so I made haste to find my gang. In the town there was a chow line from the city hall half a mile long, ten to twelve rows wide. When we finished one meal, it was time to line up for the next one. We were told that there were some 60,000 men there. After a few days, we were sent out to Flat Foot Farm, about 400 of us. When we got there, they said there was no room for us. We were told that we would have to make a camp by ourselves. We marched about four miles out into the country. The officers with us said that platoon tents would be sent up to us. But night time came and we still had neither tents nor supplies, and we had to pair up and make pup tents with our shelter halves...

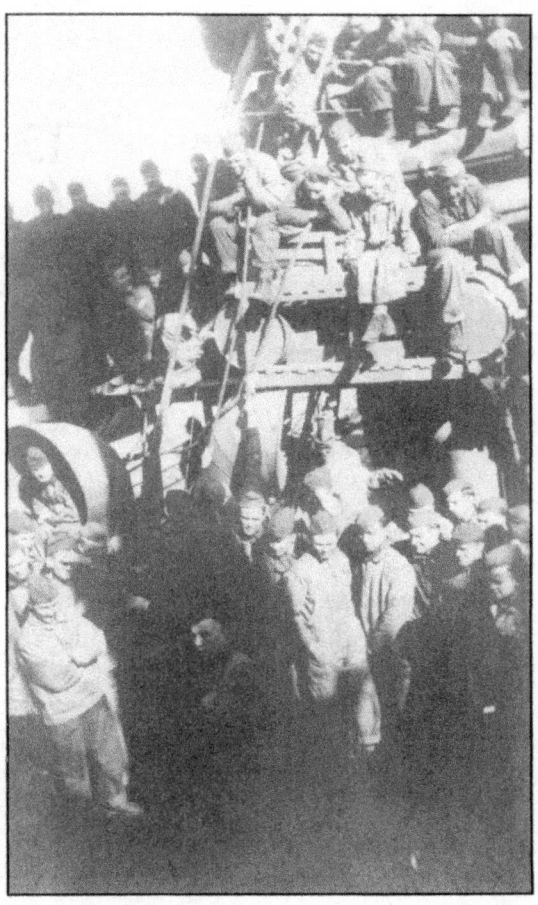

Aboard the _Nausemund_, coming home from France. (Fox)

January 4, 1987

Dear Buddy Vail:

I read with interest, of your being at St. Agony. You notice, I said St. Agony before I said St. Agnes. St. Agony was more fitting at the time than its real name, as anyone who had the misfortune to be there can attest. I note you were there about Christmas, I arrived there at the stroke of eleven o'clock on the morning of the armistice. However, as I read the morning's bulletin board, it advised that all operations that can be deferred will be postponed and to be continued once the patient is back in the states. I was scheduled for an operation on my left ear at ten that morning at the base in Bonn. However, a big storm came up during the night, and by the next morning there were only two or three tents left. The next day, we got our platoon tents and a tank of water. The water made us all sicker than ever, because the tank had previously been used to carry gasoline.

When it was time to go home, the officers began to call our names by states. One fellow said to me, "They have been through the alphabet several times, but my name hasn't been called." I asked him where he was from and he said, "Vineyard Haven." I told him to go and see the officer about it. The officer asked him, "Where are you from?" "Vineyard Haven," he replied. The officer thought a minute, then said, "Oh, you'll have to go home with the Colonial troupes. Vineyard Haven is on Martha's Vineyard off the south coast of Massachusetts, where I live."

But I was to get another jolt. I got orders one day to take the train to Bourgeois. It was another dark rainy night, I rode for several hours and couldn't believe what was happening. It seems that Bourgeois was the central records office. Part of the city was fenced off for the office buildings. Inside that camp, were other quarters for about 400 English WAC's (Women's Auxiliary Corp.). I was to do guard duty there. The WAC's quarters were fenced off from the rest of the camp by an eight foot high board fence. There was a main gate with a guard, and passes were required to go in and out.

It was around the second night there, that I was put on guard duty over a latrine at one corner of the camp, next to a city street. The place had no lights to speak of, and being in January, it was cold and misty. I could see little, about 75 feet, but not clearly. As I took one turn off my beat, I saw a form run from the city side of the camp to the back of a warehouse. As I looked, another figure appeared. I came to port, aimed and yelled out, "Halt, halt or I'll shoot." The figure halted, and then started to run again. I hardly had time to think what the hell to do, take a shot on the level, or what. As we were in a city, I thought, hell, this 30-30 would go through a half a dozen people, so I fired in the air. Talk about a shot heard around the world, a 75 couldn't have sounded louder. As I started to run to the spot, the officer of the day came running up and asked, "What's going on here?" "Someone coming through my post, sir" I said. "Did you hit them?" "No,"

I said, "I fired in the air." The officer had a flash light which he pointed on the hedge fence. A hole in the hedge lead to a well worn path to the inside camp. He looked at me kind of funny like, but didn't make any comment.

All this rather upset me, so much that I felt sick to my stomach and had to call for relief. As I entered the guard house, the Sergeant said, "What did you shoot at those girls for?" I said, "Girls?" "Yeah," he said, "two WAC's ran into the movie picture house, down the main aisle, and hid under the orchestra seats." I asked for a flash light and went back to the fence. Sure enough, there were tracks

Front line trench in Alsace. Note box of grenades and helmet design.

of size five or six women's shoes. Right away I felt that I was in a hell of a jam. Of course, I was right as a guard to do as I did, in fact, I could have been court marshaled for not shooting to kill. The next day at guard mount, we passed by the WAC's quarters, where about a dozen girls were sitting on the fence. As we marched by, one of them pointed right at me and said, "There's the bloody bloke that did it!" I never batted an eye lash, but I sensed that I had better get out of the place to stay healthy. I went back to the Camp Commander and showed him my black casual pay book. He said I had earned credit enough to have a little consideration. The next day, I got orders to go back to St. Agnes. Next, I was put in Massachusetts Casualty Company.

Hope you can make out my writing Buddy Vail. There were more experiences, but isn't it a fact, that a committee of Congress could listen to this and other testimony of service. WWI veterans look you right in the eye and say, "WWI vets don't deserve a damned thing." <u>320th M.9. Bat., 82nd Division, Co. D.</u>

Yours in buddyship,

Buddy Benjamin Dexter

ON THE ALBERT FRONT
Submitted by Ed Wagner

On August 9, 1918, while on observational patrol on "no man's land", accompanied by Private Greco and Baxa, we took refuge occasionally in shell holes to conceal ourselves from the bright vary lights released by the jerries. Just before daybreak we returned to our company to report our observations. The three of us felt nauseated, apparently having breathed in gas. We were sent to the first aid station for check-ups.

Our regiment was subject to heavy artillery fire of shrapnel and gas when on the Albert Front. When we got to the first aid station, there were so many men severely wounded, I did

"What for four years had been no man's land." near Avocourt, France.

like others and slipped away and returned to my company without being administered to. Greco and Baxa remained but were mortally wounded later.

I got over my nausea and dysentery in about a week leaving me without a medical record of this gas encounter.

Lt. James Dappert of my Company K and Lt. Wilbur Matthew of Company M were killed by shell fire, and Lt. Ray Preston died of the effects of gas inhaled. These were the first officers of the regiment killed on the Albert Front, but there were a number of men who were killed, wounded and gassed.

I had another encounter with gas on the Verdun Front. Our regiment was assigned to serve with the 2nd French Army. While being led to our positions on this front, by a French guide. Part of the regiment headquarters platoon and my platoon became detached in a woods. It was at night, pitch dark and no guide. This was a secret move and we did not know where we would be entrenched. I was Sergeant of my platoon and assigned three men to head out in front of us in four directions, I took the front. We were not to be gone more than five minutes, trying to discern whether the trenches were enemy, French or American. Fortunately, I contacted Sergeant Leo Boyll in charge of a prisoner chain post.

After contacting Capt. Hartell, I was given orders to remain in the trenches and to move up to the front line trenches at nightfall. We took advantage of a deep dug-out. Early the next morning there was a lot of hacking and coughing that woke me, and after checking two, found the gas sentry assigned to the head of the dugout steps was sound asleep. I sounded the gas alarm, everyone donned their masks and sent most of them to the first aid station. Again, I did not answer sick call. Several men were hospitalized but later returned.

This front line assignment, where we joined with the 408th French Infantry was a prelude to the great drive from the North Sea to Metz on September 26, 1918. Our regiment was the pivot of the drive, and we were to cross the Foyer swamp. This drive was highly successful. My platoon was without an officer. Capt. Hartell said, "Sergeant, you will be in command." He then wished me luck. After reaching our objective about 10 a.m., the regiment had many casualties and apparently though prayers, I reported all men present and accounted for, no casualties.

After our company was relieved, I was sent to Officers Training School at Langres, France for rigid training. I was one of the20 percent that passed, received my eligibility certificate. Unfortunately, I contracted plural pneumonia and spent five months in the hospital. I was treated in the hospital in Coblenz, Germany. No serums or medication to combat the disease. Ten days of only potato peeling broth, no salt. This was the death ward where they waited until 12 passed away before the truck pulled out. On the tenth day, I had puss on my lungs. When the operation was completed, I was again able to talk louder than a whisper. After one week in the recovery room, I was sent to Heres, France on the Mediterranean, to convalesce for about five months. In the mean time, all of my classmates received their commissions, except me. Primarily because we were to embark for the United States.

I believe the gas weakened my lungs. Several attempts were made to claim the Purple Heart, but each time they said they had no record. My discharge shows gassed in Albert, France on August 9, 1918.

After waiting for 64 years, I finally received the Purple Heart, and only through the diligent effort of Harold Freeland, counselor of St. Joseph County of Veterans Affairs. He has successfully helped me and many other veterans obtain service connected entitlements.

I am not in quest of remuneration, but do appreciate receiving recognition. The Purple Heart will be added to my collection with the Silver Star and other citations. My one regret was that I did not receive my commission, being one of the 20 percent that successfully completed a rigid training course. Unfortunately, I contracted pneumonia in the Army of Occupation and was hospitalized for four months and was not present when the appointments were passed out.

THE UNKNOWN SOLDIER OF WORLD WAR ONE

Submitted by Max Laycock

A lone infantryman rests near his foxhole.

There is a graveyard near the White House
Where the unknown soldier lies.
And the flowers there are sprinkled
With the tears from Mother's eyes.

I stood there not so long ago
With flowers for the brave.
When suddenly I heard a voice
It sprang from out the grave.

I am the unknown soldier
The spirit voice began;
And I think I have the right to ask
Some questions, man to man.

Are my buddies taken care of
Was their victory complete,
Or is the big reward you promised
Selling pencils on the street?

Does a gold star in the window now
Mean anything at all?
I wonder how my old girl feels
When she hears a bugle call?

And that babe who sang "Hello Central,
Give me no man's land"
Can they replace her daddy
With a military band?

I wonder if the profiteers
Have satisfied their greed,
I wonder if a soldier's wife or mother
Ever is in need?

I am the unknown soldier,
Maybe I died in vain,
But if I were alive and my country called
I'd do it all over again.

IT HAPPENED TO YOU

by C. Jones, Submitted by Earl M. Murphy

Now, Smith was a dashing young sea dog, his boast was omnipotent
brains.
He knew every inch of his U-boat, from her tanks to her engine room
drains.
Not a gauge but it's face was familiar, not a valve but he knew it by
name.
To be hailed as the "Master of Sea-pigs" was his lofty and ultimate aim.

Bill Brown was a dull, steady plodder, it cost him an effort to
think.
When he trimmed down his greasy hell-diver, things usually went on
the blink.
The laboring groan of his diesels, he hailed as their swan song of
death.
He held sway at the tail of the column, where they wheezed out their
laboring breath.

Smith rode poor Brown like a harpy, he held him legitimate
prey.
Dissected his brain in the ward room, refuted his knowledge each
day.
Hescoffed at thehard-luck Brown pleaded, gave the laughwhen
Brownverbally fluffed.
The scorch of Smith's caustic satire, kept friend Brown eternally
bluffed.

Each time that Brown's sea-pig hit bottom, each time that she
dropped out of line.
Smith fervently yapped, as he opened his trap, never happened to me
on mine.
Each "Bull" that Brown pulled, Smith exploited, gave detail with joyous
acclaim.
Inferred that Browns head was mentally dead, and defunct to the
points of the game.

Fate decreed that Brown act as observer, on Smith's record torpedo
runs.
Smith forgot his main hatch was open, the salt sea rushed in by tons,
And Brown just managed to murmur, as he gargled the foaming brine
It's happened to you on your boat, never happened to me on mine.

MAXWELL PARRY:
FORGOTTEN PLAYWRIGHT AND AVIATOR
Submitted by David Parry Rubincam

Maxwell Parry was the son of David Parry, a leading industrialist and president of the National Association of Manufacturers. Max grew up on his father's estate in the Golden Hill section of Indianapolis, Indiana. He displayed both artistic and literary talent early in life. None of his paintings survive, but two of his plays do. They evolved into The Lie Beautiful, which was produced on Broadway and received good reviews from the critics. Max also organized the Little Theater in Indianapolis. He numbered the poet James Whitcomb Riley and the author Booth Tarkington among his friends.

On the Parry estate stood an Alaskan Indian totem pole, a friend's gift to Maxwell's father. Max placed a message atop the totem pole in 1914, a kind of time capsule. Among his predictions were that the estate would be subdivided, and that all of the family would be alive and well five years hence. Little did Max know that this last prophecy would fail; his father would be dead in one year, and he himself in four.

In August of 1917, Maxwell Parry went to Chicago and enlisted in the Aviation Section of the Signal Enlisted Corps. Later that month he reported for active duty at the School of Military Aeronautics at Columbus, Ohio. In February of 1918, he accepted a commission as a 2nd Lieutenant in the Air Service Signal Corps. He shipped out for the war in March and became attached to the 147th Aero-Squadron.

Maxwell Parry was among the first American aviators to reach the line of battle. He shot down his first enemy plane on July 4; several others followed in quick succession.

On the July 8, 1918, his patrol sighted a baker's dozen of German planes over Chateau-Thierry. After chasing them a while the patrol turned back—all but Maxwell Parry. He was last seen climbing for position in order to dive down on the enemy. Later it was learned that he was shot down and killed. Maxwell Parry was posthumously awarded the Croix de Guerre and the Distinguished Flying Cross. He is buried in France.

Max was not married and left no direct descendants. Moreover, his family's business failed after his death. As Max had predicted, the estate was subdivided. The name of Parry faded from public view. Even the totem pole vanished, rotted from weather and termites. Maxwell Parry, playwright and aviator, was forgotten by all but his family and friends.

But now he is once again being honored, thanks to the efforts of Richard Feldman of Indianapolis. Several years ago Feldman, and his family moved to a house on a street mysteriously named Totem Lane. Feldman learned after a long investigation how the street got its name; he also learned about Maxwell Parry. Through Feldman's efforts an historical marker now commemorates the site of the long-vanished totem pole. Though the marker mentions David Parry and not Max (it was his father's totem pole, after all), Feldman dedicated the marker to the memory of Maxwell Parry at a ceremony on May 13, 1992.

"He was a marvelously adventurous and romantic person," said Feldman before a crowd of neighbors and honored guests, one of whom included Susan Bayh, the wife of the Governor of Indiana. "Maxwell Parry was a man of immense talent and creativity," Feldman went on. "He was one of those people that everyone loved and admired. He was full of spontaneity and charisma. He was one of those people who radiated personality. He became one of America's gallant World War I aviators." Feldman also quoted from a letter from Booth Tarkington to my father, genealogist Milton Rubincam. The famed author said of his friend: "If Maxwell Parry had lived, he would surely have become one of America's great playwrights."

Maxwell Parry didn't live; but he is no longer forgotten.

The Sopwith Dolphin, 1918, England. (Kelley)

MEMORIES OF THE TEXAS
Submitted by Lewis G. Ross

When war broke out in 1917, I tried to enlist in the Navy, but was told I was underweight. About three months later, on June 9, I called the recruiting office again, and they said to come on down. I was sworn in that evening and shipped out the next morning to the Naval Training Station at Newport, Rhode Island. September 13, I was sent to the Naval Training Station at Portsmouth, New Hampshire for a short time until I reported to the USS Texas on September 29, 1917.

Just before the 6th Battleship Division was to leave New York for England to join the British Grand Fleet in the war zone, we were circling Block Island when the Texas cut too close and hit a rock that penetrated both bottoms. Stores of ammunition and everything else was thrown overboard to keep her from sinking. She went into dry-dock at the Brooklyn Navy Yard. It took four months for repair. During this time we had plenty of liberty in New York. We were invited to wealthy people's homes for weekend parties, many times overnight. We also did a lot of marching in war bond parades in New York. During the time the Texas was in dry dock, 60 of us reported on board. A man with a pencil and paper interrogated us. One question was, "Do you know anything about the German language?" My answer was, "Yes!" My senior class in high school had voted to study it the last semester. He said, "Stand over there." That put a V.I.P. on my record I didn't know I had until I was assigned to the radio office. When we joined the Grand Fleet I became part of the communications office on the Texas.

I had a messenger who took the messages to the proper officers concerned. We had three and five letter codes which changed every day at midnight. There was a captain's orderly stationed outside our door who took each message to the captain. Admiral Rodman was a very strict man. Our Captain Blue was a mild mannered man. They had some differences before the war. As it happened now, the Texas in navigation followed the New York, Rodman's ship. Consequently, he could see what happened aboard the Texas. We joined the Grand Fleet early one morning in January, having left New York the day after Christmas. We received a grand welcome from the Grand Fleet. They day was spent preparing for action. A Marine Captain was in charge of the ship when we left, but he neglected to remove the lifeline, did not remove the small boats, and in general did not prepare the deck for action. About midnight we were called out for action along with the entire Grand Fleet. About the middle of the next morning, I received my first message from Admiral Rodman: "Where do you think you are going, to a Sunday School picnic?" I never heard, but no doubt the Marine Captain was penalized, and all penalties in the war zone were doubled.

Our next trip out with the Grand Fleet was in the morning. The New York

Captains inspection of the Fifth Division, USS Susquehanna (I.D. No. 316). (Felty)

sounded two blasts which meant a sub on starboard. About a half hour later the Texas sounded one blast...sub on port side. I sent my messenger out to look. He came back in and said, "It's a big one!" By now our five inch guns were in action, and sunk that sub with no survivors.

There was a meeting on board the Queen Elizabeth, Admiral Beatty's flagship of the Grand Fleet. All American ship captains were invited. On order from Whitehall, London, where the brains of the five nations met, it was ordered that the fleet should cover mine layers and mine an area south of Norway and Sweden which reach the northern part of Germany and the Kiel Canal where the water was very shallow. Admiral Beatty who thought our ship might run aground, decided not to make the trip. Admiral Rodman piped up, "I'll make the run with my division if you will give me covering destroyers." Admiral Beatty thought for a moment then said, "Oh, O.K., I'll give you the destroyers." Captain Blue of the Texas called the crew back after one morning. He got up on turret four and announced, "We are going on a trip tonight. The chances are 100 to one you will not come back. I want you all to write a letter home. Make it a cheerful one, as it may be your last letter. I will see that they are mailed today." There was a real quietness of the crew as they left. Later, it was learned that Admiral Beatty had taken the whole fleet and followed us. Next morning, the Wyoming was not n her position. She seemed to be floundering. She did not answer any messages sent to her. When she finally came to her position, it was learned her captain had gone berserk. The captain had told us how to die fast. The second you hit the water, inhale water through your nose and mouth. My messenger and I were guessing what time we would jump into the water. We were to reach the place about midnight. We had a clock in our office and our eyes were fixed on that clock. Nothing happened. The German patrols missed us because the fog was real thick.

England's grand fleet, had six battleship divisions, five ships in each division. They had two large battle cruisers, the Renown and the Repulse. Then came the heavy cruisers and light cruisers, and quite a large number of destroyers. The fleet was divided into two sections. The first section had one battleship division and one division of cruisers and supporting destroyers all under the command of

Admiral Beatty. Their duty was to locate any large units of the German fleet. The second section would follow at a distance under the command of Admiral Jellicoe.

I will enlarge on the Grand Fleet's two battle cruisers, Renown and Repulse. Their speed was 35 to 37 knots. Germany and England at that time were building identical ships. Germany had two battle cruisers, the Hindenburg and the Ludindorf. The Texas had a running fight with the Hindenburg. She was too fast for the Texas, and just walked away with her speed.

One day about noon, Admiral Beatty ran into the whole German fleet just off Jutland, Norway. Both went into action. The Germans being the strongest, really battered Beatty's ships. Beatty was on the cruiser, Tiger, which was one of the ships sunk. He was transferred to another ship. In the meantime, Beatty sent a message to Admiral Jellicoe to come up fast. However, Jellicoe did not respond fast enough, and when he did appear, the German fleet had sunk a number of Beatty's ships. When the Germans saw the main grand fleet, they turned and fled towards their base in the Kiel Canal, resulting in a running battle which lasted until darkness. There were heavy losses on both sides with many ships being sunk. After Whitehall had considered all the facts, they decided Admiral Jellicoe was at fault. He was demoted. Admiral Beatty was then promoted to Admiral of the Grand Fleet. This information was given me by two lieutenants who were on Beatty's staff. They had been sent to educate us on the English communication system. Due to the heavy losses of the English ships, Uncle Sam sent a division of battleships to strengthen the fleet. This was the largest fleet ever under one command.

I don't know too much about Queenstown. Four battleships were there plus numbers of destroyers. The Nevada was with the Grand Fleet. When we joined,

USS St. Louis at Honolulu. Arrow points to radio room. (Brandis)

she was sent to Queenstown. The Wyoming replaced her with the Grand Fleet. We had a major problem at Queenstown. There were a great number of German subs waiting for the supply ships headed for France. We were training a number of radio operators. They would be shipped aboard supply ships, and many were lost on supply ships. One night when I had finished my watch, as I was walking, I noticed someone standing in a corner. I went over to see who it was. It was a fellow in my division. I asked what was wrong. He said he just didn't feel well and had the strangest feeling that something was going to happen. I took him up to the top deck and we walked about, watched a couple of ships come in, then went to bed. Within a month he was transferred to a supply ship as a radio operator. That ship was sunk with no survivors. That was some premonition.

The North Sea was known for drizzle, fog and rain. I don't believe I saw the sun the whole year I was there. Most of our engagements were at night. I would be on duty in my tightly closed office, but could hear all the sounds of heavy guns. Sometimes the gun fire was so fierce, I thought the ship would capsize. I might add here, King George chose the Navy for his military service. England's kings at this time had to serve in one branch of the military for a certain period. King George and Queen Mary visited the Grand Fleet three times. The Queen didn't come on board. The Prince of Wales also visited the fleet with his father, and King Albert (from Belgium) and his Queen visited, both coming on board. These people were very nice. They were so grateful we were over there helping. England and Scotland were very proud of their Grand Fleet. The general feeling was...England ruled the seas. When people learned my ship was with the Grand Fleet, it raised my popularity.

The Texas was the only ship at that time with airplanes on board. They could take off for reconnaissance, but had to land on nearby fields ashore. They were returned to the ship on a smaller boat and hoisted back up on deck by a crane.

The Texas had three small spotter airplanes on board. One was set up on turret two, by a loading crane. The other two were stored aft ship. The pilot would start the engine while about six to eight men would hold on to it. When the pilot thought he had the engine running fast enough to take off, he would holler at the deck crew to let go, lie flat, and he would take off. One Saturday during "captain" inspection, our division was standing at a position so we could see the pilot (McDonald) cutting capers. All of a sudden he started to spiral and came down in the Firth of Forth River. He and the plane were not recovered.

Here is one story I happen to remember. I don't know who thought up this brain storm idea. Of course, it had to pass Whitehall. A cruiser was loaded with TNT. One man had to volunteer to run it up the canal where the German fleet was based and jump off when it got near the fleet. He was cut down by machine gun fire. The only report we got was that some of the German ships had been damaged and would be repaired. They were delivered to us when the fleet surrendered.

For a time we were in dry-dock on a river in Scotland. The New York had been there just before us. News had gotten back to us that the New York's sailors got into a battle with the local boys. New York boys had left word, "Wait until the Texas comes, they are tough." Our captain ordered all of us to be armed with billy clubs. When we went ashore we had them concealed in our dock, there was a large saloon. The bar must have been 75 feet long and had ten bartenders. I talked with one who told me the Americans were shipped all the poor Scotch whiskey, since they kept the best in Scotland. The hall was full of girls, but no local boys. I met one girl who begged me to take her back to the United States on board my ship!

On the 4th of July, all Americans were given four hours liberty in Kingston, Scapa Flow. I visited a general store and bought five pounds of well aged goat cheese. When I left the store a group of Texas sailors helped themselves to my cheese, but did save a slice for me. That was part of the life of a sailor. We didn't get to stay four hours, but were called back to duty early. I went ashore on several islands. One was where we left our comrades who had died from the flu on board. I was lucky enough to recover when it hit me. I was one of the chaplains aides when I was off duty, and took part in burial detail. It was a sad duty that needed to be done. On another island no one had ever left to go to the mainland except the one person who went to London once a year to pay the taxes. I remember they had a number of Shetland ponies and lots of sheep.

One liberty took me to London. My first night there they had an air raid. There must have been about ten planes. They bombed houses, and whole blocks were flattened. They had a huge net over the Bank of London for protection. There was a vast shortage of food in London. The restaurants didn't have anything to serve. Another sailor and I went to a grocery store and bought a can of peaches to share for our supper that night. There was a place called the "Eagle Hut", which was a military tent. One could get a cot to sleep on there. The next day, I took a tour on a double-deck wagon with horses. The first stop was Buckingham Palace. We passed through the main hall. All doors to the rooms were open. If a room had red walls, everything in the room was red. When we got to the kitchen, the cooks had large pans of cookies, coffee or milk for us. Then we toured the stables with horses of every color. This one the Prince rode in the morning, and that one he rode in the afternoon, and so on. There were two fine coaches, one had a large amount of gold on it. It was only used for coronations. The other was used for celebrations. Next we went to the House of Parliament and Westminster Abbey. We also saw the prison with it's guillotine and some other things they used to kill people. We visited the Thamses River where the London Bridge in Havasu, Arizona came from. We had a joker when we visited Westminster Abbey. He called to one of the tourists, "Hey, you're standing on someone's grave." The person jumped just to land on another grave, as the whole floor had people's nameplates. Our guide said the place was all filled up with graves.

The next day I went to Edinburgh, Scotland. I took the train to Sterling. The seats on their trains were the width of the coach with a door at each row of seats. At Sterling, I got acquainted with a couple from Switzerland. They said they had relatives in Minnesota and wanted to know how far that was from Chicago, where I lived. We went through the highlands, past the Lady of the Lake, and also to the place where Fitzjames and Roderick Drue had met and agreed to stop fighting each other. (The Trochish Hotel where we had lunch). It was a beautiful trip through the mountains. The hotel was on the banks of Loch Lomond. There we boarded a boat for Glasgow.

Loch Lomond is a famous lake which is said to have areas where there is no bottom. In Glasgow, I went to the YMCA. The clerk asked what he could do for me. I said my train didn't leave for Edinburgh until evening. I had just sat down to look at a magazine, when an Admiral of the British Navy came up and invited me to go with him to see where they were building sub-chaser boats. We also toured the port and visited his office where we had tea and crumpets. Then he drove me in his limousine to the depot. He was very much interested in what the fleet was doing. Glasgow is the home of the Scottish ballet and opera. The Burrell Collection in Pollock Park houses over 8,000 art objects. The city is built on 14 hills.

Back in Edinburgh, I visited the Edinburgh Castle towering atop a volcanic plug known as Castle Rock. At the foot of the ridge stands the palace of Holyrood, the Queen's official residence in Scotland. Princess Street is the main street in Edinburgh. Sir Walter Raleigh's statue was on Princess Street. The Scottish band gave us a concert with bagpipes at the Edinburgh Castle. The castle also had an enormous display of jewels.

November 11, 1918 did not end the war for the Navy. The next day intelligence advised us the fleet would be gassed. We were issued gas masks which we had to carry days and sleep with them at night until the German fleet surrendered to us on November 21, 1918. We set sail for home in December. When the Atlantic Fleet entered New York Harbor, we were met by an enormous number of all kinds of small boats, plus a large fireboat that sprayed water high in the air to salute our ship. There were bands and all kinds of noise makers on the small boats to greet us. The day before we were to land, we received a message that the Victory Parade would be the day after Christmas. We had to anchor near Long Island. To our surprise, on Christmas Day we received a complete turkey dinner. The next day we got up at 4 am to prepare for the parade.

All of the Atlantic fleet were in this parade with the 6th Division battleships in the lead. As we cruised past the Statue of Liberty, one could hear a number of low voices saying, "We're home." Our position to anchor was up the Hudson River along Riverside Drive. We were taken ashore in small boats and had to climb up a high sandy bank. We all got our shoes full of sand and everybody had to sit down and dump the sand out. After a long wait, the command, "Forward, march!" finally came. It was early in the morning and not very many had come to watch, but as we got nearer downtown, more and more were standing along the side. Because I was tall, my position was next to the curb when we marched.

All of a sudden a woman grabbed me sobbing, "My son, my son!" I finally got loose and told her I wasn't her son. I was about a half block from my position and had to run along side to get back in rank. Now the crowd was getting larger but for some reason were very silent. The crew of each ship had a large banner with the name of their ship. When we got downtown where the tall buildings were, a loud cheer went up..."Texas, Texas!" Remember, the Texas crew had been in New York for four months the year before with it's 1400 sailors, and we had met a lot of girls. There were about four girls in every window and they were throwing things down to us.

My leave started when the parade ended. I ran to the depot and got a ticket for Chicago. The depot had about nine long trains all for the sailors. There were two engines on each train and in a short time they were loaded and ready to roll. The first stop was Buffalo, but there were not many people there to greet us. Next stop was Cleveland, and the news had spread. There were people for blocks, waving and cheering. It was about 4 am and they had coffee and doughnuts for us. The next stop was Chicago. I again was stopped as I elbowed my way through the crowd. By now it was late in the evening. I took the subway, then made my usual shortcut to my sister's home. I looked through the back door to see her standing by the stove cooking. When she turned her back, I sneaked in. As she saw me she screamed and threw her hands up. I grabbed her because she was standing by the hot stove. The first thing she said was, "My God, I thought you were a ghost!"

When I returned to New York after my leave, I took my two sisters with me. I was allowed to take them on board the Texas and also showed them around New York City. During the last part of my Navy career, our ship sailed down to Cuba, and as far south in the Caribbean as Barbados. I really got to "see the world". I was discharged in June of 1919, at Great Lakes Naval Training Station in Chicago, as a Yeoman 2nd Class.

Caterpillar train, San Antonio, TX. (Marston)

THE LIFE OF RILEY

by C. Jones, C.E., U.S.N., Submitted by Earl M. Murphy

Now gather all ye mariners and listen to this tale.
Ye've sailed thru many a ragin sea and weathered the wintry gale.
"Twould seem serene and peaceful as the froth on a soup tureen
To leading the life of Riley on a greasy submarine.

I've reefed many a royal top gallant and hauled on a weather trace
And in reevin' a line thru a stun'l eye, I've met death face to face.
But when you flood all ballast tanks and sink to depths unseen
Then you lead the life of Riley on our hell-diving submarine.

The hero of this tale, me lads, is tall, morose and thin.
He talks just slow and peaceful like, we call him plain "Jack Binns".
To hear him speak thru his eagle beak he doesn't seem so mean
But he leads us the life of Riley on our hell-diving submarine.

And then came the day we sank, lads, down where the sea spans creep
Nesting our hull on the ocean's bed, 1200 fathoms deep.
Deemed were we for the neither world, close hauled for hell's dark shades
All but Jack, of the lord-like life, who was smiling and unafraid.

We lay on the ocean's bottom for about a day or more
When Jack hit on a daring plan to reach the distant shore.
Then all gathered 'round him, including old Sam Steen
Who had led the life of Riley on our damned old submarine.

"I have a war nose on this head, it's all ready for setting,
I'll tap it with a hammer thus, for instant satisfaction."
"As it goes off the sea comes in, it leaves an opening wide
Jump right thru it, rise to the top, and float in with the tide."

We waited for the hammer tap to free us from our prison.
To our surprise, we did not rise, but went thru hell a 'whizzin'.
We ricocheted thru hell so fast, the devil never seen us.
And landed at the pearly gates, Saint Peter waitin' for us.

"How now? What's This? and Who are you?" Saint Peter then demanded,
And after calm reflection this "Bull" to him we handed.
"We're just the E-1s crew, sir, we come from depths unseen.
She's scattered on the bottom, sir, in water cold and green."

"Who of this crowd, he sternly asked, has claim to heavenly station?"
When out stepped our old shipmate, Binns, near bursting with elation.
"Now tell me, friend," Saint Peter asked, "can you get thru the gates?"
And out speakes Jack in accents clear, as old Saint Peter waits.

"I've traveled 'round the world, dear Pete." thus spoke our bold Jack Tar
"But I have lived as Jesus would, on board a man-o-war."
"Advance," says Pete, "and enter there the gates are now ajar
But just for those who've lived as Christ, on board a man-o-war."

Then turning to our company, says slow and solemn like
"This is no place for all you bums, I guess you'd better hike
In heaven's streets of glistening gold the man was never seen
Who'd led the life of Riley on a greasy submarine.

Army ovens, Camp Travis, San Antonio, TX. (Marston)

THE RAINBOW DIVISION
by C.W. McGee

The following account of the "Rainbow Division" is excerpted from a letter addressed to Mrs. Lucy Lien and written by C.W. McGee. The letter was written Nov. 18, 1979 — 61 years after the signing of the Armistice...

At the hospital, we learned that the Rainbow Division had been selected and designated as one of the divisions to go into the Germany Occupation Army. With two soldiers from the 165th Regiment, New York Infantry, the regiment that had Father Duffy for Chaplain and about whom the great movie, "The Fighting 69th" was made, I got an early release from the hospital and the three of us got a truck ride back to the front where units quit fighting on the eleventh.

This was on November 14, and the next day, November 15, we started marching through Belgium, Luxembourg and into Germany. Our division's starting point was Sedan, France, about five kilometers from Cheherry, where I had been wounded the 7th of November. Sedan was a city of great historic importance; for it was there that the Army of France surrendered to the German Army in the Prussian War of 1870. There was a large bell in a cathedral there and the Germans rang it continuously until it cracked. After the war ended, France got the bell and while I was privileged to visit Lake Annecy on a leave, there in the renowned Packard Family Foundry and Bell Manufacturing plant I saw and touched that famous bell. The French were having the bell repaired and were going to put it back in the same belfry and after peace had been signed, they were going to ring it until it cracked again. This Packard family had been building bells for over 400 years and all the big important bells in the entire world had been built there. Annecy, France was the birthplace and home of the famous painter that painted "September Mom" and the location was in the edge of beautiful Lake Annecy. From here one could look over into Switzerland and see Mount Blanq, the highest mountain in the Swiss Alps.

I am very proud that I was privileged to serve my country as a soldier in the "Famous Rainbow Division." And famous it was, made up by combining military units from 26 different states; it was named "The Rainbow" by Mrs. Woodrow Wilson, the President's wife.

Our infantry brigade, the 83rd, was comprised of the 165th New York Regiment and the 166th Ohio Regiment. The 84th Infantry Brigade was made up of the 167th Alabama Regiment and the 168th Iowa Regiment. One very interesting fact is that the 165th Regiment, formerly the 69th New York and the 167th Regiment, formerly the 4th Alabama Regiment, were formed before the Civil War and these two units fought against each other in several important battles during that great war. After the war was over, neither regiment was ever mustered out but retained that same identity until they joined the new Brigades in the Rainbow Division.

Now that the war was on, The Rainbow was the second complete division to be sent to France, leaving Hoboken, New Jersey, on October 19, 1917, my 22nd birthday.

Going to France was the last time that the Rainbow was second in anything. Once there, we were the first complete division to enter the front lines, in February with eight inches of snow on the ground. The division gained more ground and drove the Germans back more kilometers than any other division. Although General Pershing tried to give that distinction to the Second Regular Army Division with their two regiments of Marines. Of doubtful distinction was the statistics; more killed and wounded and the need of more replacements than any other division. The division fought in every major battle than any American Division was engaged in. We were in one great battle, the Champagne, in which we were the only American Division engaged; the rest, many thousands were all French and one Polish Division. This battle, the Champagne, was one of the greatest battles of the entire war. For here it was, that the Germans were making their greatest and what turned

Thomas Kussurelis, 1917-18, 42nd Infantry Division, France.

out to be their last great effort to drive into Paris and win the war before the Americans could get enough men over there to make any significant difference.

There were two outstanding features of this great battle. One, that it was fought on the Great Chalk Plains of Chalons. Miles and miles of chalk that could not even grow grass and the very same battlefield that Atilla the Hun was defeated on in the third and last great Teutonic Invasion, several centuries ago. The second, one of the bravest and most tragic acts of all wars and one that makes me ever proud that I was in the Rainbow Division, was when elements of two of our companies and a like number of two French Companies volunteered to man the very front line trenches, which the Germans had reason to believe were our strongest position, but in reality, were entirely abandoned in the final few hours except for those volunteers that were to shoot their guns and fire off many distress rockets of all colors to indicate to the Germans that the line was desperately being held. As a result of this ruse the front line trenches held by these volunteers were

US Army Band, 22d Engineers. (Baker)

subjected to the heaviest shelling and bombardment in the war. Very few escaped and those that didn't were buried alive as the trenches caved in upon them, their bayonet rifles sticking up through the dirt and chalk. The French Government has erected a beautiful monument here, honoring those brave men that died so gloriously and still lie beneath the soil they were so gallantly defending; still holding their rusty rifles and waiting for their final mustering out.

"Greater love hath no man, that he would lay down his life for his friend." Because of these men making the sacrifice that they did, and because of the strategy of our great commanding French General, Henri Gouraud, hundreds and thousands of our men were spared being killed at and in that battle. Knowing just where the German troops were concentrated in their greatest numbers ever, and we the Allies, had the greatest concentration of artillery and other armaments that the world had ever known. This has not been duplicated since. Because of our great shelling and bombardment, there were several German Division that never left their starting point, being completely decimated.

The German Infantry attack had been planned for 4 a.m. on July 15 and from 11 p.m. on July 14, they had been subjected to a terrific shelling of artillery, trench mortars and machine gun fire, while they were waiting on their front line positions. At 4 a.m. and daylight, they started their advance and at this point of time and in the battle all the rest of the allied guns that were waiting for this advance started firing on their advance. From forward observation posts, the Germans could be seen forming in waves to advance to the attack, only to be met by our deadly fire. As one wave was killed, the next wave formed, advanced, climbed over their dead and they became the dead. Nothing could get through that line of fire. Any that fell wounded was likely blown apart by the next shell. And still they came on, wave after wave, until they were killed. Bravery is usually accorded to the defenders, but in this case, words are weak in describing bravery the Germans evidenced here as they walked forward into certain death.

At this point, after we had been killing them for ten hours, and had attained a great victory, it was a logical time for our Allied force to attack; but there was not any force there to attack; they were mostly all dead.

General Henri Gouraud, Commander of the Fourth French Army, with whom the Rainbow Division was a part in this great Battle of the Champagne, stated that the French soldiers on the entire front were very enthused and revitalized by this great victory and it was the turning point in the war. From this Battle of the Champagne, the last big offensive drive of the Germans in their last great drive to capture Paris, the Germans fought defensively only in every sector were driven back toward their homeland; with the Rainbow Division in each and every one and being used as a shock division. This means that the Rainbow Division was right in the center to break all the assaults from now until Armistice Day. On July 15, they started us overland for Chateau Thierry, then the Ourcq, The Vesle, St. Mihiel, The Argonne and finally, The Army of Occupation. You might say, "We never had a dull moment."

General Henri Gouraud, severely wounded in a battle in the Crimeara, was very impatient and anxious to return to the battles then going on. The doctors at his hospital explained to him that if his left arm were to be saved, he would have to remain in the hospital for weeks, perhaps two or three months. General Gouraud ordered the doctors to take his arm off at once so he could get back to the front. The doctors took his arm off and he returned to the front in two weeks, besides this the General had a very severe wound in his hip and thigh, but the General was the "Bravest of the Brave."

Men of the Rainbow organized into the Rainbow Divisions Veterans and each year meet in come city in America on the anniversary of the Champagne Battle. On this anniversary in 1924, when we met in Indianapolis, Indiana, we were honored by having General Gouraud as our honored guest. After making the principal address, breaking down several times because of the great emotional stress as he remembered and spoke of that greatest of all battles of the war, the General insisted on greeting each and every one of us that were there with a very personal greeting. This started out with a hearty handshake and usually ended with a big hug with his only arm. All this while the General was frequently making remarks to us in French about our battle together and what it meant to the French Nation, to have us there. Again and again he would break into uncontrollable sobs. The General loved France, he loved the French Army, and the General loved the 42nd U.S. Rainbow Division. Every remaining year of his life he sent anniversary greetings to the Rainbow Division Veterans, wherever they might be meeting. General Gouraud worked for and saw a beautiful monument erected and dedicated at Navarin Farm for a memorial to those soldiers, French and

American, who offered and gave their lives in those front line trenches, as part of the awesome strategy that was planned by the General and carried out with such marvelous success. That the battle was won and Germany was started down the road to ultimate defeat.

Every year that the General lived after the dedication of the memorial he attended the services on the date of the battle; now that the General has passed on to glory, his nephew, Philippe Gouraud, who also is a General of a younger generation, does the honors. There are usually several hundred civilian visitors attending the services besides the 1918 French soldiers that are still alive and some of their relatives. Also, our representatives from the National Headquarters of Rainbow Divisions Veterans at Arlington, Virginia report that there are usually some American soldiers brought to it to pay honor to those brave soldiers that lie beneath the monument, still holding their rifles as they were buried there alive.

When General Henri Gouraud died, he could have been buried near Paris with or near General Foch and many other great French heroes and Kings in that very special cemetery reserved for the great. Instead, he chose for his last resting place, a single solitary grave site in Suippes, France, near the monument he had erected at Navarin Farm and one of the places to receive the heaviest German shelling on July 14 and July 15, 1918. From my own position at that time, as a member of Battery F, 149th Field Artillery, I could look about one half mile south and a little more than one mile east to see Suippes, as it was at that time; just a name and a mark on the military road leading from Chalons to Paris, built by Napoleon. Shelled into oblivion.

This grave of the General's is now enhanced by a most beautiful tomb, furnished by the French soldiers that served under him, by the French Government and some contributions from the Rainbow. It can be called a fitting tribute to the Rainbow Division because it is about the very center of our battleground area.

The General's tomb is visited by many dignitaries of French Army and Government people on this day, honoring his memory for his great victory over

A World War One cemetery.

possibly the greatest Army the Germans had ever amassed in their drive to win Paris.

In writing this story and reliving those three days of the battle, which were enough for one's whole lifetime, I wonder if the General is privileged to look down from the battlements of heaven and see where those young American soldiers, previously untried in a battle of this scope, importance to the Germans and of a terrific fierceness never before equaled by either side, never gave up one inch and astounded their French comrades by bravery the veteran French soldiers said they never had witnessed before. The Germans were so sure of a great victory here that they had laid great plans for the take-over and occupying of all lands and properties all the way to Chalons in this one drive. The General knows now, what he hoped for at that time, if the Germans reached Suippes, like they had climbed over the thousands of their own dead, they would have had to walk over the dead bodies of the entire Rainbow Division.

Because of the great historical significance of this battle, the first great victory for the French, the first great defeat of the Germans greatest Army, fought on the same battlefield where Atilla the Hun had been defeated, this battlefield has been left very much like it was then and I am sure that if I were there again, I could find the places where we were and pick up a shell case right where I laid it down sixty-one years ago.

WORLD WAR ONE MEMORIES

Submitted by Charles Gerwitz

In the year of 1918, my Uncle Sam sent me to France.

We left for overseas the first of May with a convoy of thirteen ships. The ship that I was on, was a British cargo ship converted to a troop ship, called the Excelsior. When we were about eight days out, we had a terrible wind storm; the waves came over the deck all the time. We were all below deck playing cards, when all of a sudden there was a awful crash which startled everyone. They hollered, we were hit, so everybody rushed for the stairs which were about six feet wide. It had a railing on both sides, but it was built crossways the ship. When the stairs were all filled with men, the ship rolled back and the stairs were straight up and down, and it dumped all of them on a heap on the floor. Some of them lay there quite a while before they could get up. Then the guard said that the anchor had come out of the hold so far that it swung and hit the side of the ship and that all was well. The first land we sighted was Ireland.

We later landed at Liverpool, May 13, 1918. Each one received a card of welcome and greetings from the King and Queen. We got off the boat at 8 a.m. and boarded a train for Worchester. The country was very pretty; trees were in blossom, the fences were all hedges, it looked exceptionally good after having been on water two weeks.

The people in England were unfriendly and acted as though they were doing us an honor to have us there. We had a great many fights with them the few days we stayed.

While we were in camp, there was a shortage of water. The water was turned on at mealtime, then shut off again. The English said it cost too much to pump the water to have it on all the time.

We left for South Hampton across the English channel. The boat was very crowded. All standing room was filled. After dark, the boat started out. By morning, most of us were piled on the deck floor, some went to sleep, then other would fall over them. It seemed unnecessary to be treated that way.

By daylight, we docked at La Havre, France. We were very glad to get off the boat, but it was hard to walk after taking such punishment. We stayed there an hour and had English hard tack and coffee. We left carrying a full pack for a long hike. We landed in a camp at 3 p.m.

That night at retreat, we were told that they have air-raids very often and when we hear the signal, we should all come out in the groups we were in. Each group should go into a different direction so there wouldn't be too many in one spot.

At 1:00, when everyone was nestled on mother earth sound asleep, the whistle blew and we heard several airplanes and saw searching lights looking for the airplanes. Anti-aircraft guns were popping out. The group I was with was to the airplanes. Anti-aircraft guns were popping out. The group I was with was to leave at the west-side gate. The officer heading our group would blow his whistle every little way so we could follow him. He started out and ran about one and a half miles with us running after him. We sat down to rest; then returned to camp. On the way back, there were many soldiers laying on the ground that had dropped on account of sore feet.

When we got to camp most of the other men were sound asleep, and those that were awake asked what had taken us so long to get back. They went out of camp a little ways and waited till the air raid was over, then went back. Our Lieutenant had tricked us and had given us a good run.

On top of Conisbrough Castle. Kelley, Trexler and Reed, 1918, England. (Kelley)

"JOURNEY TO FRANCE"

Submitted by Charles Gerwith

We were at the first camp in France a few days, when we were sent to Camp LaCourtine. We boarded regular French passenger trains. The coaches were partitioned off in three sections, there was a running board along the outside and it had a door on each side of the sections. A plank seat running across on each side had room for four on a seat or eight to a section. We were on the road for three days and three nights. We used our blankets for pads on the seats. Even then, the planks could be felt through the blankets. At night the only way we could lay down was to lift one of our buddies up into the baggage racks and sleep one on each seat, two in the aisle and one under each seat. The smallest ones had to get under the seats and into the baggage racks. I had to get under a seat. One could just lie flat on his back because there wasn't hardly room to move. Even now, I often dream that I am in such a position and can't move.

We took our shoes off, but one of the fellows had such bad feet that we couldn't permit him to leave his shoes off. He took his socks off and tied a string to them and hung them out of the door to air out. They sure got a good airing, because when he opened the door in the morning all that was left of them was the knot from the string.

For meals, the train would stop and bread, coffee and hardtack were served. We did not care for the hardtack so we would throw them out to the French children who flocked around and fought for them. They called them bisques. Whenever the train stopped, we would jump out. The train could not make a fast getaway, but even so, some would miss their coach and catch the one further back. Then they would climb on the top of a coach until the train stopped again. There were usually 25 sitting on top of the coaches. Throughout the sections were big vineyards and plenty of wine could be gotten at any house.

Camp LaCourtine was a big camp with stone barracks; they were roomed off to hold about 16 soldiers. They had iron bars along the wall, two feet from the floor. Eighteen inches from the walls were planks hinged to those bars. They had standards on the outer end for legs so when not in use they were tilted up against the wall.

In the little town called De La Courtine, a place near the city of Lyons at the Alps Mountains, I went to the artillery school and had target practice, shooting at the mountains, and believe me we could hit them. The people there lived in stone houses. Their cows, oxen, hens and hogs live in the same place they do. Most of the houses had stone floors and stone fireplaces. The tables were rough boards, their chairs were benches or stools like milk stools. They had brooms made of fine brush, tied together to a stick. They wore mostly wooden shoes. The smaller children had shoes with leather tops with wooden soles and they sure could make some noise when they ran down the street. They had no fences, so when the let the stock out, one of them would have to watch the animals while they were eating. When they bring them to the house again at night, they milk the cows.

In the United States, we had been practicing with three inch guns, and now we were given the French 75 millimeter, which were much different. We went into the Vosges Mountains, also called the French Alps, for target practice. It was quite a distance, so we would stay for several days at a time. There was some brush much like hemlock where we pitched our tents. We cleared a spot several hundred feet and piled the brush on a pile 200 feet long and as high as we could throw.

When the Marines took Chateau Thierry in the middle of July, it was the Americans first drive, so we lit the pile of brush at night to celebrate. There was

A German machine gun. It was captured in the St. Mihiel Drive by the 5th Division. (L to R): Cpl. N. Panelilo, Pvt. O'Brien and Pvt. Otto McCamish.

a breeze to help make the flames reach out so we had to move tents, guns and horses back to keep them from burning. It was the biggest fire I had ever seen. The French people for miles around, were very excited and wanted to know what the fire was for.

By the end of July, we were fully equipped and loaded, everything on the train. As the cars were small, only eight horses and 40 men could fit in a car, which crowded them and was very uncomfortable. When the train stopped, we had to get off and push to get it started again. The men sat on the floor of the car (which had many cracks), so that when the car swayed from side to side, many got pinched; we sat on our packs to make it foolproof.

After three days, we arrived at a small village near Chateau Thierry, called Orle. We camped here for several days because horses were bruised up badly and some had to be killed. The first night we were there, the German gun called "Big Bertha" fired its last shells into Paris. We could hear the report of the gun and hear the shells whiz over us and the shell explode in Paris. We were in reserve lines of Belleau Woods. The next day "Big Bertha" was captured by the Allies. We marched toward Chateau Thierry, which was badly torn up and also the nearby villages.

The Germans had tunnels dug through the ground from house to house and under, through the streets, so one could go through the whole city without being seen. The houses had holes knocked through the walls, five feet from the floor and two feet apart in all the houses. It was built like a fort, the houses all had to be leveled down before they surrendered it. Some places were covered with machine gun and rifle bullets. I picked up some and still have one. Many of the civilians were digging away at their houses looking very unhappy; all that we could understand was "books bash", which meant much war.

When the train came, we loaded up and pushed off again, no one knew where to. We passed through wonderful places; the homes of Joan of Arc and of Julius Caesar, and saw the most wonderful cathedral in France. The cemeteries in France were big and interesting. Some grave stones dated back to the 19th century. The graves were decorated with flowers made of tin and beads. There were monuments built like churches, four feet high and eight feet long, which had alters, candles and flowers inside.

The next night at ten o'clock, we landed in Toul and had to unload at once. The wind was blowing and it was raining. We hitched the horses on the guns, caisson and supply wagons and went up a long hill to a camp that Napoleon had built and no doubt it was operated ever since. At least many of the boys were pestered with creeping dandruff, seam squirrels and pants rabbits.

"THANKSGIVING"

Submitted by Rev. Howard E. May

We're thankful for the glory of the old
    Red, white and blue,
For the spirit of America that still is
    staunch and true,
And Thankful that our harvests wear no
    taint of blood today,
But were sown and reared by toilers who
    were light of heart and gay;
Thankful for the plenty that our peaceful
    land has blessed,
For the rising sun that beckons every man
    to do his best.

Today, we're thankful for our pilgrim fathers'
    religious fight,
Which brought them to America to spread the
    gospel light,
We're thankful that here, religious freedom
    is known,
Because the Gospel of Jesus Christ then
    was sown;
Thankful unto God, the giver of every good
    and perfect gift,
Who gave His Son Jesus, this sinful world
    to lift
From bondage of greed, of sin and Spiritual
    Depravity,
Back to God, his loving care, and Glorious
    Liberty.

AIR RAID
by Charles Gerwith

There were plenty of air raids every night. Aerial bombs are very powerful. When dropped on a house, it would almost level it to the ground, the stones would scatter a good ways around. The Moselle River was about one mile from camp and every night we had to go down to learn to swim.

After ten days, we moved into the second line at Lousy. An aerial bomb struck a church and made a hole through the roof and into the floor without exploding. That was the only one I had seen that did not explode. We took up our positions in an old gun pit already dug by the French. The French dugouts for the gun crew were 40 feet into the ground and it was none too deep and had plenty of rats. One night we were playing cards and a rat came and grabbed a lighted candle and ran away with it.

It was damp and cold in the dugout, so we built a fire in it and wore the gas masks. It took out the dampness but it was unsatisfactory, so we scouted around and found some tin to make a stove pipe and had a five gallon can for a stove which worked very good. We were at the crest of a hill, and over the hill was a prune orchard. The prunes were quite green and a Turk, by the name of Vossil Angelo, liked them. He was a hearty eater and ate so many the first time, that it nearly killed him. He lay on the floor in such pain that we thought for sure he would die, but he didn't.

There were many people on the road leaving their homes what were in ruin from air raids. Some had two-wheeled carts and wheel barrows loaded with their belongings. Some carried big bundles and small children who were begging for food. When it rained they would get under the trees or other shelters for an all night stay.

The artillery received its direction of firing or data from airplanes and observation balloons. In front line trenches they would watch for enemy machine gun nests, artillery concentration of troops and supply trucks. They were pointed out to the battery commander who would give us the range. The guns were set my means of a compass. An imaginary circle around the gun, a circle has 360 degrees which starts pointing north so whatever number is given in this circle was the direction to point the gun. The range was given in the same way. A circle was fastened to the gun, only the circle was in an upright position and got by means of a level starting at one pointing forward. The gun could not be fired when the range over 45 degrees was set because it would pump into the air and get too far out of position for rapid fire. For night firing, we had a light the size of a flashlight which was usually 50 yards in front of the gun and wired so it could be controlled from the gun pit. A small telescope was fastened to the gun with a cross hair to keep it lined up and the range was held by instruments on the side of the gun barrel which was to be set and all the gunner had to do was to keep the cross hair on the target or light and the bubble level. Then the gunner would raise his hand which meant ready to fire. When the gun is well settled into position it does not move much, so we could fire from 10 to 15 rounds per minute.

My score on pistol shooting was 80 percent out of 100, the 13th highest in our company of 250 soldiers.

Not all American squadrons flew the DH-4, DeHavilland, British designed, built aircraft. Here is a Salmson 2A2 airplane of the 12th Aero Squadron. This unit was equipped with the French built-designed Salmson.

"REMEMBERING"
by Albert E. Powis Sr. Submitted by Benjamin D. Dexter

It was a hot sunshiny day on the 20th of July 1918, as we came to the hill above the valley where the town of Viersey, France was situated.

We were driving towards Rheims and the French were driving towards Soissons according to our lieutenant. We had 20 miles to go and four days to do it in and we were in seeing distance on the third day and had not eaten any food from the 18th of July when we started the drive. We were moving too fast for our kitchen to keep up. All that was in our area was artillery and infantry. As we came to the valley it was quite wide, I would say about 3/4 of a mile and down the middle of it was a small stream and it had quite a bank of white rock. Looked like lime rock. The Germans were moving over the hill. On the opposite of the valley, there was a good bunch of trees and brush on both sides of the small stream so we advanced as skirmishers down to it and at that time the Krauts started to shell the area. They were using 88 Wisbangs. We called the Austrian 88 artillery, Wisbangs because when you heard them they had hit and exploded. Our men in the ditch where they took cover to get out of the shrapnel that was flying in all directions and some were taking wounds as they were calling first aid but our artillery started to shell their gun area and they quit shooting. Then a machine gun in the edge of town opened up on us. It was situated in a large factory chimney; they had a large hole broken out of the chimney and were firing down towards our area and we were getting some casualties. So Captain Wm. Crabbe told the second squad who had two French Chauchet machine guns that used half moon clips that held 20 French label ammo with a copper bullet. In the squad was me and Leon Perry who had the Chauchets. Also Dick Seselga, Bernard Yokum, Cpl. Bickely, Caviness Trigg Nye, they were equipped with bag of clips and a Springfield Rifle, plus an extra bandoleer of ammo. We looked for cover of the brush and headed out to hit the town about half way through the town. There was a large hill and we moved around it in single file. When we got into the edge of Viersey we moved towards the Big Chimney and when we got there, I covered one street and Perry, the others and Big Dick Seselga let the lever go on a grenade and at the count of three, threw it into the hole in the chimney. IT EXPLODED as it entered the chimney and made quite a racket but the gun was silent! I went over by the door that was at the bottom of the chimney and blood was dripping so I gave the platform a good supply of Chauchet ammo.

Then the rest of our Platoon and Captain Crabbe came up and he was giving us our new orders when a voice from an opening at the side of the hill facing us cried he wanted to surrender in fairly good English. So I moved over to cover the door from my side and Perry did the same from his side. Someone hollered, "come on out and throw your rifle in a pile," and out came a lieutenant and he had his Leuger and belt in his right hand and he handed it to Captain Crabbe who was dressed the same as us privates and the amount of men who came out was 1,000 men. The Marines lined them up four abreast and Private Fisher our German interpreter told them, "if you have any more guns you had better drop them now because if you sue them, we will shoot down the bunch of you Germans," they marched them towards the rear and several were walking to Captain Crabbe when a little plane came over us and they threw out a small bomb or a grenade and it hit Captain Crabbe in the knee and he went down. I got a small piece that scraped by forehead and I lost a little blood, but I saw Captain Crabbe when we landed in New York City and he had a stiff right leg.

We entered that area at 11 o'clock, made our four day drive in two and a half days instead of four days and we were relieved at 4 o'clock and went to try and find our kitchen so we could eat.

So ends five hours in Viersey, France by the Old Devil Dog, Albert E. Powis.

NO PARADE AFTER THE WAR

World War I veteran Harold Fetherhuff was to attend a parade honoring all veterans on Monday, Nov. 17, 1991 at Aberdeen, South Dakota. Below are some of his thoughts and recollections.

"I don't remember any parade after the war, ... I went straight home after the war. I don't believe there was a parade of any kind."

He recalls one German attack in 1918. "What a racket it was,... It was a big convoy of 13 ships sailing from Halifax, accompanied by a British cruiser. We were attacked once on the way over. I happened to be on the lower deck at the time the guns went off." Excerpted from Aberdeen American News, Sunday, Nov. 10, 1991, Aberdeen, SD. Used with permission.

World War I veteran Harold Fetherhuff.

WORLD WAR I:
"WORK-OR-FIGHT"

While "Remember the Maine" was the rallying cry during the Spanish-American War, "Doing one's bit" was the motivator in WWI. On May 23, 1918, the War Department ordered all able-bodied young men to find "essential" jobs by July 1 or be ready to serve Uncle Sam.

Though not considered essential to the war effort, major league baseball players were exempt from the "worked-or-fight" order until September when the season ended.

Many farm boys among the pros simply returned home to do their part. But steel mills, shipyards and other industries lured approximately half the pro-players onto their payrolls for pseudo-essential jobs. It usually amounted to little more than playing ball for the company team.

Babe Ruth, "Dutch" Leonard, Rogers Hornsby and Eddie Plank were some of the more prominent players who hid in the "Safe Shelter League," while many of their former teammates were on the battlefields of Europe.

Ban Johnson, then American League president, criticized the slackers: "The American League will never object to a ball player shouldering a rifle and will do everything to encourage such a practice, but we do not think it is fair to take our players and put them in industrial plants where they are wanted mainly to play ball on the side."

Johnson even recommended that any pro player in the Safe Shelter League "should be yanked into the Army by the coat collar." Many athletes also despised the league and joined the military willingly.

Ty Cobb was exempt from service, but still turned down offers to play for several of the steel plants or shipyards," he said, "For such work would keep me in this country, and the line of service which I desire is to be 'over there.'"

He enlisted in the Army Chemical Warfare Service in 1918 instead and was eventually shipped to France.

Cobb was well-known for his rough tactics on the base paths and his willingness to spike an opponent who dared to get in the way. One officer who'd learned that Cobb had arrived in Europe at war's end lamented, "I wish the war had lasted long enough for old Ty to go into the Kaiser with his spikes high."

Other players interrupted their paths to the Hall of Fame to serve alongside the Doughboys in the trenches of France.

Boston Braves catcher Hank Gowdy was the first ball player to enlist, and served with the 166th Infantry Regiment, 42nd Division. He had the unenviable job of scooting along the lines to sniff for gas, making sure it was safe for the rest of the troops.

Another catcher was Gabby Street of the Washington Senators, who also served in a gas unit and was hit by shrapnel at Saint Mihiel.

Philadelphia Athletics second baseman Eddie Collins joined the Marines, and Tris Speaker, outfielder for the Cleveland Indians, enlisted in the fledgling naval aviation. "Rabbit" Maranville, Burleigh Grimes, George Sisler, Rube Marquard and Casey Stengle all donned uniforms during the war.

Tragically, two of baseball's stars (Christy Mathewson and Grover Cleveland Alexander) suffered debilitating injuries that cut short their pro careers.

Mathewson, the sensational New York Giants pitcher, was gassed in the trenches of France. He contracted tuberculosis and severely damaged his lungs, abruptly ending his baseball career.

Alexander had been with the 89th Division's 342nd Field Artillery Regiment when it came under heavy bombardment. The experience left Alex deaf in one ear and suffering from epileptic seizures for the rest of his life.

All told, 144 American Leaguers and 103 National League players served in uniform during WWI.

WORLD WAR ONE VET KNOCKS OUT NAZI ANTI-TANK GUN

Sevelen, Germany—With a bridge blown behind them, a Negro tank battalion task force staged a miniature "Bastogne" in Sevelen yesterday, mauling Nazi parachute units in savage street fighting while cut off for 18 hours.

The 784th Tank Battalion was fighting its first offensive action beside the 35th Infantry Division. The battalion won a place in the hearts of the men of the battle-hardened 35th Division, who had fought from St. Lo to Venlo and beyond, by the battle it put up here and the spearhead fighting it did to get here.

Sgt. Walter "Pop" Half, a 47-year old veteran of [the Great War] from Little York, Il, who came back in this war as the commander of a tank bulldozer, was called out under fire to fill craters in a road. He went on to knock out a German 88-millimeter anti-tank gun.

G.H.Q.
AMERICAN EXPEDITIONARY FORCES

My Fellow Soldiers:

Now that your service with the American Expeditionary Forces is about to terminate, I can not let you go without a personal word. At the call to arms, the patriotic young manhood of America eagerly responded and became the formidable army whose decisive victories testify to its efficiency and its valor. With the support of the nation firmly united to defend the cause of liberty, our army has executed the will of the people with resolute purpose. Our democracy has been tested, and the forces of autocracy have been defeated. To the glory of the citizen-soldier, our troops have faithfully fulfilled their trust, and in a succession of brilliant offensives have overcome the menace to our civilization.

As an individual, your part in the world war has been an important one in the sum total of our achievements. Whether keeping lonely vigil in the trenches, or gallantly storming the enemy's stronghold; whether enduring monotonous drudgery at the rear, or sustaining the fighting line at the front, each has bravely and efficiently played his part. By willing sacrifice of personal rights; by cheerful endurance of hardship and privation; by vigor, strength and indomitable will, made effective by thorough organization and cordial co-operation, you inspired the war-worn Allies with new life and turned the tide of threatened defeat into overwhelming victory.

With a consecrated devotion to duty and a will to conquer, you have loyally served your country. By your exemplary conduct a standard has been established and maintained never before attained by any army. With mind and body as clean and strong as the decisive blows you delivered against the foe, you are soon to return to the pursuits of peace. In leaving the scenes of your victories, may I ask that you carry home your high ideals and continue to live as you have served—an honor to the principles for which you have fought and to the fallen comrades you leave behind.

It is with pride in our success that I extend to you my sincere thanks for your splendid service to the army and to the nation.

Faithfully,
John J. Pershing

BIOGRAPHIES
OF THE VETERANS
OF WORLD WAR ONE

BOYD ABRAMS, born 1895. His parents are Henry Dudley Abrams and Rosa (Kave) Abrams.

He was a member of the 89th Division, 342nd Machine Gun Co. and the Army of Oc. Cobenz, Germany.

He received disability from enemy gases.

PIO CRESPO AGUILAR, Rio Rancho, NM, 87124. Born July 12, 1896, at Sigma Capiz, Philippines. His parents are Francisco Aguilar and Francisca Crespo.

He entered service during WWI on July 19, 1917 to June 30, 1921 in France. Also serving in WWII from Aug. 10, 1942 to Jan. 18, 1946 in the Philippines. He was a member of the U.S. Navy and achieved the ranking of Chief Petty Officer.

In WWI he was awarded the Great War for Configuration Medal and the Good Conduct Ribbon. In WWII he was given the American Theater Campaign Medal (1941-45) and the Asiatic Pacific Campaign Medal (1941-45).

He belonged to the Veterans of WWI, VFW, NARFE, K of C and Post Commander of VFW 1063 in Philadelphia, PA

His memorable experiences were Barracks 117 Commander, Dept. Chaplain, Region 9 Commander, and Nat'l Deputy Chaplain.

He was a postal employee in Philadelphia, PA. He retired from the post office after 32 years of honorable service as clerk-in-charge. He was married to Rosalind F. Littana, daughter of Gen. and Mrs. Liberato E. Littana of the Philippines.

JOHN ALEXA, 183 Ind. Park Rd., Crystal Falls, MI 49920. Born on Apr. 11, 1897 in Amasa, MI. He joined the service on Apr. 29, 1918 and was discharged in 1919.

He was a member of the Co. D, 310 Engineers, 85th Div. at Camp Custer. His most memorable experience was serving with ARF, July 22, 1918 in the Battle of Argone, France.

His wife, Mary, is 85 years old and disabled. He is now 95 and still cooks, shops and cleans.

ALBERT W. ANDERSON, 5333 N. Sheridan 23L, Chicago, IL 60640. Born on Nov. 2, 1901 in Chicago, IL. He joined the service July 31, 1918 and retired Oct. 6, 1919.

He was in the U.S. Navy and achieved the rank of Shipfitter 2C. He also served on the *USS Illinois* Battleship.

His most memorable experience was saving shipmates who could not swim.

He has six children, three boys and three girls. His brother also served in WWI in France. He is now retired as Dept. Supt. of Police in Chicago.

ARTHUR M. ANDERSON, 1204 Davenport Street, Sturgis, SD. Was born at Stanhope, IA on Oct. 27, 1896 and passed away Oct. 16, 1989 at Fort Meade. SD.

He enlisted in Btry. B, 13th Regt., FARD Camp Jackson, SC on Aug. 15, 1918. He was discharged from Camp Sherman, OH on Jan. 7, 1919, No. 34 812 77.

Following his discharge he worked for the Chicago Northwestern Railroad as an Agent in Deadwood, Phillip, St. Onge, Whitewood and Sturgis, SD. His character was rated as excellent. He was a member of the American Legion, WWI, The Masonic Lodge and Shrine Temple in Deadwood, SD.

ELMER THOMAS ANDERSON, was an American who loved his country and proud to help preserve its liberty. He was born Sept. 26, 1893 in Fenton, MO. He enlisted in the WWI Army, Dec. 14, 1917 at Fort McDowell, CA. He attained a ranking of Quartermaster Sgt. under Brig. Gen. Hutcheson at Newport News, VA and served until Dec. 3, 1918 when he was honorably discharged at Presidio of San Francisco, CA. During WWII he was too old to be inducted into the armed services so he lied about his age and volunteered for the Seabees in the Naval Reserve at the age of 50, Feb. 15, 1943. He served in the Munda Islands as a Storekeeper 1st Class until he was wounded and had acquired malaria. He was honorably discharged Dec. 1, 1944.

Upon returning home to Snowflake, AZ he

helped organize Boys League Baseball and umpired many years. He was instrumental in forming the American Legion Post #37 in Holbrook, AZ and the Standifird Hunt Post #55 in Snowflake, AZ. Both he and his wife Hazel Ramsay Anderson were active in the American Legion, serving as Cmdr., District President and other positions until his death, Mar. 23, 1972. They were also active in Veterans of WWI, USA Barracks #3267.

Deceased Veterans have been honored with flags and poppy wreaths on Memorial Day from 1945 until now; his wife and daughters carry on the tradition.

He is survived by his son, Robert Prentice Anderson, a retired U.S. Air Force Capt., his wife, three daughters, 15 grandchildren and 21 great-grandchildren.

JOHN GRAHAM AGNES, Rockbridge Co., Colbreistom, VA. His wife is Vernie and he has two boys Eugene and John Jr. He has now passed away.

ANTHONY (TONY) BADAMO, IL Veterans Home, 7079 N. 12th St. Quincy, IL 62301. He was born on Sept. 17, 1895 at 4th Hampton St., Quincy, IL. He joined the service on Jan. 4,1918 and retired March 24,1919. He was a member of the 28th Div., 109 Infantry, Co. K and achieved the ranking of Private.

His most memorable experience was being wounded in the left thigh by a machine gun bullet on Nov. 11, 1918 at 6:30am. He received the Military Order of the Purple Heart.

He got married Sept. 21, 1923. He now attends all Legion meetings and convetions. IL past Dept. Cmdr. in 1958. At present he is Cmdr. of 138 Badge of Honor Post 37. He has held several offices in Boys State and has been Director for 56 years. He is a Past Faithful Navigator of the Knights of Columbus in Quincy, IL.

CLYDE WALLACE BAKER, born April 19, 1894 in Lismon, KY. Died Aug. 31,1984 in Murphysboro, IL. PFC 2012921, Co. 22 Engineers in WWI. He enlisted on May 24,1918 in Providence, KY. He left the United States on June 23, 1918 and retired in the United States on June 22, 1919. He was discharged July 3, 1919 at Camp Zachary in Taylor, KY. He was stationed at Meuse Argonne from Sept. 26-Nov. 1918.

He came home on the *USS Princess Matoika* which was shown in the *Torch* in September 1982 with its history.

He was a member of the Lisnon Presbyterian Church in Lismon, KY and later joined First Baptist Church in Murphysboro, TN.   His met his wife through another veteran at Camp Hutchins Veteran's CCC Camp at Jonesboro, IL. He went from there to Jefferson Barracks and worked in Biet Kitchen Salvage Warehouse where he worked German POWs during WWII. Later when John Cochran Hospital was built, he was first storekeeper and received everything there.

At that time they had their home two acres east of Murphysboro, IL. He had six years before retirement and he would come home every Friday after work at John Cochran and go back on Sunday evening.

His last days were spent working on the yard and graden. He suffered a heart attack in 1977, but improved for a few years. He had another attack later and was in and out of John Cochran and Marion VA until Aug. 15 when he came home to die on Aug. 31, 1984. He and his wife had over 42 years together and she is now 88 years old.

JOE A. BARBER, born March 15, 1898 in Chicago, IL. Attended high shool at Lewis and Clark. He enlisted in December 1917 in Roundup,

MT in Air Corps. He went to Ft. Wright in Spokane and there was turned down for poor eyesight. He was then returned in April and accepted in SOS (Service of Supplies). Their moto was "Mother take in your service flag-your son's in the SOS."

He went overseas about May 1, 1918 on the *Frererick der Gros*, an old German captured ship renamed *Huron*. His unit was the Truck Co. stationed just north of Bari in Clichy. He delivered supplies of all kinds, usually individual trips to supply stations back of the frontlines.

His most unique experience was that 35 of them were moved into Paris after the Armistice to drive Cadillacs for the American Peace Commission from November 1918 to Nov. 9, 1919. He drove all the big wigs daily from the Hotel C. He was dicschaarged in November 1919 in Presidio, in San Francisco.

WILLIS E. BARNES, 3450 SW Antelope Ave., Redmond, OR 97756. He enlisted in Portland, OR at age 17. He enlisted in Co. D 318th Combat Engineers, 6th Div. He had all his training at the Vancouver Barricks in Vancouver, WN. One of the best Army posts in the United States. After three months of training they left for France where they took part in the Meuse Argonne Battle and the Geradmer Sector.

When the war ended he went into Germany. After 13 months in France and Germany they were sent back to the US to be discharged at Fort Lewis, WA. He was in a base hospital, No. 15, in Shaumont, France.

ROBERT C. BARRETT, born May 24, 1886 and died March 28, 1985. He lived in Aliquippa, PA 15001. He joined the service on July 25, 1917 and was discharged Feb. 2, 1918. He served in the U.S. Army as Wagoneer Supp. Co., 117 Infantry.

He was awarded the Victory Medal w/clasps.

His wife Mary lives in Aliquippa, PA. He had five daughters, ten grandaughters and five great grandchildren. He had one sister.

WALTER R. BATTLE, 1543 So. 13th St., Terre Haute, IN 47802. He was born March 21, 1895 at Green Castle, IN. He joined the service in 1918. He was located at St. Levere, France.

He has a wife, Mary, and four stepsons. He is not able to work today due to arthritis in both knees.

HENRY LEO BAUER, was inducted into the US Army on July 23, 1918 at Center, NE and was honorably discharged on June 9, 1919 at Camp Dodge, IA. Having been born in the rural area of Bloomfield, NE, he seemed to find the Army life a real change and quite the challenge.

He passed away at the VA Medical Center at Grand Island, NE on May 11, 1973.

He spoke fondly of his buddies with whom he served and enjoyed telling of some rather unusual stories. Having been of German descent he became an interpreter while stationed in Germany, and he was promoted to Sergeant on Oct. 16, 1918. Being an interpreter had its drawbacks. He used to laugh as he told how frustrated he was when he was trying to obtain a waffle iron for the Capt., and could not think of the translation.

He also spoke of how beautiful the Cathedral was at Koln, Germany and how excited he was to see Paris. It was not all fun and games, however, and he never spoke of why he had been hospitalized for at least a week.

Having served his country, he returned to the United States on the beautiful *Santa Teresa*. After this journey he would never eat baked beans again. It would seem that beans decorated the entire ship.

He settled down when he married Clara Belle Howard on Dec. 18, 1921 in Sioux City, IA. She loaned him the $2 for the license. They farmed in Page, O'Neill, Royal and Brunswick, NE before saving enough to purchase their farm north of Plainview, NE in 1944.

To this marriage of over 50 years, three daughters were born: Dolores Bauer of Denver, CO, (a former WAC); Bernadine Bauer Taylor of Banning, CA, (a former USAF, WAF and USAF retiree's wife); and Edna Bauer Barnes, (a former USAF, WAF and USAF retiree's wife). Edna is the Director of the County Veterans Service Office of Solano County, CA. His only grandchild, Ted Barnes, has recently earned his Ph.D in Electrical Engineering.

ROBY LA FAYETTE BEDSAUL, was born June 22, 1893 in or near Galax, VA to Colombus and Ellen (Hanks) Bedsaul. He came with his folks to South Dakota in the spring of 1896, settling on a homestead near Tilford, SD, where he went to school and grew to manhood. He worked for farmers near home until he married Effa Amburn in 1917. They moved to her homestead in Harding County.

He was drafted into the Army where he served from Aug. 26, 1918 to Jan. 30, 1919. He was in the Quarter Master Corps and served all his time at Camp Funston and Camp Forsite near Ft. Riley, KS. He was in service while the flu was bad and helped so many men that had the flu. He also helped prepare many who died for burial to be shipped home.

After coming home he had to start all over again buying stock and working for the railroad. They had three little girls when his wife died April 1, 1923. His mother took the children and cared for them till they were old enough to live with their father on a farm furnished by the farmer he worked for.

He married Florence Keffeler Schuster on August 13, 1947. He moved to Sturgis, SD and worked for a lumber company for 5 years and then at the Black Hills National Cemetary, near Sturgis for five years. He then retired. He also worked for a contractor building houses.

He was a 61-year member of the American Legion and a 24-year member of WWI Barracks. He helped organize the local Bear Butte Barracks. He also was Color Bearer for funerals at the National Cemetary for years.

He died August 17, 1986 at the VA Medical Center, Ft. Meade, SD after being there for almost two years.

JOHN BENO, born March 20, 1895 in Studlov, Val. Klobouky, Moravia, Europe. He arrived at Ellis Island on Dec. 3, 1913. Sailed from Bremen, Germany on the ship *Frederik the Great*.

He worked at various jobs in Wisconsin and Illinois. He was drafted in Barrington, IL and entered the service on Sept. 7, 1917.

He started as a cook at Camp Grant, IL, then transferred to Camp Hancock, Augusta, GA. He rated PVT 1st Class. Not being a citizen he was not sent to France; instead was sent to work as a cook near Vancouver, WA for 28 men that worked in a logging camp. He was discharged Jan. 9, 1919, 8th Sqd., First Regt. ASAP.

He married on May 12, 1919 to Mary Fischer. He has two children. His wife died Dec. 4, 1940, remarried in 1941 and moved from Scappoose, OR to St. Helens, OR where he worked in the lumber industry from 1923 until his retirement in 1965. He has lived alone since the death of his wife in 1974 until August 1991 when he moved back to Scappoose and is living with his daughter and son-in-law. He enjoys reading, writing and visiting. He is in good health.

JOHAN BERGMAN, 762508 Pvt. 1st Class, Medical Dept. He enlisted in the U.S. Army in 1917 at the age of 19. He was sent to Jefferson Barracks, MO. He was put in the Motor Transport Division and sent to the Army-Navy General Hospital in Hot Springs, AR. Later he was transferred to the X-ray Div., Medical Dept. He was honorably discharged on March 7, 1920 from the Army-Navy General Hospital. A Bronze Victory Medal was issued to him.

Bergman spent the war as a hospital worker in Hot Springs, AR. After the war he went to work for the Studebaker Co. and worked there for 40 years until his retirement in 1963. He maintains that Studebaker was the best-made car in America.

He fell into the Medical Corps in a very unusual way. In those days, photography was one of his hobbies. He would borrow a camera from a friend, take pictures, and then do his own developing. When he went in to the service he started out in motor transport. He was 19 then, and his job before he left was driving a bus from the Radisson Hotel in Minneapolis to the St. Paul Hotel. It was a privately owned bus co. and he drove back and forth on University Ave. So they put him im motor transport, and when they wanted a truck driver and an ambulance driver down in Hot Springs, they sent him. At the same time he was driving, he was taking pictures for the serivices. If a training plane fell down, they'd have him take pictures of the plane in two direction. He had a government camera that took 6x8 plates. He would develop those plates in the x-ray laboratory, and they caught him in there and then had him transferred to that section. So he took instruction on it for a few months, and he did the x-ray laboratory for the rest of the war. The hosptal they were at was for people who were hurt real bad. Men were flown from France with a lot of shrapnel wounds and bullet wounds. He took x-ray pictures of them to locate the shrapnel or the bullets so the doctors could take them out.

GLENN BERRY, U.S. Navy, Serial 1116592. USS Huntington and USS McCall, 1917-19. Both Grandfathers were Civil War veterans, one walked with Sherman to the sea, one a scout being one-fourth Cherokee Indian and a Captainancy earned the hard way.

His Father was a cowboy, miner and early pioneer of Western Colorado. His father died when he was one year old. His Mother was a pioneer school teacher who taught Gen. Eisenhower in Abaline, KS, and with another school teacher made the famous Cherokee strip run that settled Oklahoma.

He was born in Hastings Mesa, San Miguel County, CO on Oct. 15, 1901. He went to work at the Vanadium mines when he was 12 years old. He enlisted in the US Navy on April 16, 1917 at the age of 15. He was the youngest WWI soldier as of that date. He participated in the destroyer escort service during the war, and was discharged June 26, 1919.

He has since ran a cattle business and mining business together with Automobile Agency Steel Fabrication. He has also written several books which include *Active Legionnaire and WWI*. He married Norva Welsh on Dec. 8, 1920 and she still looks across the table at him. They raised a son and daughter whom are both now deceased. He resides at 714 Niblic Dr., Grand Junction, CO 81506.

REV. CHAUNCEY BIFFLE, born April 7, 1900 in Carter County, MT to Robert Lee and Henrietta Biffle. He was a graduate of the Baker

High School in Baker, MT and later had four years of Methodist Seminary study. On June 2, 1922, he was married to Josephine Howell in Baker.

He worked as a grocery clerk, bank clerk and teller in Lewistown, Harlowton and Baker, and a bookkeeper in Ekalaka. From 1933-35 he was manager of the Emergency Relief Adm. at Baker in 1935 served as manager of the National Re-employment Service in Miles City and Billings and was state director of War Manpower Commission in Helena.

He served as manager of the State Employment Service in Polson from 1948-65. In 1948, he became pastor of the Bigfork Methodist Church in Bigfork and was ordained while serving in Bigfork. In 1972, he became associate pastor of the United Methodist Church in Kalispell, serving until his final illness.

He served in the U.S. Army in France during WWI, and was a charter member and state commander of the American Legion (1944-45) in Helena. He was also a charter member and state commander of the Veterans of WWI (1955) in Polson, and was a life member of the VFW.

He passed away on June 13,1989. He is survived by his wife, his son, Robert P. Biffle, a sister, Mrs. R. G. Wheeler, seven grandchildren and 12 great-grandchildren.

He enlisted in the army and went to France in 1918. He had enlisted in April and arrived in France by July. He was in the Army exactly 10 months and was discharged in February of 1919. He was stationed between the front lines and the rear lines in France. There were just a few Americans attached to the first unit he was in.

WARNER MACDOWELL BLAKESLEE, born Feb. 11, 1899 in Muncy, PA. Parents were Dr. Talbert Washington Blakeslee and Christiana Springer. He married Eliza E. Belding in 1920 and they had two children ,Warner MacDowell Blakeslee Jr. and Edna Jean Blakeslee. His son served in WWII and was killed during a battle in Italy.

He volunteered for WWI service on Jan. 10, 1918. He signed up for the U.S. Army in Cleveland, OH and was then sent to Fort Thomas, KY. He was then shipped to England on a cattle boat called *Anselm*. While in England he was trained in first aid at Liverpool and then to Knotty Ash and Fort Arundal, England.

There was a major flu epidemic and many deaths resulted. He was determined not to contact the flu so he went to the nearest pub and consumed ale rum. He returned to the barracks and took a dose of quinine. The next morning he didn't have the flu. He returned on the *Queen Mary* and was kept busy taking care of more flu patients and the wounded.

He had a romantic encounter in England with Hilda Blunden. They wrote to each other and all of a sudden he no longer heard from her. In later years he discovered that her sister was destroying Hilda's letters.

He also served in WWII in Military Police, 3rd Service Command from Aug. 11, 1942 to Jan. 19, 1944. He is a member of the Veterans of WWI and the American Legion.

He is one of seven children and six are deceased.

ORVAL S. BOWER, 1816 Gourley St., Boise, ID 83705. Born March 25, 1901 in Lynn Creek, MO. He joined the service June 30, 1918 and was discharged July 30, 1919.

He was a member of the Marine Corps, 4th Regt. He was located in Parris Island, SC, the Dominican Republic and Washington, DC. on a hospital ship called *Solate*.

He received the Expert Rifleman Award and the Good Conduct Award.

EMERSON W. BOYCE, born Dec. 13, 1892 and died on April 3, 1980. He married Iva Purkey on March 24, 1920. They are the parents of 10 children; Gladys Boyce McVicker, Rebecca Boyce Bavely, Olive Boyce Balliger, Ida Boyce Mayer, Albert Boyce, Betty Boyce Boylen, Martha Delores Boyce, Patricia Boyce Moats, Robert Boyce and JoAnn Boyce Tucker.

He enlisted on Mar. 15, 1918 at Grafton, WV. When he enlisted he was 25 years old and was an electric welder. He was honorably discharged on Dec. 28, 1918, at Camp A.A. Humphreys, VA.

He retired from the B & O Railroad with 50 years of service. He is buried in Wesley Chapel Cemetery in Grafton, WV.

ALFRED ROSS BOYD, 445 S. 7th St., Hebron, NE, 68370. He was born on June 29, 1890 in Reynolds, NE. He joined the service on Aug. 9, 1917 at Fort Logan, CO, and was discharged Jan. 24, 1918.

While serving he achieved the ranking of Corporal of the 476 Aero-squadron of the regular Army. He was an overseas chauffeur and his most memorable experience was being overseas with the American Co. 27115. He was entitled to wear the WWI Chevron.

JAMES W. BRADLEY, was inducted into the Army on July 22, 1918 in Meade Co., Sturgis, SD. He reported to Camp Dodge, IA as Pvt. 1st Class with the Casual Dd. 104 Demobl. Group. They left the U.S. on Oct. 22, 1918 and returned on July 2, 1919.

While in France, he took care of the horses. Many of them returned in a shocked condition as well as wounded. They were very close to the front lines.

He was born in Ochedean, Oceola Co., IA. When he was very young the family moved to Omaha, NE. He was a newsboy on the streets of Omaha and when he was older worked as a hotel house man. In the spring of 1908, the family moved to Meade Co. where they farmed and raised cattle.

He married Julia Higgins in November 1934 and they had six children. He moved to Sturgis, SD in May 1946, where he was employed at the Ft. Meade Veterans Hospital. He started as a mess attendant moved to a elevator operator, ward attendant and then a nursing asst. He retired with disability on May 3, 1960.

When he was 71, he had a severe stroke. He lived for seven years and the last three years he was cared for at the Veterans Hospital in Ft. Meade. He died Feb. 28, 1978 at the age of 87.

FRED A. BRANDIS, from San Jose, CA enlisted in the U.S. Navy Radio Dept. at San Francisco, CA in December 1915 at the age of 18. He was stationed at Mare Island, CA. After graduating as 2nd Rate Wireless Radio Operator, he joined his ship,, the *USS St. Louis*, at Bremerton, WA, on July 10, 1916. He sailed from there to Honolulu where nine months were spent in cruising among the islands and in various kinds of war maneuvers. The ship was ordered to San Diego, CA in April 1917.

On this cruise he picked up a distress signal coming from a fellow vessel which had gone aground on an island off of the Mexican coast. The *USS St. Louis*, with another ship assisted in the rescue. Early in June, when the *USS St. Louis* was about to go through the Panama Canal, he was transferred to Darien Gatun Lake radio station which was 50 miles from Balboa.

On Jan. 1, 1918, as chief electrician, he was sent to Punta Mala, Panama, to install and be in charge of all the receiving instruments in the large station. He and his six-man Navy personnel team survived the remote jungle headquarters in style. Panamanian natives kept them in fresh fruits and vegetables. He and his men hunted for fresh meat. Once, he and two of his buddies, armed with rifles stalked a wild boar and shot one. Suddenly out of nowhere 20 boars rushed to surround them. Dropping the rifles, the men scrambled to safety up a tree, but only to find dangling just above their heads was a huge boa constrictor. They could jump from the tree to the waiting boars or they could sit with the snake. He didn't want to do either one. The snake met the skill of his knife.

For a while fish became their primary meat source. He utilized the outpost's 40 ft. boat for fishing. The motor-sailor, as it was called, met the Navy's supply ship from Panama once a month. Mail was taken by horseback from Panama to a small jungle town eight wilderness miles away. Tired of walking, he bargained for a native's small horse and he rode it bareback on the trail. Mail was important to Brandis, for there was always a letter waiting from his high school sweetheart, Mildred.

Brandis was out on his horse collecting orchid plants when a huge black snake slithered between the horse's hooves. The horse reared and crashed through dense vegetation. He hung onto the mane and managed the wild ride, besides finding another unique orchid plant for his collection. He hung plants around the barracks where the blooms fascinated him and orchid growing became a lifelong hobby.

At Punta Mala, maintaining the three tall antenna towers was a challenge, he wouldn't allow his crew to do anything that he couldn't do so he devised a boatswain seat. After scrambling up the 200 ft. tower and entering the six ft. space, he swung out to the seat and then lowered himself down the guy wire protecting it from the salt air with a coating of grease. This feat then was repeated by the other men.

He took many photos of his jungle home and of the Panama Canal. In the humid environment, film processing was difficult resulting in streaks on many of the prints. Photography has remained another hobby of his.

Upon his discharge from the Navy in December 1919, Brandis continued to work for the government in a civil service capacity. He worked out of Mare Island, inspecting the radio apparatus of any and all ships utilizing the port and returning to sea duty. In 1920, he married his high school sweetheart, Mildred, and settled in Berkeley, CA.

He installed a ham amateur radio station in the couple's home. Using his station, he participated in the famous Admiral Byrd Antarctica Expedition, relaying messages from the Antarctic to key points in the United States.

He quit his civil job and along with a few former shipmates, opened a radio store which later lead him to an executive position with a large furniture company in Oakland, CA. He retired from the firm in 1965 and moved to Sacramento, CA with Mildred to be near their only daughter.

Recently, he at the age of 93 became a crusader for the WWI Veterans Eagle statue and monument to have it restored and relocated in California. The American Legion and public officials are now working on this project.

At 95, he resides at the Carmichael Convalescent Hospital in Carmichael, CA. His wife of 72 years visits him everyday. He can't walk but can talk about his Navy days in the Panama jungle and about his many trips and hobbies.

DAVE W. BRIGHT, was born Oct. 2, 1895 at Duluth, MN. He served in the U.S. Army in WWI and saw action in France.

In 1920, he moved to Montana where he became associated with Pacific Hide and Fur Co. in Great Falls, Butte and Browning. He established the branch office for that company in Kalispell in 1946 where he was manager at the time of his death.

He was married to Nellie E. Archibald, Aug. 29, 1945, and she survives him at the family home. He is also survived by one son, Bruce David Bright of St. Louis, MO, a step-son, Harold R. Archibald and a step-daughter, Teresa L. Cooke.

He was a member of the Elks Lodge of Kalispell and the American Legion and VFW. He died Nov. 17, 1969, in Kalispell.

CLARE E. BRIGHTHAUPT, born Aug. 3, 1892 in Sugarloaf, PA. Joined the service on May 27, 1918 with the 60 Co., 15 Bn, 155 Dep Brig. until June 20, 1918. He was discharged on June 6, 1919, as COE 131st Infantry.

He was stationed in Meuse Argonne, Bois Detorges and defense of Verdun Sector. He received the Purple Heart award.

His first wife was Letha Spaide Brighthaupt who died in 1952. His 2nd wife was Mae Singley Brighthaupt. He died on Aug. 25, 1973. At the time he entered the service he was a gardener and carpenter. Later, in civilian life he owned and operated a country store and U.S. Post Office in the small town of Sybertsville, PA. His hobbies were hunting and fishing.

EDGAR JOHN BROCK, 4101 9 Mile Rd., Masonic Home, Richmond, VA 23223. Born May 14, 1896 in South Hampton Co., VA. He enlisted on Feb. 8, 1917 and joined the VA Militia. On March 23 he went to Newport News for guard duty and then transferred to Anniston, AL and Hampstead, NJ. He later shipped from Philadelphia to England.

He served as Pvt. 1st Class in NE France and as an MP on troop trains. He was not in combat. He had an honorable discharge on June 2, 1919 at Ft. Meade, VA.

After the discharge he was an engineer at Power Station in New Port News, VA and later farmed. He joined the Masonic Order in 1944. He lost his vision during cataract surgery in 1979.

BERT BROUILLIER, born Sept. 15, 1889. Passed away March 2, 1969. His wife was Helen Dorothy.

He was a member of the K. Co. 125th Inf., 32nd Div. in France from May 11, 1918 to May 1919.

ORVAL S. BROWER, 2220 El Rancho Circle, Hemet, CA 92545-1607. He was born March 14, 1895 in Sedgwick, KS. He joined the service on June 5, 1917 and was discharged on June 14, 1919.

He was a member of the 1st Regt. Band, U.S. Marine Corps. He achieved the ranking of Corporal-Technical. He saw no combat. He was located in Philadelphia and New York. He played the baritone horn in bond drives to support the war. Near the end of the war the band was sent to Quantanamo Bay, Cuba.

He achieved the Expert Rifleman Award four times before being advanced to Corporal.

He has one daughter, Betty Jane Larson, two grandsons, Richard L. and Paul Ray, as well as four great grandchildren, Amy, Kristi, Amanda Marie and Christian. He is now living in a nursing home. In October 1983, a car pulled out of side road and plowed into him. He was taken to a Riverside Hospital. He had a fractured left hip. In March 1986, while putting down new carpeting, he accidentally backed up into the rug stretcher, and fractured his right hip. He again was hospitalized. He walked many years with a walker and cane. He had a slight stroke that affected his speech. In January 1990 he became more helpless in his walking. Since February 1990, he has lived in the nursing home. He is very strong for a man almost 97 years old, from his waist up, but the two legs just do not work anymore.

HOMER S. BROWN, when 19 years of age, went to Davenport, NE where he enlisted as a Pvt. in the WWI U.S. Army. He was indoctrinated at Ft. Logan, CO on June 1, 1918 and was there about three days, then was moved to Camp Jackson, SC and was in training there for 30 days. He later sailed from New York to Liverpool on July 1, 1918 with Btry. F, 6th Field Artillery, 1st Div. to Germany and France.

His duties were on Liaison detail, carrying messages from post camp to post camp on the front line in France. He was wounded with shrapnel and onion and mustard gas while there. He was in the front line hospital for three weeks, which was later bombed and all records destroyed on Oct. 30, 1918. He fought in all of the major battles in France and Germany including, St. Miehel, Ansarville and Meuse Argonne.

He was in Mesves, France Hospital Center and left there on Jan. 26, 1919. He marched to Cannes, France and was placed in Co. G and later in Co. F. He slept in a hayloft in a barn.

On Jan. 31, 1919, some snow fell and drilled one to two hours some days through March 16, 1919. He then left Cannes for La Sous on a train about 4 pm on 48 cars for Brest, France. At Brest, France went to Camp P for inspection of equipment through March 24, 1919. Left Camp Brest about 10 am on March 25, 1919. Loaded on the *Leviathan* the afternoon of March 25, 1919. He was bound for Hoboken. The seas were rough and they passed ships every day, then on April 2, 1919 he landed at Hoboken. He went to Camp Upton on Long Island.

At Camp Upton, Long Island the food was good and stayed waiting for train transportation. He was discharged April 21,1919 at Camp Dodge, near Des Moines at 11 pm.

After discharge he went to Norfolk, NE and went to work for the C&NW Fireman until Nov. 10, 1919.

LEROY H. BROWN, was born in Wayland, NY on June 5, 1896. He enlisted in the National Guard in Rochester, NY in 1917. His Co. H, 108th Inf., 27th Div. had their basic training at Camp Wadsworth, SC.

He went overseas from Newport News, VA and landed in Brest, France. His outfit hiked all the way to Belgium, where they held the country against the Germans. The fighting was all trench warfare and artillery.

While in France, he went to Officers Training School and got his 2nd Lt. Commission while stationed there. He also was appointed a town major when the Armistice was signed.

He stayed overseas in Belgium to entertain the troops with a show troop called the Gloom Killers, until he returned to the United States in 1919.

He was married in Buffalo, NY in 1919, where he and his wife remained and raised a son and daughter. He was employed in the laundry business. Upon retirement at age 70, they moved to Florida. He is now 96 years old and is a resident of the VA Nursing Home in Gainesville, FL.

HENRY J. BRZEZNIAK, 515 Monroe, Apt. 901, South Bend, IN 46601. He was born on Dec. 27, 1989 in Manistied, MI.

He joined the service on May 7, 1977 and was discharged on July 19, 1919. He was on the ship the *USS Montana* as a Seaman 2nd Class.

He has retired.

DAVID WILLIAM BUNDRICK, 928 E. Bear Creek Rd, DeSoto, TX 25115. Born on July 27, 1891 in Troupe, TX. He joined the service in 1918 and was discharged in 1919. He was a member of the U.S. Army Supply Co. 332 and achieved the ranking of Pvt. 1st Class

He made rope for tying down Army equipment on railroad cars in Dijon, France. Sailed from St. Nazaire, France on June 14, 1919. Was barracked in Newport News, VA.

He married Odette Cowart in 1920 in Dallas, TX. Has son, David, and daughter, Mary. He has five grandchildren and eight great grandchildren. His wife passed away in 1984. He lived in his home place until April 1991. He then moved in with his son and family. He loved TV, music, flowers and visiting with family. He exercised by doing yard work. Flowers were a part of his life until a heat stroke at age 95 slowed him down. He passed away on March 17, 1992.

FRANK BURNS, was born Oct. 1, 1899 in Columbus, OH. He joined the service and participated in WWI. He was discharged in 1945.

He retired from civil service in 1963. He was in the Navy and achieved the rank of chief petty officer. He was stationed in the South Pacific.

Burns memorable experiences include meeting his only son, a Seabee, in the South Pacific. *Submitted by his daughter F.M. Wagener*

JOE E. BURNS, 2809510, proudly followed a Burns family tradition by volunteering for military service in McKinney, Collin County, TX, on April 28, 1918. The unmarried, 23-year old Joe Burns was a Pvt. in the 359th Inf. of the United States, Co. H. His grandfather, William W. Burns, also volunteered in McKinney for service in Co. H at the beginning of the Civil War. Co. H, a Cavalry unity, dismounted in 1863 during the early years of the Civil War. William's grandfather, John Burns, fought in the Revolutionary War at Guilford County Courthouse in North Carolina. The family motto is, Where there is a war, there is a Burns to volunteer!

He went to New York City with the other soldiers in his company where he boarded a ship for France. He fought in WWI in Gen. John J. Pershing's European Theater during the most fervent battles of the war with no time off from Aug. 24 to Nov. 11, 1918. He was engaged in the following battles: Villers en Hay Sector from Aug. 24 to Sept. 11, 1918; Saint Michiel from Sept. 12-16, 1918; Venelli Sector from Sept. 17 to Oct. 10, 1918; and Meuse Argoune Forest from Oct. 22 until he was injured by mustard gas on Nov. 11, 1918.

During the intense fighting in the Argoune Forest, the men in his company fought so fiercely that many were caught off-guard by the sudden attack of mustard gas. He was one of the men not wearing a mask. He fell to the forest floor overcome by the severe burning pain in his chest. He lay there dying. A soldier quickly put his mask on him, threw him over his shoulder, and carried him to safety. If it had not been for the quick acting soldier, by the name of Kellow, he would have died there in France.

Pvt. Burns spent some time in the hospital suffering from the damaging effects of the mustard gas before being sent back to the United States at the end of the war. He was honorably discharged from service at Camp Bowie, TX, on June 24, 1919. He received a pension for his service connected disability throughout his lifetime. His discharge papers were signed by Col. E.K. Sterling, 359 Inf. The papers show he was of excellent character, never AWOL, never absent, a farmer by occupation, blue eyes, red hair and ruddy complexion and 5 ft. 8 in. in height.

On Dec. 17, 1921, he married Vergie Glendi Stibbens in Parker, Collin Co., TX, in the home of her parents, William T. and Bertha Drain Stibbens. He and his wife's first daughter, Geneva Lois, was born on March 5, 1924, in Allen, TX. She married Pvt. Dwight L. Smith, U.S. Army, in Tyler, TX, on Feb. 12, 1944, just a few days prior to his being

shipped to Europe during WWII. Geneva and Dwight are the parents of Dwight Craig and Joe Gary. Craig, born in McKinney on Dec. 5, 1944, followed the family tradition and volunteered for the U.S. Air Force and served in Vietnam. He married twice and is the father of Michelle, Bryan and Kevin. Michelle is married to Robert Spencer, U.S. Navy. They are stationed in San Diego. Joe Gary, born in Dallas on July 26, 1948, has not been in the military. He and his wife, Linda, are the parents of Joanna and Megan.

Joe and Vergie's second daughter, Brenda Joan, was born in McKinney on Nov. 7, 1940. Brenda is an author, historian and genealogist. She and Robert Strong Kellow married in Dallas on March 3, 1961. Robert's father, James Campbell Kellow Sr., served in the U.S. Navy during WWI. Brenda and Bob's first daughter, Monique Renee, was born in McKinney on March 13, 1963. She married Marc A. Quattromani in Dallas on April 21, 1990. Marc's father, Anthony Quattromani, retired from the U.S. Army in 1984. Bob and Brenda's second daughter, Veronique Elizabeth, was born in McKinney on March 15, 1965. Elizabeth is an attorney at law in Dallas.

Joe E. Burns died in Plano, Collin County, TX, on April 29, 1977 at age 84. He is buried in the Plano Mutual Cemetery. His grave, marked with a bronze marker, notes his service as a veteran of WWI. Vergie, age 84, is alive and lives in Plano.

WALTER RALEIGH BUTTERTON, was born Sept. 9, 1898 in Merry Hill, NC. His parents were James Thomas and Lena Taylor Butterton.

He enlisted in the U.S. Army on October 29, 1915. at Ft. Slocum, NY. He then was sent to Camp Harry J. Jones, in Douglas, AZ. He later attended U.S. Horse Cavalry School at Ft. Bliss, TX to become Horseshoer 1st Class. During this period he participated in the Mexican Border Campaign against the notorious Pancho Villa. He was assigned to Btry. A, 10th Field Artillery of the famed 3rd (Rock of the Marne) Div., he sailed from Hoboken, NJ on April 23, 1918, landing in Bordeaux, France on May 7. Following artillery training at Camp Coetquedon, his unit was dispatched on a three-day march to Chateau-Thierry on the Marne River to immediately engage the Germans. Later, he participated in the Aisne-Marne Offensive, St. Mihiel Offensive and the Muese-Argonne Offensive. He received five campaign medals.

Serving in the Army of Occupation, and stationed in Kruft (near Koblenz), Germany from Dec. 17, 1918 until Sept. 21, 1919. He sailed from Brest, France on Sept. 27 aboard the *SS Prinz Freiderich Wilhelm,* arriving in Hoboken, NJ on Oct. 4. He was discharged at Camp Pike, Little Rock, AR on Nov. 6, 1919.

He was married to Nellie Gray Lawrence on May 18, 1921. They raised two sons and two daughters. Retiring from the Atlantic Coast Line Railroad as Capt. of Police on Sept. 1, 1963, after 36 years. He continued in WWI veteran affairs. He died at age 92 in Jacksonville, FL on May 28, 1991. An older soldier who served his country well.

W.C. BYNUM, 1413 W. Main St., Waxahachie, TX 75165. Born Dec. 9, 1893 in Ellis County, TX. Joined the service on Sept. 15, 1917 and was discharged on June 24, 1919. He was a member of the Army Co. D, 359th Inf., 90th Div. He achieved the ranking of Sgt.

He was located at Camp Travis and participated in the battles of St. Michael and the Meuse Argonne. His most memorable experience was being in action on the front line at Waen Armistice on Nov. 11, 1918. He was awarded to Victory Medals and the Silver Star Medal.

He has two daughters. He worked in a post office from 1916-1961. Today he is in a rest home in Waxahachie, TX.

JOSEPH T. BYRNE, was born in Dubuque County, IA on June 30, 1892. He spent his entire life as a farmer in Vernon Township, Dubuque County, IA. His parents were Eugene Byrne and Mary Ann Lynch. He married Marcella B. Maloy of Bernard, IA. They had 2 children, Roger Byrne and Grace Byrne Mark.

He was drafted into the U.S. Army on Oct. 31, 1917. He was an only son and was much needed by his father to help with the farm work, but his

number was drawn, and he went to service feeling this was his duty. He served in France, and fortunately returned home with no injuries. All his life he was extremely proud of the fact that he had been in the service. His wife, Marcella, kept his khaki uniform and woolen dress uniform in perfect condition for years and years. She cherished them and told her children how proud she was of their wonderful father. Marcella used to sing songs such as Over There, My Buddy and Pack Up Your Troubles as she washed the dishes. That spirit of love and pride is alive in Joe and Marcella's children today.

He passed away in Dubuque, IA on Oct. 25, 1959.

COLOMBO M. CALEFFIE, born Aug. 15, 1892 in Belle Vernon, PA. Served in WWI with the American Expeditionary Force, in the 87th Div., 347th Inf., Co. 61, 16 Bn., 153 D.B. He played in the Army band.

After basic training, he was sent overseas, embarking from New York on a British cattle boat called *The Star of Calcutta,* a barely seaworthy ship. The ship became grounded on a sand bar for three days, off of Coney Island, NY, and they missed their convoy. The next convoy had a very dangerous crossing due to storms and floating ice bergs. They landed safely in Southampton, England and then on to Le Havre, France.

When peace came, they went home in style on the *USS Mauretania.* He was honorably discharged at Camp Dix, NJ in April 1919. He then became a U.S. Civil Service worker and then retired.

OTTO CARD, Idaho St. Vet. Home, 320 Collins Rd., Boise, ID 83707. Born on Feb. 18, 1900 in Austin, PA.

He joined the Army on July 3, 1918. He achieved the ranking of Corporal before being discharged on Dec. 8, 1918. He entered in Pennsylvania and was discharged in Alabama.

He worked as a farmer, restaurant business and as an aircraft mechanic. His wife, Ruth, still lives in Parma, ID. He now lives at the Idaho St.

Vet. Home and attends WWI meetings with the Sawtooth Barracks #217.

CARL CHESTER CARLSON, 5719 Hwy. Place, Apt. 14, Everett, WA. Born Aug. 4, 1891 in Elgin, WA.

He joined the Navy on Jan. 18, 1918. He achieved the ranking of Quartermaster 2nd Class before being discharged on Feb. 6, 1919.

JOHN F. CARLUCCI, one of the Italian U.S. born. Joined the U.S. Army during WWI, and mustered on Dec. 12, 1917 at Ft. Slocum, NY.

Before the end of this month, a group of soldiers were transmitted to Kelly Field, San Antonio, TX. The coaches of the train they rode on, must have been of the primitive cars manufactured. They didn't have much to eat on this journey, so arriving at Kelly Field, he was hungry as a dog.

After their arrival, an Army officer asked if anyone would like to be a cook. He then thought this was a good opportunity for an empty stomach. He immediately raised his hand for this choice of being a cook. Whether he had any experience or not in cooking, he soon had schooling in Army cooking. This ended with a diploma. From that moment on he had no more problems with hunger. Being a cook in the Army was a wonderful circumstance. He enjoyed a King's life because of the freedom he enjoyed with the issuing of a permanent pass card, which enabled them to go out of camp without reporting.

In France, he had one day on and one day off. The day off, he could rise from his bunk any time he wished. However, when on duty, he had to work from 4 am to about 7 pm. In France, he was in the 656 Aero-Squadron.

On his conduct report from the discharge certificate, he was rated excellent. During his last flight, he received a certificate from American Airlines.

JOHN A. CHAMBEY, was born to Rowland and Margaret Chambey on Sept. 12, 1893 near Egan. He lived on a farm when he was young. His father was a veterinarian at Coleman. He went to veterinary school and was drafted from Chicago.

He joined the service in Oct. 18, 1917. He was a Pvt. in the Medical Corp. He was in a camp in Chicago when the war was over.

He married Marjorie Luby and had one child who died when she was 11. His wife died and he remarried Anna May Miller in 1942. He worked as a veterinarian in Artesian, SD. In the 30's he worked for the Burer of Animal Ind. He came to Rapid City in 1953 and in 1954 he worked in Sturgis, at the Sales Ring. He built the Sturgis Vet. Hospital.

He died on Mar. 18, 1987 and is buried at the Black Hills National Cemetery.

FRED CHRISTIANSEN, was born Feb. 13, 1897 in Mauston, WI. At the age of 20 he worked for a bank in Wisconsin for one year.

Fred joined the army during WWI conflict. He was stationed in Camp McArthur, Waco, TX. Because of his clerical ability, he did office work there. He was honorably discharged with a ranking of Sergeant Major. He had a twin brother, Frank, who saw action in France for two years.

After his discharge, he worked in a Wisconsin bank for two years. He moved to Rapid City, SD, and worked nine months for Allen Abstract Co.. A friend, Harold Walker, had purchased the Bear Butte Valley Bank from a Chicago syndicate. He moved to Sturgis and worked for Walker in banking for 35 years.

He was married twice and had no children. He is now a resident of Sturgis Community Health Care Center in South Dakota.

JAMES W. CLAYTON, 2492206, 6703 Elm Court, Tampa, FL 33610. Parents were H.M. Clayton and Mary Clayton. Born March 12, 1892, in Jackson, TN.

He joined the service on Dec. 14, 1917, in Jacksonville, FL. He left the United States with the AEF on May 10, 1918. He landed at New Port News, VA on July 4, 1919. He was discharged on July 13, 1919 at Camp Gordon, GA. He achieved the ranking of Pvt. with the 29 Co., 20th Engineers. He trained at Ft. Scriven, GA. He sailed from New York in April 1917, and landed in Brest, France. The convoy had 16 ships and about 50,000 on board.

He belongs to the WWI Barracks 17 and the American Legion. He retired.

HARRY G. COATES, 985 Canyon Rd., Ogden, UT 84404. Born April 16, 1897 in Holosborough, Manchester, England. He joined the Troop L, 11th Cav. on March 22, 1918. He achieved the ranking of Pvt. before being discharged on June 29, 1919.

He served with the Mexican Campaign. He was sharing guard duty at a bridge with another sentry. In an attempt to prevent a group of Mexicans from crossing the bridge to the United States side, the other sentry shot a Mexican, killing him. The rest of the group became very angry and threatened violence. The sentry asked him to take over while he went for help. He managed to keep control until back-up arrived.

In another incident, the mounted cavalry rode single file up a narrow mountain path for the benefit of movie cameras. The film being made was "The Border Wireless" and the star was Bill Hart.

He was raised an orphan after the death of his father in 1901. He married Gertrude Miller in 1923. She died in 1940 leaving four children. He married Barbara Bunn in 1949. They had four sons, the youngest born when he was 61 years old. The youngest grandchild is six.

ALBION B. COLLINS,

of the 26th Yankee Div. was the first full division that landed in France under Gen. Edwards. They were engaged in five defensive sectors, Soissons, Champagne, Marne, Aisne Marne, St. Mihiel and Meuse Argonne. The 26th Div. relieved the 1st U.S. Div. and the 42nd Div. The 26th Div. was awarded the Victory Medal.

He enlisted in Co. B, National Guard at Fitchburg, MA on March 4, 1917. He was soon federalized and stationed at South Boston Curnard Docks, where he did guard duty. Then shipped to Camp Devens, Ayer, MA for training. Then transferred to Hartford, CT being assigned to the Supply Co., 102nd Inf., 26th Div.

In September 1917, he was stationed at Newport, VA and assigned as a wagner, called Mule Skinner. On setting out for France with the convoy, a very devastating thing happened. The ship's rudder broke and they were steered by hand pulley at the stern of the ship under the direction of the pilot by members of the crew. All the way to France for 15 days.

An odd experience happened, he was going in the Chateau Theey Front by night. In putting his mules harness beside a tall tree, he met an old schoolmate, Jimmie Marloe, who was coming out from the front lines, who belonged to the U.S. 1st Inf.

After being deloused twice for cooties, they sailed from Bordeaux and arrived at Boston Harbor in April 1919. He was discharged April 29, 1919. He lives in Florida.

JOSEPH CONN,

was born Feb. 2, 1893, in Pleasantville, IA. His parents were Richard and Jemima Conn. He was educated in Iowa and in 1906 moved to the Flathead Valley, where he worked at sawmills and in the woods.

He entered the Army on June 24, 1918, and served in Co. K, 105th Inf., until his honorable discharge on April 3, 1919, at Ft. D.A. Russell, WY.

He returned to Flathead where he did sawmill work and then farmed north of the airport for 17 years. He also was employed with the Montana Highway Dept. in the weighing div. and as a truck driver, until he retired in February 1958.

He married Marian Jeanette Bliss in Spokane on April 28, 1923. She died on March 14, 1972 in Mesa, AZ. On June 8, 1973, he married Neva J. Lyons in Coeur d'Alene. She died on March 23, 1980.

He was a member of the Central Bible Church, WWI Barracks, American Legion and a member of the Odd Fellows for more than 65 years.

JOSEPH T. CONNOLLY,

Dubuque Co., IA 52001. Born Feb. 25, 1894 at Melleray, IA. Joined the Co. D, 326th Inf. on Feb. 22, 1918. He achieved the ranking of Corporal before he was discharged on Nov. 30, 1918.

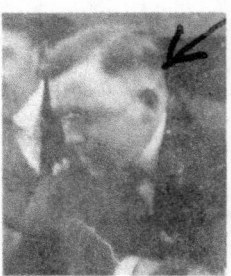

He was located at A.E.F., St. Mihiel, and fought in the Meuse Argonne Offensive, Teul Sector. He received medals and badges.

He was married. He passed away on Nov. 28, 1968.

VINCENT J. CONNOLLY,

was born July 26, 1895 in New Melleroy, IA. He joined the B 313, Sup. Tr. and Co. A, 327th Inf. on Feb. 22, 1918. He was discharged on March 10, 1919. He was in the Toul Sector, Fr. Marback Sector, St. Mihiel and Meuse Argonne battles.

He was wounded in action by gas on Oct. 9,

1918. He received medals. He passed away on Sept. 24, 1970.

JAMES W. CONRAD,

JAMES W. CONRAD, 466582, was born on July 7, 1898 in Heilwood, PA. He joined the Casual Detachment 116, 163rd Depot Brigade on March 8, 1918 in Jefferson Barracks, MO. He was also a member of Co. D, 417 Tel. Bn. He was discharged on March 19, 1919 at Camp Dodge, IA.

He participated in the Meuse Argonne Offensive from Nov. 1-11, 1918. He was also located on the Mexican Border. He sailed from the United States on Aug. 13, 1918 and arrived at port on his return to the United States on March 5, 1919.

He was married to Velma Dungan and they had four children, James Jr., Barbara, Patricia and Robert. He passed away on Sept. 16, 1966 and is buried at Wood National Cemetery.

In the 1920s, he worked as an electrician. In the late 20s and 30s he was on stage with the Oklahoma Cowboys, as a guitar player. In 1933, he was with the Bobwhite Melody Millers of Kingfisher, OK. He had his own radio programs in Oklahoma City, Ada and Enid, OK. In the late 30s, he returned to electrical work in Louisiana, Ohio and Wisconsin.

He had two brothers in WWI named, Pious Agustus Conrad, born November 1889 in Pennsylvania and died Aug. 9, 1969. Patrick Gabriel Conrad, born February 1895 in Pennsylvania. At one time the three brothers did meet in Germany.

CHARLES R. COSBY, 2874 Green Trail Dr., College Park, GA 30349. Born Jan. 4, 1900 in Washington, GA. Joined the Quartermaster Corp.

on May 1, 1918. He achieved the ranking of Sgt. before being discharged on June 14, 1919.

He was stationed at Camp Johnston, FL and Camp Humphrey, VA.

He married on Oct. 13, 1945 and had three children, two daughters and a son. His son served in Vietnam for 15 months. He has retired from Southern Railway. He is a member of Barracks 948, Atlanta WWI Veteran's Org. of which he is Quartermaster as well as State QM. Also member of Retreads, which is a WWI and WWII Org. Though they no longer hold meetings, they have 3 living members, and as State Commander, he represents Retreads in Memorial Day Services at National Cemetery, Marietta, GA. Also represents Retreads in Veterans Day Parade in Atlanta on Nov. 11.

To commemorate the United States entry into WWI on April 6, 1917, he helps organize and attends the services at Pershing Point Park, Atlanta, GA each year. In 1992, they celebrated 75 years.

DR. THEODORE SMITH CROSBY, entered the U.S. Army on June 26, 1917 at Wakefield, MI as a 1st Lt., Medical Corps. Assigned to Romania Expedition from Presido of San Francisco, CA. He was discharged from the service on Dec. 19, 1918 at Ft. Worth, Camp Bowie, TX as a Capt. of the Medical Corps.

He sailed for Jassey, Romania on Dec. 5, 1917. He returned to San Francisco after the Russian Armistice. He served in the Army Reserve as a Major from 1919-1929.

He was born at Corry, PA on Oct. 24, 1877 and died at Milwaukee, WI on July 18, 1942. He married Stella Baskisky of Chicago, IL and had two sons, Alvin (named after Alvin York) and Archibald. He was loved greatly by his wife and children. His community held much respect for him. His service in a little known theater of the great war that is categorized as "Russian Service".

SYDNEY CULLEN, enlisted in the National Guard in September 1917. The National Guard was not allowed to leave the United States so, U.S. Army officers came and mustered them in.. By September 17, he was training in Oklahoma. It was cold, so when asked if he wanted to be a cook he took the job to stay warm.

In January 1918, he and the artillery battalion were assigned to move out. They had short stops in Hoboken, NJ and in Nova Scotia. After 11 days in passage across the Atlantic, the coast of England was seen by the troops. There the battalion was trained on French guns. He was involved in the battle for the Argonne Woods and the final major battle of the war, Verdun. His job was bringing food to the front lines. Mostly bread and hard tack, sometimes huge barrels of hot soup.

He left France for home in April 1919. He was a fireman in St. Louis for over 20 years, moved to Oregon in 1944 and was a fire chief at St. Johns for more than 10 years. He then moved to the country and dairy farmed. His second wife is Isabel, and they live at the Elms Residential Retirement Community.

SELMER DAHL, was born Sept. 7, 1895 in Lake Preston, SD. A son of Albert and Mauren Louise Gulbrunson Dahl. In 1906 he moved with his family to Gackle, ND, where he was raised and educated. He was a member of the first graduating class at the high school.

He enlisted in the U.S. Navy on June 28, 1918, and served as Pvt. 1st Class with the 339th Machine Gun Bn., 88th Div. He was honorably discharged June 11, 1919.

On May 17, 1921, he married Bertha K. Dufloth in Minneapolis, MN. They farmed in the Gackle, ND area until 1951, when they sold the farm and traveled throughout the western United States. In 1953, they moved to Kalispell.

He was a member of the American Legion, VFW and WWI Barracks of Kalispell. He was preceded in death by his wife, Bertha, on Feb. 27, 1979. He passed away on Apr. 10, 1985.

ELMER MORRIS DAHLGREN, was born to Scandinavian parents, Lars Ferdinand and Ellen Oleson Dahlgren, in Ludington, MI on Aug. 30, 1894.

He enlisted in the Navy because he loved the water and boats and wanted to serve his country. That was in 1917, and he served 27 months. He entered as an apprentice Seaman on a sub chaser and reached the rank of 1st Class Machinist Mate. Part of his tour of duty was served in Panama.

He married Mary Tidholm in June 1927, and they had one daughter, Betty. He worked for Standard Oil Co. in the Motor Transport Dept. for 34 years in Seattle, WA. He retired in 1959.

He is still active at 97 years of age, outliving two wives. He bowls and golfs and does his own housekeeping.

HUBERT W. DANHAUSEN, was born in Honolulu, HI on Nov. 10, 1895. Three years later, his parents brought their 12 children to California, settling in Sonoma County near Santa Rosa.

At the age of 22, he enlisted in theU.S. Army on Dec. 15, 1975, and served in the 9th Balloon Corp. until his discharge on May 21, 1919. While in France, his company participated in battles in the Meuse Argonne, Toul, and Verdun Sectors.

In 1924, he married and settled in Sonoma County, CA where he owned a chicken ranch, dairy ranch and later was a contractor specializing in building sanitary dairy barns. He and his wife recently celebrated their 68th wedding anniver-

sary. They raised two children, a son who served in WWII and a daughter. They now enjoy six grandchildren and six great-grandchildren.

HUGH DANIELS, born to Laland Daniels and Janette Stolp Daniels on March 1, 1896 in Juanita, WA. He joined the Army Inf., Co. B, 305th Inf., 77th Div. on June 23, 1918. He was discharged on May 23, 1919.

He was located at Camp Lewis and participated in the Battle of Meuse Argonne in France. He was a Pvt.

He married Dora Kager on June 19, 1918 and was the father of seven children, four boys and three girls. After leaving the service he worked as a logger until he retired. He serves as Commander of the Everett, WA Barracks of WWI Veterans. He is the last charter member of VFW 2554 of Sultan, WA. In his honor the post named their meeting hall the Hugh Daniels Hall.

He was married 73 years to Dora, who passed away on Sept. 2, 1991.

LESLIE ELMER DAVIES, McGregor, IA 52157. Born Aug. 6, 1895 in McGregor, IA. He joined the 347th Inf. on Sept. 18, 1917 and achieved the ranking of Corporal. He was discharged on Jan. 29, 1919.

He was located at Camp Dodge, IA and Camp

Dix, NJ. He was also stationed near France where he held the position of camp cook. He remembers making pancakes for 200 men and the long, cold marches. He was awarded the Sharp Shooter, Good Conduct Medal and the WWI Victory Ribbon.

He married a neighbor girl and former school teacher. He raised two sons and three daughters. He bought the home farm and farmed for many years.

CLARENCE VALENTINE DAVIS, "BUD", born on Feb. 14, 1895 in Marl City, OH. He joined the service on Feb. 2, 1917 and discharged on June 30, 1923. He served in the U.S. Navy on the *USS Utah, Albany, Permithius,* and *Sub Chaser.* He served in the Mexican Campaign with Poncho Villa and also Vladisvostock in Siberia.

He joined the Ohio National Guard in 1913, he was discharged out and mustered into the Navy. His most memorable experience was working on sub chasers which were the granddaddy of the WWII PT Boats. He was awarded the WWI Victory Medal.

His wife Alta Palen Davis and daughter Elinor D. Tallman are both deceased. His son John Ira Davis lives in Pennsylvania. He had 15 grandchildren and about 30 great-grandchildren. One brother and sister in Ohio. He passed away on March 5, 1966.

DAVID R. DAVIS, 556367, 5030 14th W., Box 26, Bradenton, FL 34207. Born on June 16, 1889 in Hardwick, MA.

He joined the Sup. Co., 39th Inf., 4th Div. in August 1917. He attained the rank of Master Sgt. before being discharged in August 1920. He received a medal with 4 bars.

His most memorable experience was a siege at the Meuse Argonne in August of 1919. He had a large shell come close, however it turned out to be a dud.

He retired at the age of 93.

ELEA J. DAVISON, Lutheran Sunset Home, Grafton, ND 58237. Born Dec. 26, 1895 in Cherry Creek, NY.

He was a member of the A307 Bn, Field Art.,

78th Div. He was located in Fort Dix, NJ and France.

DR. FRANKLIN THOMAS DENNY, was born March 8, 1895 in Jefferson County, IN. He was a member of the Army Medical Corp.

He was in the battles at Champagne-Marne, Aisne-Marne, St. Mihiel and the Meuse Argonne. He also served in the Rencsdorf Defensive Sector. He was gassed on the front lines with mustard gas while taking the wounded back. He received a Division Patch and a Campaign Ribbon.

He practiced medicine in Indiana for 50 years. He delivered 5,000 babies during his private practice. In WWII he went overseas. He died on Feb. 5, 1974.

JOSEPH DECKER, was drafted July 5, 1918. From Rhineland, Knox County, TX to Ft. Sam Houston, San Antonio, TX. He was then sent to Camp Bowie, TX. He was also stationed at Camp Cody, NM. He was discharged on Dec. 6, 1918 and arrived home on Dec. 8, 1918 as a corporal. He is still living at age 99.

His brothers Albert and Lawrence were drafted at the same time. Lawrence was, for a time, stationed in France.

BENJAMIN DEXTER, Answered the call for recruits in April 1917. At that time, he was working on the Stone Estate. This proud young man from Brockton enlisted with the U.S. Army and ended up in Georgia training with the 82nd Div.

"They landed at Liverpool, took the train to Southhampton and crossed the channel to LeHavre."

He remembers one scene while on his way to the front "... in the Argonne, after one ... battle, they were passing a field hospital. Well, there were possibly a thousand casualties of the battle from the night before... You could hear them moaning and groaning. It sounded almost like the surf of an ocean as in a storm. It had quite an unnerving effect. The mules laid back their ears as we walked by."

He was in St. Agnes at the time of the Armistice. They departed some months later, the troops departed LeHavre, France for the journey home. They landed in New York and were discharged from Camp Dix, NJ.

Dexter can still wear his uniform from the Great War, complete with helmet and leg wraps. He wears it while marching in parades on Veterans Day, Memorial Day and the 4th of July.

NATHAN MILES DILLMAN JR., was born on Nov. 14, 1898 in Standish, MI. He lived on a farm in Standish with his nine other brothers and sisters. He had to walk two miles to school.

When he was six years old, his father got a letter saying how good the country was in Washington. So his family sold their farm, and moved up to Elma, WA in 1905. He graduated from high school in 1917 towards the end of May.

On June 7, 1917, the United States declared war on Germany. On June 11, 1917, he enlisted in the Army hoping to learn how to fly. While in the Army, he went everywhere from San Antonio, TX where he slept on a cot in an open field at the beginning of the war, to Washington, DC. where he sent sightseeing with some friends. He sailed on a variety of ships ranging from his Majesty's ship, *The Baltic,* to a cattle ship. He has been many places outside the United States including, Liverpool, England, where he was attacked by an enemy submarine, to Leon, France, where box cars had posters on them saying they could carry eight horses or 40 men.

While in Leon, he was put to work training as a mechanic. There, his French instructor took a fancy to him and they started to spend time together talking. One evening, his friend and instructor took him into the city for a drink. While sitting at the bar, a cute French dame came up and spoke something to him in French. All he could do was smile, because he couldn't understand French. After the dame left, the instructor started laughing and told Nathan that she had asked him if he would sleep with her that night.

He also worked as a canteen clerk in the Army. He and his buddies used to take francs out of the till and go have a drink of cognac. He also gave away cartons of apples that belonged to the YMCA that he was supposed to watch. He didn't think it was right that the YMCA could sell apples that came in boxes saying "donated by the Yakima Fruit Growers Association to the boys down there."

On Nov. 11, 1918, he came back to the states, home from the war. He then went down to Tacoma to visit his sister. His brother-in-law, who worked as a conductor for the Northern Pacific Railroad, got him a job as a brake man on the railroad. On July 18, 1919 he went to work at the Union Station in Tacoma, but it took him 30 days before he could get a date to start getting paid by. On Sept. 30, 1966 he retired.

A joy in his life was meeting again, an American nurse in France while on a three day pass, who had waited on his brother John, back at Yelm before the war. He was married for 56 years to his first wife, who was appointed National Musician of the Ladies Auxiliary to the Veterans of WWI. He had two sons, Jim and Jack. He remarried again on Nov. 14, 1981 to the National President of the Ladies Auxiliary to the Veterans of WWI, Ora Rickert Afdem.

WILLIAM H. DILLON, born Dec. 15, 1889 in Watrous, New Mexico Territory. He joined the U.S. Navy on Sept. 28, 1917 in Omaha, NE. He achieved the ranking of Electrician Mate 1st Class, Radioman. He was discharged on May 19, 1920 at the Bush Terminal Dock, NY. He was stationed at Great Lakes, IL and served as an instructor in Radio Theory at Harvard Univ.

He served on the *USS Melville, USS Corsair,* USN Communication Office in Venice, Italy, Naval Port Office Trieste, *USS Olympia, USS Pittsburg* and the *USS Nereus.*

He married Sibbel K. Hall in Denver, on Dec. 15, 1922. He retired from the Denver & Rio Grande Railroad in 1955. Died April 2, 1982.

CARROLL T. DISNEY, 7676 Walnut St., Omaha, NE 68124-1717. Born on Feb. 25, 1899 in Laurel, MD. He joined the Army, Aviation Section of the Signal Corp., 71st. Co. on April 13, 1917. He achieved the ranking of Sgt. 1st Class before being discharged on March 14, 1919.

He served at Fort Omaha, NE and Richmond, VA. His memorable experience was that one of the balloons got away and they chased it across country to Nebraska City.

Following employment in the Navy Yard at the U.S. Naval Gun Factory in Washington, DC., he enlisted in the U.S. Army in Washington, DC. as a machinist on April 13, 1917 at the age of 18. From Washington they were sent to Ft. Slocum, NY for induction, after which they boarded a ship for transfer to Newport News, VA. From there they boarded a train through Kansas City on the way to Ft. Omaha, NE and the 71st Balloon Co. Detached. Most had joined the service to learn to fly, so imagine their surprise upon arrival at Ft. Omaha to discover that they were in the Balloon Corps of the U.S. Army. There were no airplanes.

One morning there was a notice on the bulletin board asking for motorcycle riders, and after one of the balloons got away, and we had to chase it across country, and since he had experience with motorcycles, he decided to apply and was eventually made an instructor. Part of his duties also included going to the post office every morning to pick up the mail. From Omaha, several of us were sent to Richmond, VA where a Balloon Depot was set up in an old warehouse. All of his service was in the United States, and he was honorably discharged on March 14, 1919.

He is married and has two daughters, six grandchildren and two great-grandchildren. He celebrated his 93rd birthday on Feb. 25, 1992.

JAMES S. DONAHUE, Zwingle, IA 52079. Born on Jan. 6, 1894 in Zwingle. He joined the 674th Casual Det. in Camp Dodge, IA on July 25, 1918.

He sailed from the United States on Sept. 1, 1918 and arrived at port on return to the United States on May 29, 1919. He served in the Inf. in France. He was discharged on June 8, 1919.

He was a farmer in Zwingle territory. Had four children, three girls and one boy. He married Margaret Laughlin on Sept. 28, 1921. He died on June 21, 1977.

JOHN PATRICK DORAN, was born on April 28, 1901 at Coon Rapids, IA. He enlisted in the U.S. Navy at age 19 in Missouri on Oct. 13, 1920. He was rated as Clerk HA 2C.

At the time of discharged he was a Hospital Attendant 2nd Class, at the Navy Hospital Corp. Training School in San Francisco, CA. By order of the Sect. of the Navy and Bunay Ict., N65-JPL-UTP-12066, on Jan. 18, 1921 and Bunay Tel., 6324-1530, Jan. 24, 1921.

John married Celestine Kovarik in June 1927. They had six children. They had a grocery store and post office, where he was Postmaster for 12 years. They moved to Sturgis in Meade Co., SD in 1939. In Nov. 18, 1940, he worked at Ft. Meade Veterans Hospital as chauffeur, mess attendant and store keeper. After leaving Ft. Mead, he opened a grocery store in Sturgis.

During this time he acted as City Councilman and following this was Register of Deeds for Meade Co. for six years. He died on Nov. 17, 1973.

ORLANDO A. DRAHEIM, 876 Easy St., Medford, OR. Born on Jan. 11, 1896 in Woodville, MN. He joined the service on July 23, 1918 and was discharged on July 30, 1919.

He was Pvt. 1st Class of the Cas. Det. 1157, Dem. Group, Co. F, 3rd Pioneer Inf.. He was stationed in the Argonne Forest and the Meuse in France from Sept. 26 - Nov. 16, 1918. His memories include a lack of food to eat on the lines and being cold and lonely.

He has a wife, Cleo, two sons, Wayne and Rodney, and two daughters, Blanche and Beatrice. He has a total of 35 grandchildren, great-grandchildren and great-great-grandchildren. He has retired from a service station that he owned. Until two years ago, he lived with his wife Cleo in their own home in Eureka, CA. They did all their own work and upkeep. Then he had several strokes that left his right side mostly paralyzed. His son, Wayne, moved them to Medford, OR and found a foster home where they could be together and be cared for. They have celebrated their 70th wedding anniversary and both are still of sound mind.

AUGUST CARL DREWS, born on May 17, 1896 in Oxford, NE. He was discharged from the 375th Balloon Co. on May 3, 1919.

He passed away and is survived by his wife Margaret Drew.

DANIEL WALDO DUFFY, was born Jan. 3, 1896 to Daniel Paris and Annie Liza Weir Duffy, he was reared on a farm.

He married Floy Mcherran on June 14, 1917 and was inducted into the service on Sept. 19,

1917. He was assigned to the 342nd Field Artillery at Camp Funston, KS. On October 15, he was transferred to the 164th Depot Brigade.

He was stationed at Camp Doniphan, Ft. Sill, OK and on May 9, 1918 he left Ft. Sill and arrived at Long Island, NY. His daughter was born that morning but he didn't find out until being overseas for three months when he received his mail. On May 19, 1918, he left for England aboard the U.S. *Justicia* arriving at Liverpool on May 31. He was at Seaforth Barracks quarantined for spinal meningitis. He was able to leave Seaforth on June 15, 1918 and sent to Knotty Ash Rest Camp.

From England he went to France. He was at the following locations: Fort Conetquidaux, Reuis, Lerran, Versailles, Paris, Theirfoord, Labresse to Kruth, Wasserfall in Alsace. He was also in the St. Mikiel sector and went into action at Verdun. He also moved up the front in the Meuse-Arzonne battle. Lined up to go to Metz when armistice was signed. Got ammunition to Harry Truman's battalion before he ran out.

Awards received: Victory Medal with Campaign Clasp. He was discharged on May 5, 1918 at Camp Funston, KS. He arrived home one week before his daughter's first birthday.

He farmed for four years and then became postmaster in South Greenfield, MO, a position he held for 39 years. After retirement, he raised cattle until glaucoma impaired his eyesight.

His wife of 64 years died in 1981 and he entered a nursing home three years later. He now lives in residential apartments and is in excellent health for his 96 years.

His son-in-law recently acquired his service medal for him. He has one daughter, one granddaughter, and one great grandson who is stationed at Ft. Hood, TX. *Submitted by Eileen Duffy Douglas (daughter).*

LLOYD T. DUNBAR, enlisted into the army Oct. 2, 1917 from Dupree, SD. He reported to Camp Funston, KS with the military police, Troop B, 314th and 89th Co. He was also company barber.

Lloyd fought in WWI from June 27, 1918 to March 27, 1919, overseas. He went overseas on the *USS Prince Friedrick Wilhelm* and served in France and Germany. He was in a battle at AEF St. Mihiel, on Sept. 12-16, 1918, and the Argonne Oct. 19- Nov. 11, 1918. He was wounded while riding horseback in Germany, when a mine exploded. He returned from overseas to Camp Dodge, IA and was honorably discharged on June 9, 1919.

He homesteaded south of Faith, SD in 1912, and after service in WWI he married Daina Higgins in 1921. They had three children, two daughters and one son. They lived on this ranch until 1940, when they moved to Dupree, SD. He served as County Treasurer, Auditor and County Veterans Off. for many years. He received a plaque for being the oldest and serving the longest in the United States as Veterans Service. Off.

He served as Dupree Mayor and Councilman, was named Citizen of the Year, was a member of the Masonic Lodge, Odd Fellows, American Legion, VFW and Sturgis WWI Barracks.

In 1976, he and his wife moved to Sturgis, SD and remained until his death, Sept. 24, 1977.

LELA DURHAM, Rt. 173, VA Hospital, Hampton, VA. Was born June 12, 1895 in Norfolk, VA.

She served in France from 1917-1918. She served as a nurse in both WWI and WWII. She was trained in a New York Hospital and Medical School.

She is married to Dr. John Dawson Durham. They have no children.

HAROLD O. EARLES, Rt. 1, Box 9, Hillsdale, IN 47854. Born Jan. 6, 1894 in Findlay, OH. He joined the 5th Field Arty., 1st Div. on May 4, 1917. He achieved the rank of Cpl. before being discharged on Sept. 27, 1919.

He participated in seven offenses. His most memorable experience was when full 1st. Div. was formed at Camp Pickney in France.

He had three sons and one was killed in action in Germany during WWII. He retired from the C & EI Railroad after 50 years of service. He was a signal maintainer. He is the last living WWI veteran in Vermillion County, IN.

JOHN ELBERT EARLY, 30887, was born May 19, 1892, in Loves Valley, OK, and died Sept. 5, 1982. He joined the service on Aug. 14, 1917 and was discharged on April 18, 1919.

He was in the Army's 640th Aero-Squadron, Air Service. He obtained the rank of Sgt. He was stationed in Issoudun, Indre and France. His most memorable experience was being an Aircraft Gunner. He received the Bronze Victory Button.

His widow is Catherine G. Early, and he had one daughter, Mary E. Dishner.

FREDERICK JOSEPH EGGER, is a vet-

eran of WWI and WWII. He was born in 1896. He married Oral Elizabeth Champion Race on Nov. 12, 1983 at Emmanuel Baptist Church in Penn Yan, NY.

FRANK A. EICKERT, was born June 22, 1888 in Chicago, IL. He was the son of William and Bertha Eickert. He was educated in Chicago and moved to Harlowton in 1907. From 1907 to 1912 he worked in the bridge and building div. of the Milwaukee Railroad. He worked until 1932 when he was injured on the job and was forced to retire.

He married Mildred M. Toombs on April 2, 1920 in Harlowton. The couple moved to Kalispell in September 1934. He farmed in Evergreen until 1950 and also built homes.

He was in the Army 147th Co. Trans..

He was a member of Trinity Lutheran Church and Barracks 362 of WWI Veterans. He had two sons, Bob and Richard, one sister, Mrs. Meta Ortgies, 12 grandchildren and seven great-grandchildren.

JOHN W. ELCO, 511 Chestnut Hill Apt., Washington, PA 15301, was born on July 1, 1899 in Manown, PA. He joined the service on May 14, 1917 and was discharged on June 1, 1951 in Mississippi.

He was a member of the 111th Inf., 28th Div., 19th Eng, 56th Cav. and also the 110th Inf., 28th Div. of which he was a Major. He served in France and the United States wherever he was needed. He served the people of the United States above and beyond the call of duty. He received a few medals and some ribbons. He received a letter of appreciation from the Sec. of Army.

He had a wife and four children, two boys and two girls.

CHARLES M. ENGEL, enlisted in Btry. A, 1st Mi. F.A.N.G., on June 15, 1915. He served on the Mexican Border, El Paso from 1916-17, WWI from July 15, 1918 to May 15, 1919, 32nd Div. (Red Arrow), Wisconsin and Michigan National Guard. in 199th FA.

He sailed from Hoboken on the H.M.S. *Olympic,* torpedoed off the Irish coast, missed by 20 ft. sub. Sank or chased off by subchasers and landing in Liverpool, crossed channel from South Hampton to La Harve and to Camp Coetqudon where they received their French 75s. Trained there and entered first defensive sector on June 11, then Alsase where they were the first American troops on enemy soil. Then to Chateau Thierry and drove the enemy back across the Marne. Next to the Soisson Offensive where they supported the French Foreign Legion and 1st Moroccan Div.

Next they hiked seven nights to the Argonne as they had only 827 horses left, barely enough to haul their equipment. First barrage started on September 26 and followed through to the last big barrage on November 4 that spelled the end of WWI.

Their 57th FA Brigade spent the longest time of any American FA Brigade in France, steady that is, for five months. Received eight French medals and landed in the United States on May 2, 1919.

He is 96 years old and spends summers in Michigan and winters in Florida, still drives back and forth.

Works for the veterans, is on his County Veterans Affairs Committee. Is life member of the VFW, WWI Veterans, past Department Commander of his VFW post, instrumental in organizing same. Also, a member of WWI Barracks, 32nd Veterans Assoc. and 119th FA Association, past president. He is also a member of the Detroit Red Arrow Club. His motto is "Wear out, don't rust out."

HERMAN ENGSTROM, was born Feb. 22, 1896, in Wilton, ND. His parents were one of the first families to homestead in Burleigh County in central North Dakota. He was one of ten children born to John and Christina Engstrom. The family spoke Swedish at at home and the children did not learn English until they went to school. He grew up and attended school in rural North Dakota. After that, he helped on the farm.

He served in WWI in France. In 1927, he married Agnes Thor, a neighbor girl he grew up with. They farmed until 1939, when they moved out west with their two daughters, Sylvia and Audrey. They stopped near Kalispell to visit and ended up making their home there. Agnes taught school for many years at Ashley Lake, Helena Flats and then at Evergreen until she retired. He worked for the State Forest Service for several years. He then was a sawyer for the American Timber Co. and later he worked at Lost Creek Saw Mill until his retirement.

He was a member of the Btry. D, 65th Art. from Dec. 19, 1917 until Jan. 21, 1919. He is a member of the WWI Veterans and the Bethlehem Lutheran Church.

LAMBERT N. ERPELDING, 921 E. Washington, Boise, ID 83702. Born Aug. 13, 1893 in Leonardville, KS. He joined the service on Aug. 7, 1918 and was discharged on Feb. 18, 1919.

He was a member of the Co. F, 62nd Inf. of which he was Corporal. He was stationed at Camp Fremont, CA and Long Island, NY. His memorable experience was awaiting transport to France to an overseas camp, until the armistice was signed.

His wife is deceased. He has one daughter in Boise, 11 great-grandchildren, five great-great-grandchildren and three grandchildren. He is still living in his own home, but is legally blind.

JAMES HOLBERT EVANS, born July 23, 1896, in Crimora, Augusta County, VA and died on July 1, 1988. He joined the Army A.E.F. in 1917, and achieved the ranking of Corporal before being discharged in 1919.

He was stationed in France, England and Belgium where he was wounded. His most memorable experience was the Doughboys were presented to the King and Queen at a reception at the palace in England. He also met one of his old friends on the battlefield. He achieved the France Campaign Medal, other VA state recognition's and city medals.

He and his wife, Bessie L. Evans, have been married 70 years. They have one daughter, Dolores E. Matze, who is a musician, a son-in-law, Wm. J. Matze, who served in the U.S. Navy during WWII and a grandson, Wm. J. Matze II, who is a member of the U.S. Marines. After 50 years at N & W Railroad, he retired.

CLARENCE EVENSON, was born Dec. 27, 1891, in Northwood, a son of Herman Gustav and Karine Evenson. He received his schooling in North Dakota and as a young man moved to the Flathead Valley.   In 1917, he was married to Mabel Lee in Kalispell.

On Aug. 14, 1918, he entered the U.S. Army in Kalispell and served until receiving his honorable discharge on Feb. 6, 1919, at Fort Logan, CO.

He then returned to Kalispell and was employed as an automotive mechanic for the Flathead Motor Sales for over 30 years. He was then employed as a meter maintenance man for the City of Kalispell for over ten years prior to his retirement.

He was a member of the Bethlehem Lutheran Church and the American Legion.

He and his wife had one son, Neal Evenson of Longview, WA, one daughter, Mrs. Howard (Phloris) Dixon, of Spokane, WA, five grandchildren, and one great-grandchild. His wife passed away on Jan. 31, 1971 and he passed away on Feb. 27, 1978.

ROBERT J. FAGERING, born Oct. 12, 1895 at Castlewood, SD. His mother, father and two brothers, came to settle. The family had moved from Christandsun, Norway in the late 1890s. They farmed in Castlewood until he was about nine years old. He and his Mother went back to Norway, when her father passed away.

His father went to work on a large farm or ranch in Whitewood Valley. He homesteaded on land about 11 miles out between Whitewood and Vale, SD. He and his mother came back from Norway and stayed with relatives in Pettibone, ND, until the home was built on the farm.

He finished his schooling in a small school about three miles from his home. He walked to school every day. Both of his brothers were in college in Augustana College at this time.

He left home and worked on ranches around the country. He liked working with horses, so he bought a small place near Edgemont, where he raised and broke horses.

He enlisted in the Army on March 18, 1918 as No. 2559530, and was stationed at Camp Dodge. He was a member of Co. C, Bat. 1 Development. He never got to go overseas, because he came down with either scarlet fever or typhoid fever on the ship over and was sent back. He was discharged from Camp Dodge on Jan. 15, 1919.

He came back to Edgemont, sold his ranch and went to work for a couple near Lincoln, NE, putting big electric lines throughout the country.

He came home at his father's death in 1927. He stayed with his mother until her death in 1928.

He married on Dec. 13, 1933 and stayed on the farm until 1936. They moved to Whitewood and worked putting in the water lines in Whitewood. He and his wife and two daughters lived in a home they had bought in Whitewood. In 1938, he went to work for the Chicago Northwestern Railroad. He continued his work there until his health failed and he had to retire in 1962, after 35 years.

He liked to garden, fish and hunt. He was active in the city, church, legion and WWI. He was a deputy sheriff of Lawrence County for several years and was on the police department in Whitewood.

He, his wife sold their home and moved to Sturgis, SD after his retirement. He passed away at home on March 19, 1973. He is buried at National Cemetery. His wife, two daughters, 13 grandchildren, 30 great-grandchildren, and one great-great grandchild survive along with one son-in-law.

HAROLD E. FALES, Elks National Home, Bedford, VA 24523. Born on Sept. 28, 1897 in Boston, MA. He joined the service on April 13, 1918 and was released from duty on May 15, 1919.

He was an officer at the U.S. Naval Training Station in Rockland, MA. He was in the U.S. Co. 105. and sailed on the *USS Martha Washington*, a transport ship. His most memorable experience was leading the Armistice Day Parade as head of the military contingent in Rockland, MA on Nov. 11, 1919.

His wife, Mrs. Marion Fales, is active in WWI Auxiliary. He has one daughter, Mrs. Pennie Hargrove of St. James, NY. He is a Past Commander of Barracks 485 of the Veterans of WWI in Daytona Beach, FL. He is now retired.

RAYMOND O. FATIG, Apt. 419, 340 Eastern Ave., Newark, OH 43053-6569. Born April 12, 1898 in Lancaster, OH. Joined the 4th Ohio Inf., Ohio National Guard on July 4, 1915 and was a member of the Headquarters Co. Band. He was discharged on May 19, 1919.

He served on the Mexican Border from August 1916 to March 1917. Regiment made into federal service as 166th U.S. Inf., 42nd Div. on July 1917. On Oct. 30, 1917 he landed at St. Nazaire, France and in February 1918 went to the war zone and trenches.

He fought in the Battle of the Champagne from July 15-18, 1918, the Chateau Thierry, 2nd Battle of Marne from July 26, to Aug. 3, 1918, the St. Mehiel Salient from Sept. 12-16, 1918, the

Argonne from Oct. 12 to Nov. 1, 1918 and the Meusse from Nov. 5-8, 1918. He was in the Army of Occupation from Nov. 11, 1918 to April 6, 1919. He was discharged on May 19, 1919 at Camp Sherman, OH. He received a Good Conduct Certificate.

He returned to high school in September 1919 and then attended Ohio State Univ. from 1920-1926. In April 1963, he retired from Ohio Power Co. at Newark, OH. He is now a widower.

FRED FAWCETT, born July 3, 1897, and died on Feb. 24, 1971. He is buried in the Woodsdale Memorial Park. He was born in Grafton, WV.

When he enlisted he was 19 years old and was a pipe fitter. He was stationed at Camp Meade, IN on July 15, 1916. He was discharged on June 25, 1919.

BENJAMIN FELTY, was born July 29, 1890 at Teges, Clay County, KY, to parents Daniel and Amanda Felty. He served in the U.S. Army as a Pvt. in 22 RCT Co., Gen. SVC Inf.

He was married to Minnie and they had three children. He died on Dec. 30, 1921.

GEORGE W. FELTY, was born on March 19, 1901, in Clay County, KY, one of five brothers. Four served in various branches of service during WWI. He joined the Navy on July 10, 1917, and served until Oct. 12, 1919 on the troop ship the *USS Susquhana*, making 15 trips to France. He achieved the ranking of 1st Class Seaman.

In 1926, he married Maggie Marcurm and

they had three daughters. He has lived in Jackson County, KY most of his life, and is retired as the Jackson County Sheriff, and later the Jackson County Master Commissioner. Today he resides in Sand Gap, KY, and is 91 years of age.

JAMES A. FELTY, was born March 13, 1889 in London, KY. He was stationed at Ft. Bliss, El Paso, TX.

He married Molly Jane Sparks on June 7, 1905, in Clay County. They had two daughters, Martha Dew Hellard and Eunice Salonen. His parents were Daniel and Amanda McCollum Felty. He died on Jan. 17, 1958 and is buried at Ft. Bliss Cemetery in El Paso, TX. He served as a barber for a while in the Army.

JOHN FELTY, was born March 11, 1893, at Teges, Clay County, KY to parents Daniel and Amanda Felty.

He served in the U.S. Army as Pvt. in 80th Co., C.A.C., Key West, FL, from Nov. 27, 1911, to Nov. 20, 1914. He also served in the U.S. Navy from Nov. 21, 1914 to Sept. 11, 1919 with rank of B.M.I.C. He served at Key West, Florida, Camp U.S.S., Georgia and overseas.

He married Provie Ann Powell on Oct. 17, 1921, and they had five children. He died Sept. 10, 1962.

WILLIAM FELTY, was born March 10, 1896, in Clay County, KY. His parents were Daniel Felty and Amanda McCollum.

He served in the U.S. Army from Dec. 28,

1912 to Dec. 27, 1919 as Sgt. He served in the Mexican Campaign.

In 1925, he married America Riley and in 1927, joined the Cincinnati Police Force. They raised their daughters in Cincinnati.

He served in the U.S. Navy from Oct. 9, 1942 to Oct. 10, 1945 as 1st Class Petty Officer. He was authorized to wear the Mexican Campaign Ribbon, Good Conduct Ribbon, American Area Ribbon, WWI Victory Ribbon and the WWII Ribbon.

He belonged to the VFW, Vet. of WWI, FOP and Masonic Order. In 1955, he and his wife moved to Tampa, FL, and were very active in the Sulphur Springs Tourist Club. He died on Dec. 5, 1991 at the age of 95.

ALBERT E. FERGISON, 1602 Cedar St., Elkhart, IN.

He was born Dec. 24, 1899 in Goshen, IN. He joined the 11th Regt., Supply Co. on July 2, 1918. He achieved the rank of Pvt.

He was stationed at Camp Monterchaum, Brest, France. He achieved the Expert Rifleman Award.

He retired from the Loco. Engineers, NYC Railroad in Elkhart, IN. He has five brothers and three sisters.

HAROLD L. FETHERHUFF, enlisted at Aberdeen, SD on Jan. 15, 1918.

He was discharged at Ft. Dodge, IA on May 7, 1919. He served in Btry. B, 2nd Trench Motor Btn. He was 18 years old when he enlisted and a senior high school student.

He served in France, left the United States on May 29, 1918 from New York on the transport ship the *USS Cordinshire,* carrying 3,000 men. He landed in Liverpool, England, then to Moone Hill in Winchester, England for first encampment for training. He then went to Brittany, France, Vitry, France and on to the front at Alasas Lorraine, France. He spent his encampment in tents. He was at the Front Ponta Mousson when the Armistice was signed. He was in the battle on Lorraine Front from Oct. 16 to Nov. 11, 1918 with the 4th Corp., 2nd Army.

He arrived in the United States on April 20, 1919, and was sent to Ft. Dodge, IA for honorable discharge on May 7, 1919. He then took a train to Aberdeen, SD and again by train to his home in Hecla, SD.

He completed high school and graduated from Dakota Weslyn College in Mitchell, SD and taught school several years prior to becoming a Federal Employee for 30 years. He served as a Postmaster in Herried ,SD. He is now past 92 and in good health. He served as State Legion Commander for South Dakota from 1959-60.

ROBERT FISHER, was born Sept. 12, 1893, in Gregg Co., TX as eldest child of McBee Fisher and Juan Minerva Bumpus.

He died on May 5, 1967 in Longview, TX. He is buried in Grace Hill Cemetery. He married Colista Davis on July 7, 1923 in Longview, TX, and they had one child, a daughter, Grace Fisher DeuPree, of Dallas, TX.

He enlisted on May 25, 1918, and trained at Camp Cody, NM. He was a Pvt. 1st Class Sharpshooter and was assigned to Sniper and Scout Squad, Co. D, 141st Inf., 36th Div., A.E.F. From Ft. Dix, NJ, he left the United States on Oct. 17, 1918 aboard the *Olympic*, 883 ft. long, stood 60 ft. out of the water and had 9,500 soldiers aboard. He arrived in France, on Oct. 25, 1918 and was sent to Chase and Lagesse, southeast of Paris. He was sent later to Torce, west of Paris. He left France on May 22, 1919 on the *SS Troy* with 6500 soldiers aboard. They arrived at Camp Mills, NY on June 3, 1919. He was honorably discharged from Camp Travis, Austin, TX on July 3, 1919.

EUGENE F. FITZPATRICK, enlisted on April 3, 1917 in the 5th Regt., Maryland National Guard, Baltimore, MD, at the age of 16.

He was first assigned guard duty at Baltimore's Lake Montebello Filtration Plant, then Cape Charles' Chesapeake Bay Ferry Terminal, Virginia. After induction in the U.S. Regular Army, 29th Inf., Co. H, he was involved in establishing Camp McClelland to train expeditionary forces and then transferred to Ft. Wadsworth, Spartansburg, SC to form the 1st Pioneer Inf.

He arrived in Brest, France in July 1918, and after the Armistice, was part of the Occupation

Army in Germany. He was discharged at Ft. Lee, VA in July 1919.

He then enlisted in the U.S. Navy, gaining experience and qualification as a licensed engineer, Motor Vessels Unlimited Tonnage. After serving eight years, he commenced a career that served Standard Oil Co., the Arundel Corp. in Maryland and the Engineering Experimental Station in Annapolis for the Department of Defense before retiring in 1963.

He and Margaret O'Leary were married on June 4, 1930. After 61 wonderful years, Margaret died on Sept. 15, 1991. He enjoys an active retirement at Charlestown Community in Baltimore, MD, where he has lived since October 1985.

REGINA FORD FITZGERALD, born Jan. 30, 1900 in Newport, RI. Joined the U.S. Navy on April 19, 1918 as an Yeoman 2nd Class. Was discharged on April 27, 1920 as Yeoman 3rd Class.

From 1920-21 was in a one-room schoolhouse in Portsmouth, RI. In 1922, had a job in the library at War College, Newport, RI. With that experience and help from the librarian, she took an exam for Library Asst. In 1924, got a job as Library Asst. at Bureau of Fisheries in Washington, DC. Sent material during the year to the experimental stations in Beaufort, NC, Fairport, IA and Woods Hole, MA. Went to each place for about two week to put the libraries at these stations, so they would be ready for professors from colleges to research work summers.

In 1928, she married Gerald A. Fitzgerald, S.A.T.C., M.I.T. 23. They moved to Gloucester, MA where Clarence Birdseye was pioneering in the frozen food industry. Her husband was offered the job of Chief Chemist in his laboratory. The laboratory was eventually taken over by General Foods. They had three children, Gerald A. Jr., a free lance writer, David F., a lawyer and Richard T., a lawyer and Judge of Probate.

Her first job in the Navy was in the enrolling office, writing up the enrollment papers. Her last job was Secretary to the Chaplains, Fr. Burke and Chaplain Machair. In 1952-54, she spent two years in Iran. Her husband was sent there by the government to help them with their fruit and especially date industry. She is now living in her own apartment and trying to keep up. She is active in the church and belongs to a prayer group that meets once a week.

RICHARD L. FOLEY, was born in Piedmont, WV on Sept. 23, 1893. He enlisted in the Army on March 11, 1918 in Grafton where he was living. He served until Jan. 6, 1919.

In February 1923, he married Mamie Eickelberger at the St. Augustine Catholic Church, by the Rev. Father Michael J. Hannon. He was very active in the VFW and was continually working with the members in all phases. He worked for the Baltimore and Ohio Railroad his entire life, and retired at the age of 65.

He lived in Grafton during the rise of the town and his memories were filled with all the good times even though his wages were sparse and his struggles many. He passed away at the Clarksboro, WV Veterans Hospital in November 1965. He buried in the National Cemetery in Arlington, VA.

ANDRE (ANDY) T. FONTES, 5861 Moraga Ave., Oakland, CA 94611. Was born April 16, 1898 in Oakland, CA. He joined the service on Jan. 18, 1918 and was discharged on April 3, 1919.

He served in the 190th Aero-Squadron and was transferred to the Regular Army, 104th T.M.B., 29th Div. in France. He was discharged on April 3, 1919 as Pvt. 1st Class.

He has been married for 57 years to Margaret A. Fontes and they have three daughters and grandchildren. He is still active in clubs, organizations, gardening and general activities. He is a life member and founder of the Lake Merritt Breakfast Club. Also the East Bay Zoological Society, WWI Vets Barrack 258 in Santa Rosa, CA, East Bay Police and Firemen's Div., Post 2727 in Oakland, CA, 29th Div. Headquarters, Post 8, WWI Washington, DC and the Disabled Veterans 7 in Oakland, CA.

JOSEPH WYLIE FORD, was born Sept. 17, 1889, in Green Castle, MO to George and Phoebe Ford. He received schooling in Green Castle and in May 1906 moved to Columbia Falls.

In Jan. 14, 1950 he married Nellie Mae William's in Kalispell and she preceded him in death in December 1959. In June 1961, he retired from his life-long career as a farmer. He was a member of the WWI Barracks and Farmers Union.

MUNRO FOX, was born Dec. 8, 1896 in Saginaw, MI. He enlisted on Feb. 24, 1918 in the 56th Engineers, Search and Lights. He arrived in the Washington Barracks, as it was named then, present sight of War College on March 1, 1918. New companies were being assembled for training. He was assigned to the 18th Plt., Co. D and was appointed Corporal about March 20, 1918. He was appointed Sgt. on May 1.

He left for France from Hoboken on May 10, 1918 aboard the *Dwinsk*, which was sunk by submarine on the return trip. He arrived in France on May 22 at Brest Harbor, and arrived at Ft. Shrennes, just outside of Paris, about May 30. He was shipped to Is-Sur-Tille about June 15 to protect supply depot while working with anti-aircraft artillery. He was appointed Supply Sgt. about June 15. He stayed for the duration of the war, leaving Dec. 8, 1918 for home. He sailed on the *Nansemond*, a captured German freighter which was made of all steel and bad for our job of nail shoes.

He was discharged on March 10, 1919 from Camp Chister, MI.

WILLIAM T. FRAYER, joined the U.S. Army as Pvt. on Sept. 21, 1917, and was stationed in Camp Custer, Battle Creek, MI. He was assigned to Co. C, 338th Inf., 85th Div.

After a short time, he was transferred to Headquarters Co. and made a Pvt. P1C. and mounted orderly for Col. Wells, the Commander of the 358th Regt. It was the rule that when the officers had no need for their horses we orderlies gave them exercise by riding them out on the country roads outside of camp. One day, they were riding quite a good clip and was in the middle of the string looking over the countryside, when he felt his horse turning and not the saddle. He couldn't stay on, so he fell off under a lot of the horses hoofs and he thought he was done for. He came out of it with only a sore head.

In July 1918, the 85th Div., went to New York and then shipped out for Liverpool, England, which took two weeks. From there to South Hampton, English Channel to La Harve France. After arriving in France, they are loaded in boxcars for a long ride to Sancerre on the Loire River. While there, if they wanted a bath, they had to go down the hill to the river.

They kept on moving, not staying in one place for long, and he remembers after dark seeing red steaks in the sky and hearing a little noise from the artillery. One day, he saw a German spy plane shot down, while looking for a place to eat lunch. The pilot came down in a field and was captured. Some of the men brought back a piece of the motor crankcase and he made a charm for his watch chain out of it.

It was only a few days after this, the news came of the Armistice. The war was over. They now moved slowly back to the coast of France and the city of Brest where they boarded the largest ship afloat at that time for a weeks trip to New York, Camp Dix and Camp Custer.

He was discharged on April 12, 1919. He is now 96 years old and lives in Lansing, MI.

DOROTHY FROOKS, born Feb. 12, 1899 in Asbury, Saugerties, NY. She is a lawyer, publisher and Judge in the Small Claims Court she founded in the early 1920s. Her first job as a lawyer she became the attorney for the Salvation Army at their

National Headquarters in New York City. Through the head Evangeline Booth, she arranged to have legislation drawn up by Professor Wood and Parkinson of Columbia University, and for several years became the Small Claims Court signed by Mayor Fiorello LaGuardia.

She has all the law degrees and the highest educational degrees. She served as Yeoman in the U.S. Naval Reserve in WWI and in the Judge Advocate's Office in WWII. She authored; *The American Heart, Love's Law, All In Love, Over the Heads of Congress, Lady Lawyer,* and pamphlets *Wills, Labor Courts/Outlaw Strikes,* and *Small Claims Court.* She published *The Murray Hill News* for over 50 years.

HUGH THOMPSON GALLOWAY, was

born Aug. 21, 1897 in Shelley, ID. His parents were Curtis and Harriet Galloway. He grew to adulthood in the Shelley and Blackfoot, ID areas. During his teen years he did extensive trapping, an occupation he followed for most of his adult years.

He entered the U.S. Army on Oct. 5, 1916, and served in the Philippine Islands. He broke horses for the cavalry during this time. In 1920, he received his honorable discharge and returned to Idaho, where on Sept. 12, 1923, he married Mary Leah McGary at Rigby, ID. A short time later the couple moved to the Milk River country in northeastern Montana where they farmed. They then moved to the Big Hole country where he trapped coyotes, beaver, mink and fur bearing animals.

He was preceded in death by his wife, Mary in 1971, a daughter, Leah Ann, and two sons, Hugh Jr. and Donald Paul. He is survived by six sons, John, Calvin, Kenneth and Dennis all of Kalispell, Edwin of Great Falls and Lawrence of Columbia Falls, one daughter, Irene Wyman of Alaska. He had 35 grandchildren and 40 great-grandchildren. He passed away on May 29, 1980.

HENRY GATES, served in France from 1917

to 1919 in the 362nd Inf. He married Thora Tufte on Aug. 27, 1919. Gates died Aug. 8, 1947.

FRANCIS J. GERLACH, was born in 1895

and joined the Minnesota National Guard in June 1916. He served on the Mexican Border during the Revolution, was released January 1917, and called back in February 1918 for WWI. He served in the 35th Div. 140th Inf. Harry Truman was in the same division in 129th Artillery as a captain.

He received a Purple Heart for a wound in the Argonne.

His diary of military experiences is in the U.S. Army Military History Institute, WWI Survey Collection, the permanent collection of personal papers from soldiers for the Great War.

As their only boy, he inherited his parents farm in Austin. When he retired at the age of 65, he passed the farm to one of his boys. He has seven sons, two daughters, 35 grandchildren, and 20 great-grandchildren.

His wife Irene died in 1988. Francis moved into a retirement community in 1991 and is doing fine.

ROBERT L. GILBERT SR., was born in

Lawrence, KS on Dec. 30, 1898. He served in the U.S. Naval Aviation, WWI, October 1917-July 1919. He spent one year in France as crew member and machinist mate in the Navy Seaplane Bombing Patrol; ROTC, University of Kansas; BA, journalism, UK, 1923; Postgraduate, Southwestern Institute, Dallas, TX, 1956. He worked in journalism and in advertising as well as a variety of other jobs.

Was married to Mariam Meader on Oct. 27, 1923, and they have a son and a daughter. They were divorced in September 1936, and he married Josephine Gill on Sept. 2, 1939. He has eight grandchildren and five great-grandchildren.

He is a member of Delta Upsilon Fraternity and WWI Veterans Association. He is a Methodist and Republican. He only stopped flying on Feb. 6, 1979 due to being grounded for an irregular heartbeat.

ANTONIO O. GIROUX,

was born Jan. 28 in Canada, one of 11 children. His parents were Arthur and Georgia Anna Giroux. The family moved to Terryville around 1902 and he grew to manhood there.

He enlisted in the Navy on Dec. 13, 1917 and was discharged in August 1919 in San Diego, CA. He achieved the ranking of Printer 1st Class. He was a photographer and went on flights to take pictures.

He was a miner in the Homestake Gold Mine at Lead, SD. He went to college in Missouri for a while then got married to Margaret and had five children. He retired from the mine and continued to live in Lead until his death. He is buried in Lead.

PAUL NELSON GIROUX,

was born in Canada and moved with his family to Terryville. He met his bride to be, in Lead before joining the military.

He never got out of the states. He got the flu and nearly died. He came back to Lead and worked in the mine.

He had two children and went to the Casper Oil Fields. He was still working when he became ill and died around 63 years old. He is buried in Casper.

FREDERICK H. GLAUERT,

230 S. 2nd St. Shiloh, O'Fallon, IL 62269. Was born Feb. 11, 1894 in Plum Hill, IL. He joined the service on June 24, 1918.

He was a member of the Army Veterinary Corp. and achieved the rank of Pvt. He was discharged on Aug. 30, 1919. He served in France. His most memorable experience was camping out in all extreme weather conditions and suffering broken bones when a motorcycle messenger ran into their formation as they were returning from the front line.

He received his training at Camp Lee, VA. He went overseas aboard the *USS Agamemnon*, a 720 ft. long boat with four smoke stacks and traveled at 23 knots. Because they were loaded with horses, feed and water they had smooth sailing. While overseas in France, they took care of the horses, supplying fresh horses to the front lines as needed.

He was married to Margaret, had one daughter, Evelyn Shelton, and two sons, Melvin and Vernon. He had a brother, PFC Henry F. Glauert and a half brothers, Pvt. John Siegmann. Henry was with a heavy artillery unit that went through some of the major battles.

HENRY F. GLAUERT,

was born on June 18, 1892 in Washington Co., Plumhill, IL. His parents were Henriitta and William Glauert.

He served in the U.S. Army from April 29, 1918 to May 27, 1919 as Pvt. 1st Class. He served in France the St. Mihiel, the Argonne Sector, and Grand Pre

In Sept. 6, 1917, he married Louise Schuette. He was a foundry worker in Belleville, IL. They had two daughters, Irene Schanz and Marilyn Eulli. After his discharge he worked on Eckerts Fruit Farm growing peaches and apple trees in the rural area of Freeburg, IL. The rest of his life, he belonged to the VFW and the American Legion. He was a very hard working man and was liked by every one. He died on Oct. 6, 1976 at the age of 84.

HAROLD B. GLAZIER,

was born Nov. 18, 1895 in Estelline, SD to Aaron Glazier and Hannah Gustane Burk. He married Olga Kicker on March 26, 1928 and they had two boys and one girl. He had a homestead.

He served from 1917-18 in France, 23rd Engineers. He had livestock and farmed. Also ran a mail route for ten years. They moved to Kalispell, MT. He died Aug. 5, 1958.

CHARLES GLIOZZO,

was born Jan. 21, 1896 in Italy. He was in the 12th Amminusion Train, Co. F, Heavy Artillery from 1917-18. He trained at Ft. Dix.

His most memorable moment was going to Canada to Montgal to take a boat. After ten days out, a submarine caught up with them and started shooting. A sub from England, *the Chasher*, came to help. They saved two cargo ships. He landed in England before they got to France. They met King George. They marched single file and saluted the King. After eight days a whistle blew and everyone went to the deck. The bugle began to blow, one soldier had died and was being buried in the ocean.

He now lives in Helena, NY. His wife is Nancy, and they have one son, Gino, and one daughter, Tina. His daughter lives in Cheasapeake, VA. His son lives in San Diego, CA.

WADE GOFF, 3168571 born Nov. 2, 1892 and died June 17, 1985. He was born in St. George, WV. He was enlisted at the age of 25 and was a farmer by occupation.

He was a member of the Co. A, 47th Inf. and served as a Pvt.. He was honorably discharged at Camp Dix, NJ on Aug. 2, 1919. He was stationed in the Toul Sector from Sept. 4 to Sept. 12, 1918, the St. Mihiel Offensive from Sept. 12 to 16, 1918, the Meuse Argonne Offensive from Sept. 26 to Oct. 19, 1918. He sailed from the United States on July 18, 1918 and arrived back in the United States on July 27, 1919.

WILLIAM J. GOFF, was born June 11, 1895 in Tucker Co. WV. He died on March 13, 1964 in Ravenna, OH.

FRANK E. GOODNOUGH, served with the U.S. Marines in battles throughout France, such as the Meuse-Argonne drive. He was a machine gunner with the 6th Machine Gun Btn, 5th Marine Div.

He was a replacement after the decisive Battle of Belleau Wood, where the fierceness of the Marine attack caused the Germans to call them "Devil Dogs." He says that for all the ground he covered in France, he saw very little of the country because he and his unit were either moving quickly or were dug in. Toward the end of the war, he was in trenches along the River Seine. He lost 23 of his buddies on the banks of that river, when they were ordered to attack across it just hours before the armistice was announced.

After the war, he finished high school and then graduated from DePauw University, in Indiana. He then finished the School of Theology at Boston University and went on to Harvard University.

He served as Methodist minister for Harvard students for four years.

He moved to the Northwest in 1927, where he rebuilt St. Paul's Methodist Church in Tacoma. He finished his ministry in 1962, after being director of the Methodist's Wesley Foundation at the University of Washington for 23 years. When he and his wife retired to Whidbey Island, they bought the Ivy Inn, south of Langley and tore it apart and rebuilt it for a home.

HENRY ALBERT GOSSMAN, was born July 13, 1896, in Dubuque County, IA. He attended the one-room country school. He helped with farm work until he enlisted in the Army on May 31, 1918 at the age of 21.

He served in WWI as a Horseshoer Btry. 6, 72nd Field of Artillery. He was honorably discharged from Camp Knox, KY, on Feb. 6, 1919 with high esteem for his honesty and faithful service.

He married Catherine O'Hea on Nov. 20, 1929, at St. Joseph's Church in Key West, IA. They had one girl and three boys. He worked as a molder at the Adam's Plant in Dubuque, IA.

In the later years of his life, he had both legs amputated as a result of poor circulation. He died on Sept. 19, 1976.

ANNA JOSEPHINE DAVIS GRAY, was born July 1, 1894 in New Orleans, LA. She joined the service in November 1917 and was discharged on July 11, 1919.

She wanted to serve her country because she had no brothers to do it. So when, Gen. John J. Pershing, A.E.F. head in France, issued a request for American women fluent in English and French to serve as telephone operators overseas to relieve soldiers for combat, she answered the call.

She spoke fluent French because of her family's French background. She applied for a job at the South Central Bell Co., because she wanted the experience of operating a telephone system. She was chosen to serve and was the only young woman from the entire Southeast in the first group of 33 to leave. She arrived in Tours, France in March 1918. She served 12 months in Tours, then assigned to Coblenz, Germany.

While in Coblenz, she married, Lt. Samuel W. Gray on June 15, 1919. He was a pilot and aircraft mechanic. In July 1919, they returned to the United States and settled in Indianapolis, IN. At the end of the war, members of the Signal Corps Female Telephone Operators Unit, were released from service but never given a military discharge. In May 1979, the military decided that the women who served in the unit in WWI, should be recognized as active military personnel and receive a honorable discharge and benefits. She proudly received her honorable discharge on September 1979, at the age of 85.

She passed away on Dec. 30, 1991 at the age of 97. She had three daughters, Dixie, Frances and Betty. Betty served eight years in the Waves during WWII as Navy Aerographers Mate.

LOUIS G. GRAY, enlisted in the Army 60th Inf., 5th Div. on Dec. 2, 1916 in Indianapolis, IN. On his way to Ft. Bliss, for training, he became sick and was isolated in Kansas with the black measles. He recovered, and the cargo ship, *Herschey,* took him to Liverpool, England and he was assigned to Supply Co., 8th Inf. He later was transferred to Supply Co., 16th Inf. as a cook on May 19, 1917 and then as a Wagoner on Jan. 10,

1918. He was overseas from June 15, 1917 to Aug. 30, 1919.

He was in the battles of St. Mihiel, Argonne, Belleau Wood, Verdun and Bois de Remourlle. As a wagoner at Bois de Remourlle, France, after moving his team to safety the field was suddenly shelled. He hurried back into the barrage and from the shelled area, with other teams, he saved at least ten teams. On his own, he organized a small group of litter bearers and assisted removing the wounded. He also took charge of a few men to repair under fire, a road which enabled the field train to move to safety.

In the Battle of Argonne, his horse was shot from under him, and he had both legs broken. He awoke at the Walter Reed Hospital to find he had been considered missing in action, with all his records destroyed.

He received a Silver Star Citation, Orders No. 2, Gen. Headquarters, AEF France on June 3, 1919. He received a Division Citation (silver star citation superseded by citation from General Headquarters) Gen. Orders, No. 4, Headquarters 5th Div., A.E.F., on March 6, 1919. A Brigade Citation (silver star citation superseded by citation from Gen. Headquarters) General orders, No. 11 Headquarters, 9th Inf. Brigade on Dec. 31, 1918. He also received a citation certificate for gallantry in action on March 27, 1919 from John J. Pershing.

He is a retired minister of 97 with a wife of 92. They had eight children and six are still living. He has received honors from the American Baptist Association for 52 faithful years. They reside in Putnam Co., IN.

SAMUEL WILLIAM GRAY, was born Aug. 26, 1886 in Rushville, IN. He joined the U.S. Army Air Corp. in 1917. He achieved the ranking of Lt. before being discharged on July 11, 1919.

He was stationed in Tours and Paris, France and Coblenz, Germany. He was a mechanic and pilot. He repaired, serviced and test flew the Eddie Ricken Backer's plane.

He was married to A. Josephine Davis on June 15, 1919 in Coblenz, Germany. He became an engineer. While working in a machine shop, he developed several carburetors. The first was called Linkert. The next one was better. He went on to promote it. It was called Marvel Worlds finest. This was about 1925. He became President of Marvel-Schebler Carburetor Co. It was bought out by Borg Warner Corp., however he remained President and General Manager of the Marvel-Schebler Carburetor Div. until he retired in 1952.

He passed away on March 30, 1967.

HERBERT FRANKLIN GREEN, was born Dec. 8, 1898 in Columbus, OH. He received his education in Ohio and on Sept. 20, 1916, he entered the U.S. Navy in Cincinnati, OH. He served as a seaman aboard the *USS Tacoma* until his honorable discharge on Dec. 5, 1919.

He returned to Ohio where he married Mabel Carbaugh in 1920. The couple moved to the Flathead in 1925. They had also lived in Great Falls, Billings and Whitefish.

He became a member of the Church of Jesus Christ of Latter-day Saints in 1939 and was an elder in the church at the time of his death. He was preceded in death by a daughter in infancy, a son, Harley Green, in 1958, and his wife on Jan. 19, 1981. He passed away on March 18, 1981.

WILLIAM ROY GREEN, was born on Feb. 14, 1896 in Brownwood, TX. He joined the service on June 18, 1917 and was discharged in 1918.

He served with the 142nd Inf., 36th Div. as a Sgt. He was stationed in France in the Argonne Forest. His memorable experience was capturing four Germans and being wounded in the knee. He is now deceased.

BERYL R. GREENE, was born April 6, 1888 in Clinton, IL. He attended schools there. He served overseas in the Army during WWI. Following the war, he moved to Glasgow and farmed there many years.

He married Cecelia E. Dargatz in Glasgow on Nov. 28, 1923. He was a construction worker on the Ft. Peck Dam and later moved to Fairfield where he farmed 12 years. After selling the farm, they moved to Martin City and to Kalispell in November of 1969. He had been a member of the Senior Citizens in Kalispell. He died on Jan. 6, 1977.

FRANK CECIL GRIFFIN, was born July 7, 1893 in Rush Co., IN. He joined the service on Dec. 6, 1917 and was discharged on April 18, 1919.

He was a member of the 259th Aero-Squad and served as a Chauffeur. He was stationed in San Antonio, Waco and Mincold, NY in the United States and in Vatan, France. His most memorable experience was a wonderful trip over and back. He had no sickness.

He was married for 63 years and is the last of his family. He retired in 1963.

COXWIN Q. GRUNDER, enlisted in the Medical Corp. on Sept. 4, 1917 in McKeen Rock, PA.

He served as a Wagoner in the Camp Hospital #52. He passed away on March 10, 1988 and he has no living family.

WILLIAM ROYLE GUTHRIE, was a Corporal in the Co. K, 10th Inf. He was honorably discharged on Sept. 17, 1917.

He died on Sept. 12, 1961 and is buried at Woodsdale Memorial Park.

JOSEPH LANE HALDEMAN, was born Feb. 17, 1887, in Minneapolis, a son of the late Joseph Hanslip and Olive Virginia DeMoss Haldeman. A veteran of WWI, he was the oldest veteran in Taylor County.

He organized a Taylor County Barracks for Veterans of WWI, in 1958. He was Department (State) Commander of the Veterans of WWI, serving from 1961-62. He was a former commander of the Taylor County American Legion Post, and a member of Memorial City Post VFW. He is a life member of the Elks and the Moose, with a Fellowship Degree in the Legion of the Moose. He served as governor three times.

Following the war, he held several temporary jobs before taking a job with Prudential Insurance Co. He worked for the firm for 30 years. On retiring in the 1950s, he moved to the ancestral farm.

FRED F. HALFHILL, was born Nov. 2, 1898, in Greeley, IA. He joined the service on May 12, 1917, and was discharged on April 24, 1919.

He served in the Army's Co. D, 101st Inf., 26th Div. He achieved the rank of Pvt. before being discharged. He was stationed in France, and fought in the battles of St. Mihiel, Meusse Argonne and H.E.F. He received the Purple Heart and the Accolade of the New Chivalry of Humanity awards.

He had a wife, Amy, seven girls and two boys. He is now deceased.

FRANK A. HANCOCK, 634315, was born Oct. 2, 1896, in Ashley Co., AK. When WWI was declared, he volunteered for service, leaving home on April 12, 1917. He was assigned to Headquarters Co., 60th Field Artillery, trained at Fisherman's Island, Virginia.

He was shipped overseas on the *Sibony,* and arrived at Brest, France on May 6, 1918. He was put in charge of the Officer's mess hall. He traveled by truck and train (cattle cars), to front lines through muddy, congested roads, shot-up towns, heavy air bombardments and hundreds of refugees. Participated in the St. Mihiel, Defensive Sector and the Argonne Offensive, which ended the war.

Word of the Armistice was not believed and black-outs continued. After Armistice, he convoyed back to Brest for debarkation, arriving on Nov. 29, 1918. He sailed for American on Jan. 26, 1919. Arrived in New York on Feb. 4, 1919. Cheers rang out at sight of Statue of Liberty. He went through de-cootielizer, then left by train for Camp Pike, AK. He was discharged on Feb. 26, 1919.

CHARLES I. HANES, 1895-1989, enlisted in the U.S. Army on June 14, 1918, in Olney, IL. His service included training at Bradley Polytechnic Institute in Peoria, IL, where he learned automotive, electrical and instrument repair. He was then transferred to 5th Casual Co., 2nd Provisional Regt. O.T.C., Camp Hancock, GA on Sept. 14, 1918.

Later he was assigned to Co. B, Ordinance Dept., Aberdeen Proving Ground in Maryland, where he was an artillery crew member who helped proof-test heavy artillery, including 18 inch railroad guns from the Chilean government and American 6 inch guns. He recorded results from stargauging the heavy guns after firing. Pvt. Hanes received an honorable discharge on March 9, 1919, while stationed at Camp Zachary Taylor, KY.

Following his discharge, he continued to use his mechanical skills in auto and tractor repair, saw-milling, threshing and shredding. He eventually married and raised two daughters. Throughout his life, he was a quiet, confident man with uncanny keenness of mind and an unwavering love for God and his country.

HILMER WILLIAM HANSON, was born March 16, 1892, in Kandeyoki County, MN. In WWI he enlisted in the Navy and was stationed at Miami with ARIC Provisional, 170-67-17, U.S. 9th Naval District, and U.S. Naval Reserve Force, Class 5. He serviced and repaired airplanes until his discharge on Sept. 30, 1921 at Great Lakes, IL.

From a used propeller, he made a swaggart

stick, (an empty shell on its bottom and a 1918 quarter on its top), which friends sometimes used.

At home again, he responded to a call to serve the Lord and became a Methodist minister, serving 33 years in the Pacific Northwest, retiring in 1958. He married Lillian Anderson, who bore him a daughter, Lois. He then married Alice Kimble, who shared his life for 53 years, and bore him five children. He lived on Whidbey Island in fair health until his passing at 98 on May 27, 1990.

OLE HANSON, was born Dec. 7, 1888, at Michigamme, MI. He had attended schools in Michigan and as a young man, he had moved with his family to Kalispell. The family had homesteaded in the Tally Lake area for a number of years.

He was a veteran of WWI, having served in the Quartermaster Corps. Following his discharge from the armed services, he returned to the Flathead, and was engaged in logging and lumber work.

On Aug. 16, 1968, he was married to Lillian Darrow in Kalispell and is now survived by her. He died in Kalispell on Oct. 8, 1969.

CHARLES A. HARPER, was born June 4, 1894, in Templow, TN. He was a member of the Army's 114th Machine Gun Bn., Co. B.

He achieved the rank of Private before being discharged in November 1919. He was called into service in June 1916, and served on the Mexican border. In August 1917, the troop was converted into a machine gun company at Camp Sevier, SC, and began training for overseas duty.

Early in 1918, the company was sent overseas, and after several weeks of intensive training, went into the advance area on the British front as a part of the 5th British Army. Before going into the huge Somme Offensive of September 1918, which included breaking of the Hindenburg line, the outfit took front-line training in many points in Belgium. Co. B, remained in the Somme offensive for 40 days after the breaking of the Hindenburg line on Sept. 29 and 30, with virtually no relief. It suffered many casualties, until the signing of the Armistice in November.

In April 1919, this unit was brought back to Fort Oglethorpe, where men living in this area were discharged. He died on July 20, 1968.

ASBURY CARR HARRELSON, was born April 16, 1885, to Miles P. Harrelson and Sallie Beam Harrelson. The second of six children. They lived on Rt. 1, Shelby, NC in the Waco community.

On May 28, 1918, he rode the Southern Railroad train from Shelby, NC to Columbia, SC, where he was inducted into the 81st Wildcat Division at Ft. Jackson. He stayed there four weeks, then transferred to Camp Sevier in Greenville, SC, to continue training in the Motor Corp, where he became a Pvt. 1st Class. He left there late in July 1918, to go to Camp Mills, Long Island, NY. Without having a visit with his family, he left Long Island by boat on Aug. 7, 1918 and landed in Liverpool, England on Aug. 12, 1918.

His group began unloading equipment from the boat to the train at sundown, finishing at 3 a.m. They left there for Southampton, England, where they loaded the equipment from the train back onto a boat to cross the English Channel. Three boats left for Cherbourg, France. He was on the only one that landed.

They had been under fire during the night. They hiked two days to Erva. Stayed there two weeks, then hiked to Davery, France, where they stayed in the basement of an old school building. Here they received full equipment and supplies, which they delivered to the 81st Division as they moved.

On to the Vogue Mountains and then the Argonne Forest, where the heaviest part of the fighting occurred. They were here, when the war ended on Nov. 11, 1918. The Motor Corp. remained in France to supply the troops there. They left France in June 1919, on a captured German boat that had been converted to a carrier and accommodated 2,000 men. Their trip across the Atlantic took 14 days and 15 nights. During this time he worked as a meat cutter for the cooks.

Landing in Newport News, VA, the last day of June, they were sent to Camp Lee, Petersburg,

VA, for discharge on July 10, 1919. He was given a train ticket to Waco, NC.

He is the third generation on the family farm and has worked since he was eight years old, when his father became ill. Working as a carpenter also brought cash to the family. He is a fine Christian gentlemen, he is self-sufficient in every way. He drives, gardens, cooks and takes care of his own needs. His family consists of, his wife, Willie Gardner Harrelson, two daughters, Deloras H. Wood and Betty H. Helton, two sons, Dr. Lewis G. Harrelson and Dr. Michael A. Harrelson, nine grandchildren and two great-grandchildren. His wife and one son are deceased.

CLEO H. HARRIS, enlisted in the Army on April 27, 1917, at Fort Sam, Houston, TX. He was put in the 2nd Co. of the 19th Inf. Later the 19th was split into two regiments.

He was sent to Leon Springs, TX and from there he was later transferred to McAllen, TX on the Mexican Border. He was sent back later to Fort Sam, Houston, TX, to go to the cook and baker school. Three months later, after graduations, he returned to I Co., 57th Inf. at Saratoga and Batson, TX. There was an oil field strike and they had trouble from there to Beaumont, TX. They left all privates in Beaumont and because he did not get a title as a cook, this included him. He finally left for Houston, TX, where they received 200 new recruits. They were drilled for sometime and then the war was over. He was then transferred to Little Rock, AK and put into a barracks instead of a tent. One day, his Sgt. came in the kitchen and told him to come to the office. He sat there while he wrote out his discharge papers. He was discharged on June 10, 1919.

BENJAMIN F. HARRISON, was born on May 7, 1898, in Norfolk, Va. He is now living in the VA Medical Center in Hampton, VA.

EVART B. HARTMAN, was born June 12, 1894, in Mercer County, IL. He was the son of George and Effie Hartman. In 1900, he came to the Flathead Valley with his family and has lived there since.

He was a veteran of WWI, serving in France and Germany during that time. He was one of the first men to leave the Flathead Valley for the armed services. He was a member of the 91st Div., 348 F.A., Btry. C, from September 1917 to April 21, 1919.

On July 16, 1922, he married Mildred Boyd at Somers. They had continued to farm at Somers until 1943, when they moved to their home on Two Mile Drive. He continued to farm for a time and was also associated with his son in the Skyline Dairy Business. He was a member of the WWI Barracks of Kalispell and the Elks Lodge. He had two daughters, Effie Bradford Missoula and Hazel Halsey Libbey and 12 grandchildren. He died on Oct. 8, 1972.

WILLARD LOYD HAWKINS, was born March 31, 1898 in Reading, KS to James Van and Cora Murdock Hawkins. He was the oldest of nine children.

He enlisted in the services on Aug. 2, 1918 in LaJunta, CO. He served with Base Hospital #93 from Aug. 8, 1918 to June 23, 1919. He embarked for overseas duty on Oct. 20, 1918. He arrived in Mont Dore, Puy-de-Dome, France on Nov. 6, 1918. He received his first patients on Armistice Day, Nov. 11, 1918, at a hospital set up in the Hotel Sareiron.

He was transferred to Cannes on Dec. 18, 1918 to a hospital set up in the Hotel Metropole. There were 4,570 patients treated there. He left Cannes on May 27, 1919 for Marseilles and arrived in Brooklyn, NY on June 22, 1919. He was discharged on July 2, 1919 at Fort D.A. Russell, WY.

He then worked as a locomotive engineer for the Santa Fe Railroad for 43 years. His hobbies include, gardening and bicycle riding. He married Bessie May Marcellus in 1925. He has five children, 14 grandchildren and 19 great-grandchildren. He rode his bicycle in the Armistice Day Parade every year through 1989, wearing his original uniform. At the age of 91, he lives at home with his wife in Emporia, KS.

HARRY H. HEAD, was born in Aberdeen, SD on April 17, 1892. He spent his boyhood days in Aberdeen and even then dreamed of a career in the fast-growing railroad industry. His dreams became a reality, as he began working for the railroad as a young man.

At the age of 25, he answered the call to arms during WWI, by enlisting in the U.S. Army on July 5, 1917 and became Pvt. Harry H. Head, ASN #1,410,123. He served with the AEF, and rose to the rank of Corporal before he was granted an honorable discharge on April 24, 1919. Even in the service of his country, he diligently applied his talents to railroad transportation units, both in this country and abroad.

Upon returning from WWI service, he immediately began working for the Chicago Northwestern Railway and for more than 42 years, he served as a passenger train conductor while living alternately between Huron, SD and Tracy, MN with his first love and spouse, Evelyn. During this time, he proudly accepted the appointment as Chief Conductor on two historical Presidential trains as they plied their way across the plains of his native state. At the age of 67, in 1959, he chose to retire. In his words, "While he had a little time left!"

Thirty-three years later, he is still going strong. He walks several blocks daily with a spring in his walk, which draws envious ogles from many half his age. His wit and mind are sharp as a tack, his memory of past events are remarkable, and his zest for life is second to none. Now at 100 years of age, he often expresses one simple wish and that is to live at least eight more years as a centenarian, whose life-span touched three centuries. Those who are aware of Harry Head's determination and stamina best realize that his wish could very well come true.

SIGURD HENDRICKSON, was born Aug. 1, 1893 in Velva, ND, a son of Ludwig and Karen Hendrickson. He graduated from high school in North Dakota.

He joined the Army on Sept. 18, 1917 in Minot, ND, and served as a Sgt. in Btry. A, 335th Field Artillery until his honorable discharge on March 18, 1919 at Camp Dodge, IA. He then moved to Canada, where he farmed until 1942, when he moved to Kalispell.

He worked on the Hungry Horse Dam construction, Anaconda Aluminum Co. construction and was employed by Gyrion Construction Co. until his retirement. He was a member of the VFW. On Nov. 8, 1922, he married Gertrude Kendrick in Hardesty, Alberta. He also had a daughter, Evelyn, whom with his wife preceded him in death. He had three sons, George, Lloyd and Lawrence Hendrickson. He had eight grandchildren and ten great-grandchildren. He died on Sept. 7, 1983.

CRAIG S. HERBERT, enlisted on April 29, 1917. He served with the 2nd Balloon Co., A.E.F.. He participated in the Apremont, Seicheprey, Xivray-Marvoisin Defensive, Champagne-Marne Defensive, Aisne-Marne Offensive, St. Mihiel Offensive and the Meuse Argonne Offensive from Feb. 26 to Nov. 11, 1918.

The outfit, during 251 unrelieved days on the front, was attached to or operated with the artillery of the following combat divisions: 1, 2, 4, 5, 26, 28, 32, 35, 42, 77, 78, 80, 82, 89 and 90. There were 93 balloon companies formed, 36 were in France and 17 operated on the front.

After six months occupation duty in Germany, he was discharged on July 2, 1919. In 1932, he founded the National Association of Balloon Corps Veterans. It held 50 reunions in 36 cities. He wrote and edited their tabloid newspaper *Haul Down & Ease Off,* for 50 years. His history of the balloon corps was printed in the Air Force's magazine, *Aerospace Historian,* in 1968.

In 1976, he negotiated for and received a Caquot type observation balloon from England, for displaying at the Air Force Museum in Dayton, OH. In 1986, he wrote a book titled, *Eyes of the Army.*

JOSEPH HERMAN, was born on June 1, 1895 to Mathia Vincentia Dubert and Herman in Taber, SD. There were nine children in the family. They lived on a farm and he grew to manhood helping his father on the family farm.

He enlisted in the service on June 27, 1918 at Lake Andes, SD. He went to Ft. Dodge, IA and from there to the European theater. He was engaged in battles in the Hauge Alsace area. He received victory medals and buttons in April 15, 1922. He was not ill while overseas. His only comment to his wife was that it took 13 days from the United States to Europe. They ate raw fish and terrible food. Joe had gotten a supply of fruit, ate it and didn't get sick. However, there were many who died and were buried at sea.

He was discharged from the service on June 15, 1919. He came home and farmed with his father until he was 26 years old. He married Margaret Cote in Nov. 22, 1920. He farmed until he retired in 1958, and bought a home in Boulder Canyon near Sturgis, SD. He had a severe heart attack and died on July 15, 1970 and is buried at National Cemetery near Sturgis, SD.

KELSY R. HIGHSAW, was born March 31, 1898 in Belle Fourche, SD. He enlisted in the Army on April 2, 1917 and was discharged on Dec. 24, 1919 at Ft. Dix, NJ.

He was a member of the Co. A, 1st Supply Train, Q.M.C. He achieved the rank of Sergeant. He fought in the Montdidier Noyon Defensive from April 25 to July 7, 1918, the Aisue Marue Offensive from July 18 to July 26, 1918, the St. Mihiel Offensive from Sept. 12 to Nov. 16, 1918 and the Meuse Argonne Offensive from Oct. 1-12, 1918. He served in France and left the United States on Jan. 11, 1918. He arrived back in the United States on Dec. 21, 1919.

He was the youngest man to go into service from Butte County. He was in the motor supply branch of the service. It was his duty to make many trips to the front during the war and he had many thrilling experiences. After the signing of the Armistice, the government called for 500 volunteers to go to Poland, Prussia and Russia to act as instructors in the motor branch, as the United States had sold a large number of trucks to those counties and the people were ignorant of the operation of the machines. He thought he might as well see as much as possible of the 'Old World' during his stay over there, so he was among the first to volunteer for four months more service. He went through Germany and spent a day in Berlin.

He married Frances Heather on June 21, 1926 at Sioux Falls, SD. They had one daughter, Joyce Alberts who lives in Belle Fourche. He was proceeded in death by one grandson, Tom Alberts, in 1976, and his wife on Oct. 13, 1991. He passed away on Sept. 9, 1957. He had been postmaster of Belle Fourche Post Office for 22 years until he died of a heart attack.

WILLIAM HILBIRD, was born Dec. 18, 1901, in Lincoln County, OK. He moved to Vigo County, IN, in 1903, with his parents, where he had attended school at Prairie Creek Township.

In 1919, he enlisted in the Marine Corps. He served in Haiti, until his discharge in 1923. He was a member of the 2nd Regt., 1st Pro. Brigade. He came to Montana, later re-enlisting in the Marines in 1942. He was stationed at Bremerton, WA and Farragut, ID.

He married Lorna Lindsey in August of 1946, at Kalispell. The couple moved to Libby in 1946, where he operated The Maytag Store and later managed the VFW Club. He later was employed by the State Highway Dept., working at the weigh station south of Libby, until his retirement in 1963. He was a member of the VFW and the Disabled Veterans. He had two step-daughters, Marie Mueller and Donna Wittlake, two stepsons, Gordon Lindsey and Ben Lindsey and numerous grandchildren. He died on April 23, 1979.

ELIAS LOVE HINEMAN, was born Sept. 20, 1894 in Bloomfield, IN. He joined the service

on Sept. 19, 1917 and was discharged on June 29, 1919.

He was a member of the Machine Gun Regt. His most memorable experience was the boat ride across the ocean.

He married Leona Dannen on Sept. 17, 1919 and they had four children. He is a great-great-grandfather and was a farmer for 65 years. Today he is enjoying relatives and friends.

FRANK J. HINSMAN, was born June 17, 1895 in Chicago, IL. He joined the service on March 8, 1918 and was discharged on March 29, 1919.

He was a member of the motor transport and achieved the rank of Pvt. 1st Class. He participated in the Bordon, Verdun, Tulle and other battles. He remembers delivering supplies to the front lines and having to drive at night without lights, dodging the shells on the roads.

He has one brother and one sister whom are still living. He is now 97 years old and has trouble walking.

J.R. HOLLINGER, served as a member of Ambulance Co. No. 3. Enlistment for this organization was started on May 16, 1917. The company was enlisted to full war strength by June 5, 1917 with five officers and 156 enlisted. The company was mustered into Federal Service by Lt. Mankow on July 19, 1917. The company departed New York aboard the steamship *Briton*, disembarking at Liverpool, England on May 31, 1918.

The company saw service in the following locations: Artonges, Charly, Chateau Thierry, Bezu St. Germain, Le Channel, and Dravegny, as well as others. The station at St. Germain was particularly engaged in the treatment of men from both the 42nd and 26th Divisions. The company was involved with treatment of men of the 32nd Div. at Dravegny. An advanced dressing station was established at St. Gillis. Later this station had to be abandoned due to hostile enemy shellfire. Many other encounters were similar.

The company left isolation camp at St. Nazaire on April 27, 1919 aboard the USS Mongolia. They docked at New York on May 9, 1919 and entrained at Camp Dix where they were mustered out.

They arrived at Lancaster, PA on May 21, 1919. They were received with open arms and a welcome never to be forgotten. *(Extracted from "Brief History of Ambulance Company 111," and submitted by J.R. Hollinger.)*

PAUL JENNINGS HOLSEN SR, was born Dec. 3, 1899 in Mt. Carmel, Wabash Co., IL. Enlisted on Jan. 24, 1918 at the age of 18, at the Jefferson Barracks, MO. He was a student, but gave his occupation as a truck driver. He enlisted for patriotism and adventure.

He remembers the cold, wooden barracks with the coal stoves at Jefferson Barracks. He saw his first and only free lunch in a saloon in St. Louis. He trained at Camp Jackson, Columbia, SC. He curried and exercised artillery horses by the numbers for two weeks before transfer to Truck Co. 6, First Corps Artillery Park. Then it was infantry drill until May 8, 1918, when he was ordered to Camp Merrit, NJ.

After the Marines cleared Belleau Wood, he and a few other drivers were sent in with a company of Pioneer Inf. to pick up guns, packs, etc. While his truck was being loaded, he walked through the woods and saw the dead Germans in their machine gun pits or scattered out in the woods. He also found and disassembled his first potato masher, a German hand grenade. He was wounded in action on Oct. 2, 1918.

He has five bars on his victory medal; Champagne-Marne, Aisne-Marne, Chateau Thierry, Oise-Aisne and the Meuse Argonne. He was discharged on Feb. 10, 1919 at Camp Dodge, IA. He returned and completed high school in Mt. Carmel, IL. Then completed two years military school at Marion Military Inst. at Alabama. He then attended Tulane University in New Orleans for two years where he received his BA degree.

FERD O. HOMMEL, was born Jan. 2, 1896 in Needham, IN. He enlisted on April 3, 1918 and was discharged on March 22, 1919. He was a member of the Army's 67th Artillery and achieved the rank of Pvt. He trained in Ft. Hamilton, NY.

He was inducted into the service at Camp Sherman, OH, then to Camp Merrill, NJ and was there one month with the flu. He was sent to Long Island, NY at Camp Mills and then sent overseas to Brest, France on Sept. 4, 1918 on the *Mt. Vernon*. It was a three ship convoy, the *Mt. Vernon, Farland,* and the *Zyphlin*. He was then shipped to several different places in France.

After the war was over, he boarded an Italian ship in Marcelle, France. They sailed through the Spanish Straight, with a six day layover in Gibraltar for coal for the ship. He left there and docked at Hoboken, NJ, then back to Camp Mill in Long Island, NY.

The regiment was broken up and he was sent to Camp Sherman, OH for discharge. He was given a train ticket, with two cents a mile compensation to Franklin, IN. He then walked home to Needham, IN, which was nine miles.

He is presently living in the same house he was born in and tends to one or two gardens each summer. He also does some mowing with his lawn tractor. He married on May 22, 1924 and was widowed on March 21, 1928. He has one daughter, son-in-law, five grandchildren, 19 great-grand-children and six great-great-grandchildren.

JEHIRAS HOUTS, was born on Aug. 30, 1894 at Marion, IA in Linn County. His parents were Henry and Ella Frager Houts.

He served with the U.S. Army and National Guard outfit from Feb. 25, 1918 to May 2, 1919. He was in active duty in Alsass Lorraine, Argonne Territory, Verdun and St. Mahiel.

After being "chamber-maid" for the horses in Camp Dodge, IA, being in Co. 337, Division 88, he signed up to be a replacement in the Missouri/Kansas City National Guard outfit under Capt. Bill Smith and Maj. MacDonald. This was the 91st Div., 347th Inf.

He sailed from New York with the Missouri/Kansas Outfit. They took an old cattle boat across and it took 17 days to Port Liverpool, England. They were attached to the English Army for a while to get gas instructions. One of the battles, there were 240 men that went in to fight and only 87 came out. He was a lucky one.

The most memorable experience he had was when he was chosen to be a runner. Usually two or three were sent, hoping that at least one would make it with the orders. He heard shots and saw dust coming from the ground in front of him. He hit the ground and rolled into the ditch and crawled on his belly until he felt it was safe. As he continued on the road, he passed a team of horses that had four or five men on the wagon laying every which way. They were all dead including the horses.

He married Mary Wilson, a school teacher. Most of their married life they lived in Cedar Rapids, IA and raised five children, two sons and three daughters. After 45 years, she passed away and he married Lera Flitsch. After 17 years, she passed away and he married his present wife, Clara Joan Knight. They have been married for seven years. They live in Alburnett, IA and still raise a big garden every year, drives his own car, dances two or three times a week, and when he has time travels, plays cards and does volunteer work for a local agency.

CLARENCE DEWEY HOWELL, was born in Sept. 26, 1900 in Union, SC. He enlisted on July 9, 1916 and discharged on May 14, 1919.

He was a member of Co. A, 117th Engineers, Rainbow Div. He achieved the ranking of Corporal. He was in the Champagne Marne Defensive, the Aisne-Marne, St. Mihiel, and Meuse Argonne Offensive. He also fought in the Luneville Baccarut, Esperance Souain and Essex Pannes Defensive sectors.

He worked for the Texaco Co. for a while after being discharged from the Army. He married a young lady from Union, SC. She died shortly after they were wed. In January 1928, he married Della Mae Ingle from Asheville, NC. They had one daughter, Sarah Margaret, born in August 1928. He went to the Panama Canal Zone in 1929 and was employed by the Canal Zone Fire Dept. His family joined him in 1930, where he and his wife resided until his retirement in September 1957 with rank of Lt.

His daughter married and returned to the United States in 1953. He and his wife bought a retirement home in Asheville and became active in the United Methodist Church, where he was a trustee and member of the United Methodist Men. He was a mason, shriner, a member of the American Legion and VFW. Much of his retirement life was spent being active in the Veterans of WWI, U.S.A., Inc. He was the NC. Department Commander for two years and commander of the Fourth Region. His wife was also active in the organization and was the President of the Ladies Auxiliary for the state of North Carolina and Fourth Region.

In May 1982, they went to live with their daughter and her family in Winston-Salem, NC, because of ill health of his wife, Della. She passed away in September of that same year. Clarence continued to live an active life in Winston-Salem until his death on March 22, 1984 at the age of 83.

EARL CURTIS HOWELL, was born April 28, 1899 in Jackson, GA. He joined the service on Sept. 10, 1917 and was discharged on June 11, 1919.

He was a member of the 302nd Supply Co., Q.M.C. as a cook. He served overseas from Nov. 26, 1917 until June 15, 1919.

He has one son and is retired from the Post Office after 34 years of service.

JOHN C. HUBER, was born on Aug. 31, 1892, on a farm in Peosta, IA, Vernon Township, Dubuque County. He grew up while he attended a one-room school, as he worked with his family on a moderate sized farm. He developed many talents on his own, such as a carpenter, an engineer with the capability of fixing machinery. He operated a small grocery store in the city of Dubuque for many years.

Later he became a foreman at The Dubuque Container Co. as well as a maintenance man. He married Marie Lynch and their married life was spent in Dubuque where he was very helpful to friends and neighbors.

He lost one lung in the war. He suffered from shrapnel that was lodged in his left shoulder, that could not be removed. However, on his honorable discharge from the U.S. Army stated: that he did not fight in any battles, engagements, skirmishes or expeditions.

He was honorably discharged at Camp Dodge, IA on June 17, 1919. He served as a Pvt. in the 350th Inf. He died on Nov. 14, 1951 and is buried in Mt. Olivet Cemetery, Dubuque, IA.

JOHN HUGGINS, was born April 27, 1896, in the Deer Park area south of Columbia Falls. He was the second child of Logan and Nannie Huggins. He attended Deer Park School. As a young man he worked on farms, logging, river drives, cooking and fur trapping.

In 1917, he entered the U.S. Army, serving in the 46th Sprice Squadron, until receiving his honorable discharge in 1918.

In 1924, he married Grace Oertell. In the late 1920s and 30s he lived in Essex and worked on lookouts, trail crews, railroad and road construction, depending upon the season. During WWII, he worked as a carpenter at Hanford, WA and followed that trade thereafter. He worked for five years on the construction of Hungry Horse Dam.

In 1951, he married Wilma Apple, and was preceded in death by her in 1962. He had one son, Fred C. Huggins, four grandchildren and three great-grandchildren. He died on May 2, 1984.

JESSE L. HUNTER, was born Dec. 22, 1898 in Lewiston, ME. His parents were George E. Hunter and Rebecker M. Vickery.

He served in the U.S. Navy from June 1918 to June 1919. He enlisted in the Regular Navy from Portland, ME as 3rd Class Mid-Ship-man and was sent to Newport, RI for training in naval work and military format. In August, he was transferred to Framingham, MA on temporary assignment where there was an epidemic of influenza. He moved back to Newport in Sept. and then in October was sent to Boston, MA, Naval Unit, Steam Engineering Commonwealth Pier. He was assigned to the Wentworth Inst. and completed his course in June and was discharged.

He returned to Lewiston, ME and married Hester L. Bell, and raised two children. His wife is now deceased and he is living with his daughter in So. Portland, ME.

J. ROY HUTCHINSON, was born Sept. 16, 1896 in Tallula, IL, a son of Ansley and Georgietta Hutchinson. He was educated in Illinois and graduated from high school in Tallula in 1913.

In 1916, he came to Montana and worked with his brother doing ranching work in the Glendive area. In 1918, he entered the U.S. Army serving in France, until his honorable discharge in 1919.

In 1920, he came to Kalispell and was employed with the U.S. Forest Service until 1938, serving as a district ranger from 1930 to 1938. He moved to the Bitterroot Valley where he farmed until 1942. He moved to California for two years before returning to Montana, where he served as a park ranger until his retirement in 1969.

He was a member of the WWI Barracks. On April 20, 1945, he married Audrey York in Kalispell. He died on June 25, 1983.

PETER ROY IRELAND, born April 29, 1897 in Fairfax, MO. He was located in Ft. Lewis, WA and Ft. Stevens, OR.

The Armistice was signed before he had to go overseas. He remembers the flu epidemic and how bad it was.

He married Mary Markers on May 1, 1919 and they had two boys and two girls. He was a farmer and a rancher until his retirement. He is active in the Sawtooth Barracks 217. He still rides horses to check out the ranch once in a while. He loves to travel.

CALEB JACKSON, was born Sept. 3, 1889, in Sheridan, WY to Isaac and Kate Jackson. He received his education in Cody and Sheridan, WY. In 1910, he moved with his family to the Flathead Valley.

In 1917, he entered the service in Sheridan. After his honorable discharge, he homesteaded in Arvada, WY. Later, he was in charge of the Wyoming State Highway Dept. for 10 years.

On March 24, 1928, he married Alma May Smith in Sheridan. The couple then farmed in the Big Goose Valley in Sheridan for 11 years. In 1948, they sold the farm and moved to Kalispell. He then worked for the Montana Highway Dept., retiring when he was 70.

He was a member of the American Legion and the Central Christian Church in Kalispell. He was preceded in death by a daughter Beatrice Alma. He had four grandchildren and two great-grandchildren. He passed away on Sept. 25, 1985.

LOUIS F. JACKSON, son of John J. and Annie Cunningham Jackson, served in France with 35th and 30th Aero-squadrons.

While in France, his last living sister and father died. He is a Hardin, KY high school graduate of 1917. He joined the service in Paducah, KY in late April. He was sworn in May 4, 1917 in Louisville, KY. He was honorably discharged on April 23, 1919.

He hiked the hills in Ft. Thomas, KY for a short time. Maj. Carl Spatz and Bowen were in charge of the 8th Aero-squadrons 30 through 37.

He left Kelley Field in early August. He slept in pup tents at Staten Island, NY for several days. He then boarded the *SS Baltic*, on Aug. 23, 1917. He was in the Halifax Harbor for 10 days or more. During the ocean crossing they encountered a sub in the Irish Sea in Liverpool, England on Sept. 15, 1917. They crossed the English Channel during the night to Le Harve, France

He was in a small group on detached service in French Aviation Instruction Center in Lyon, France for about 75 days. After, he was sent to the 3rd Aviation Instruction Center near Issoudon, France. There he became a member of the 30th Squadron.

He assembled LeRohne rotary motors until Armistice Day. Early in 1918, Gen. Pershing, came through and later Maj. Gen. Harbourd. When the war was over he went on a generous leave to St. Malo via Paris.

All of his company officers and men were splendid. Col. Bingham, his Post Commander, was a compassionate and good man, one of the finest. He understood. Later, near Bordeaux it seemed we waited long in stock barn quarters. Finally boarded a ship, *Arizona*, he sailed a southern route. They ran into tremendously high seas for a few days. He was discharged on April 23, 1919 in Chillicothe, OH.

PAUL H. JARRETT, was born in Selingsgrove, PA on June 19, 1895. In 1901, his family moved to Nebraska. In April 1917, he enlisted in the Army.

He attended officer's school, was commissioned 2nd Lieutenant and assigned to Co. M, 166th Regt., 42nd Rainbow Div. He arrived in

France in November 1917 and was sent to British hand-to-hand combat school in St. Pol. He was later appointed Judge Advocate (prosecuting attorney), for the entire 166th Regt. He was wounded on July 29, 1918 in the Aisne-Marne Offensive. He spent six weeks in the hospital. He was gassed in the Meuse-Argonne in November. He was in Army hospitals in France and the United States until the Army discharged him on August 1919.

He went to Los Angeles, CA in 1921. He married Helen Ericson in 1930 and they had six children. He was a Culver City Clerk and then Postmaster from 1940 until retirement in 1960. He then worked at MGM studios.

He travels extensively with a house trailer. In 1988 and 89 he went to France to visit WWI Battlefields. In 1989, the village of Neuviller, named a street after me during a ceremony held in his honor.

JAMES CHRISTIAN JENSEN, left home at Minden, NE to enlist at the recruiting office in Hastings, NE. He was sent directly to Ft. Logan, CO where he was sworn in and equipped on April 15, 1917.

He was then shipped to El Paso, TX to join the 23rd Inf. On June 1, 1917 was transferred to Syracuse, NY after the 23rd Inf. was split into the 49th and 50th Inf. He drew a salary of $15.00 a month and was then raised to $30.00 a month. In Syracuse, he was assigned to the 50th Inf. as their company mechanic. There was no camp in Syracuse, so the company was put in the fairgrounds building.

He stayed in Syracuse until the fall of 1917 and because it was so cold, they were living in tents, they were shipped to Canup Green, Charlotte, NC. They stayed there until the weather was warm up north. They were then split into small sections and the section he was in was sent to Chester, PA, where he was assigned to guard duty at Sunship Building Co. They were there three months and then transferred to Camp Mills, Long Island. There he was assigned to military police in New York City. They stayed at Camp Mills in tents so when it got cold again they were transferred to South Carolina to train for overseas duty.

He was in training until the Armistice was signed on Nov. 11, 1918. He was then shipped to Camp Dix, NJ and since they weren't doing anything he put in for a discharge. He was discharged from Camp Dodge, IA on March 4, 1919. He was made Corporal on June 29, 1918 and made Sergeant on Nov. 8, 1918.

LOUIS JENSEN, was born Sept. 11, 1893, in Ringstad, Denmark, a son of Hans and Johanne Jensen. He received his education in Denmark and when he was 17 years old he came to America and has lived in Kalispell much of the time since then. He had engaged in farming operations and had also been employed with the Kalispell Laundry prior to his retirement.

He served in the U.S. Army during WWI. He was a member of Co. F, 318th Eng. from Feb. 15, 1918 to June 23, 1919.

He married Adelaide Gilbertson in Kalispell and was preceded in death by her on Jan. 19, 1973. He had one son, two daughters, ten grandchildren, two great-grandchildren and one great-great-grandchild. He died on July 5, 1991.

HARLAN JENSON, was born May 28, 1899 to James and Mary Jenson at Dells Rapid, SD. He lived on the farm and stayed on the farm until he went into the service school in Woonscocett, SD.

He joined on Oct. 18, 1917. While in the Army he became a Corporal. He was in battles in the St. Mihiel and the Meuse Argonne. He was in active combat for six months.

His medals were an overseas medal. He was wounded with shrapnel in his leg. He continued to farm and moved to Whitewood in 1943. He died in 1965. He had two children, both girls. He is buried at National Cemetery near Sturgis.

WALFRED G. JOHNSON, was born Aug. 1, 1895, at Lisbon, ND, a son of Andrew and Lottie Johnson. He received his education in North Dakota and on July 1, 1918, he entered the U.S. Army at Washburn, ND, and had served until receiving his honorable discharge on Dec. 26, 1918, at Camp Grant, IL.

On Sept. 21, 1921, he was married to Charlotte R. Runell at Dogden, ND. The couple later moved to Bigfork where he was a rural mail carrier, later moving to Hardin where he continued as a mail carrier. He retired as a mail carrier at Hardin after 34 years of service.

In 1965, he returned to Bigfork, where he had lived since. He was a member of the Bethany Lutheran Church of Bigfork, Veterans of WWI Barracks, 45 year member of the Bigfork American Legion No. 86, member of the National Rural Letter Carriers Association and the National Association of Retired Federal Employees. He had five sons, 10 grandchildren and one great-grandchild. He died on Oct. 30, 1972.

ROY R. JOHNSTON,

was born March 28, 1889 in Flathead. He was the eldest child of the late Mr. and Mrs. Reuben Johnston. He married Martha Bradley Rising on Sept. 3, 1926 in Thompson Falls.

He was a steam electrical engineer in charge of the electric dept. of McKengie-Wallace in Kalispell in the mid-1920s. During WWI, he was a 1st Lt. in the U.S. Army. During WWII, he worked for the government in Alaska. He was state boiler inspector for three years, retiring in 1963 to his home in Deer Park area.

He died on Dec. 12, 1978.

JAMES L. JOLLY,

was born Dec. 18, 1895 in Pleasantville, IA, a son of Lawrence and Nora Jolly. He later moved to the western states where he entered the U.S. Navy at Salt Lake City, UT on June 9, 1917, and served until receiving his honorable discharge at Minneapolis, MN on Aug. 25, 1919.

He then returned to Montana. On July 25, 1923, he married Bertha Shouse in Kalispell. He had been a custodian for a privately owned property at Lake McDonald in Glacier National Park for 20 years prior to his retirement. He was a resident of the Bigfork Convalescent Center. He had two sons, four grandchildren and one great-granddaughter. He passed away on Jan. 31, 1979.

JESSE F. JONES,

was born July 22, 1893 in East St. Louis, MO, a son of Harvey and Irene Jones. He was reared on a farm at St. Elmo, IL, where he received his education. In 1914, he moved with his mother, brothers and sisters to a homestead at Culbertson, MT.

In 1917, he entered the U.S. Army, where he served during WWI with the 4th Div. Regulars, until his honrable discharge in 1919. He came to Whitefish in 1919, where he was employed by the Great Northern as a boilermaker helper at the roundhous and later became a Brake-man for the Great Northern Railroad until 1946.

From 1951 to 1957, he was employed as a toolmaker for Boeing Aircraft in Seattle, until he was forced to retire due to illness. He then returned to Whitefish, where he made and repaired violins.

He was married to Ethel Baughman on Aug. 10, 1922 at Whitefish. He was a member of the Christian Church of Whitefish, WWI Veterans Barracks No. 362 of Kalispell and the Disabled American Veterans. He had two sons, three daughters, 15 grandchildren and one great-grandchild.

Courtesy of R. Fitzgerald.

ALBERT H. KADOLPH, was born Sept. 26, 1897 in Chicago, IL. He joined the service on Jan. 3, 1918 and was discharged on March 29, 1919.

He achieved the rank of Sgt. before being discharged. He participated in the Sully France and St. Mihiel Battles. He remembers sleeping in a truck the night the Armistice was signed.

He is a 74 year member of the American Legion. He married his wife Lela, in 1920 and she died in 1980. His parents were Gary and Mary Kadolph. He is a retired farmer.

ROBERT DOLAN KELLEY, was born Aug. 10, 1890 in Henry County, GA. He was a Sgt. of the 210th Aero Squadron in the Army. He died on Sept. 25, 1952.

His name was recorded wrong, Kelly, upon enlistment. He had to legally change back to Kelley after the war. He was stationed in Doncaster, England.

He attended the University of Georgia and married Nannie Pearl Morgan in Atlanta in 1924. They had two sons. He worked as a heating engineer with Randall Brothers and President of Sunbeam Heating Co., in Atlanta. He was a member of the Scottish Rite, Lions Club and active at Druid Hills Baptist Church. He died suddenly of a heart attack while calling on a customer.

WILLIAM JOSEPH KELLY, was born Nov. 6, 1898. He joined the Vermont Inf., National Guard at Ft. Ethan Allen. His final discharge was in 1922.

He served in the U.S. Army's Co. B, 103rd Machine Gun Bn. His Ethan Allen National Guard was melded into the mass group, which then became part of the famous 26th Yankee Div. He served in the Co. B, 103rd Machine Gun Bn. from Feb. 9, 1918 until Nov. 11, 1918. He was wounded in Belleau Wood on July 18, 1918.

He was awarded the Purple Heart and Silver Star, along with special recognition from his Division Commander for meritorious service on May 13, 1918.

His married Ethel Borden Kelly and they had four daughters, Elizabeth, Ethel, Patricia and Wilma, one son, William B. Kelly, 20 grandchildren and 17 great-grandchildren.

He missed the gang after discharge and re-enlisted in July 1919 for the Army of Occupation, where he was sent to the watch on the Rhine at Fortress Ehrenbreitstein in Coblenz. He attained the rank of Corporal here until his discharge in 1922. He later visited the Fortress Ehrenbfeitstein to relive his carefree days and see how Germany had changed.

He was in all the major offensives, Meusse Argonne, St. Mihiel, Aisne-Marne, Pasfini Sector, Xivray and Marvoisini Defense Sector as well as the Chateau Thierry. He sailed to Liverpool on the *Cedric*, then over to LeHavre on the *Mona's Queen*, where he learned the correct use of the ammunition from French instructors. He often told stories of their hotel accommodations being French pig pens, which they had to clean out before they could use them for bunks. He passed away in the Albany V.A.M.C. on April 13, 1987.

FRED KENT, was born on April 13, 1895, in Winterset, IA. He joined the service on July 13, 1918 and was discharged on Dec. 13, 1918.

He was a member of Co. D, 2nd Inf. and attained the rank of Pvt. He was stationed in Camp Dodge, IA

He married Minnie and they had three

children, Marie Long, Delores Carson and Dennis Kent, whom is deceased. He is now deceased and buried at Ft. Meade National VA. Cemetery.

GUY SAMUEL KEPHART, was born in

Sidney, IA on Nov. 3, 1893. He attended a one-room school and worked for various farmers before filing on a homestead claim in Campbell County, WY in 1917.

On Oct. 6, 1917, Kephart entered military service and was a member of the Co. M, 23rd Rainbow Inf. Div. He sailed to France on the *USS Lincoln*, leaving the United States on Dec. 12, 1917. He fought in several battles in France including; Vaux, July 1, 1918; Soissons, July 18, 1918; St. Mihiel, Sept. 12-13, 1918; and Champagne, Oct. 2, 1918.

He suffered a shrapnel wound to the right shoulder, while fighting with the American Expeditionary Forces in France on Oct. 6, 1918. He spent several months at a field hospital in France, before arriving in the United States on Feb. 22, 1919. He was then transferred to the hospital at Des Moines, IA, where he received his medical discharge on July 16, 1919. For many years, shrapnel exited the wound, requiring several trips to Fitzsimmons Hospital. Due to an oversight at the time of his discharge, it was 45 years before he received the Purple Heart.

After his discharge, he returned to farm his homestead. It was there that he met and married Elaine Nordgen and they had three children. In 1938, he moved his family to South Dakota. From 1944 until his retirement, he was employed for 17 years at Ft. Meade, SD Veterans Hospital. At the time of his death, Nov. 10, 1990, he was a member of WWI Barracks.

WILLIAM GUY KESLER, was born Nov. 9,

1895 in Clifty, WV. He joined the service on April 2, 1918 and was discharged on June 13, 1919.

He was a member of Co. G, 317th Inf., and received the ranking of Pvt. 1st Class. He participated in the Somme Offensive, St. Mihiel Offensive and the Meusse Argonne Offensive. He received an award for Marksman and a Victory Service Ribbon with three bronze stars.

He married on June 21, 1926 and had one daughter. He died on Oct. 31, 1965.

DARRELL A. KESLING, registered for the

draft of 1918 at Toledo, OH. He passed his physical examination and on May 17, 1918 boarded a troop train parked in the Toledo, OH railroad yards. The train headed south and all along the route, stopped to pick up soldiers. He arrived at Camp Taylor, KY. He choose to be a member of the Inf.

He was located at Camp Buregard for basic

training. On Aug. 5, he left Camp Buregard by train and headed to Newport News, VA, where he boarded the troopship, *George Washington*, and headed out across the Atlantic Ocean for France. After 12 days, they landed safe in Brest, France

They then marched to the Soissons Sector and then was ordered to the St. Aignon. While in the Army, he formed his own quartet, however was not able to reach them after the war. He boarded the cruiser *Oregon*, and crossed the Atlantic in five days to land at Hoboken, NJ. He was discharged at Camp Sherman in Ohio on March 15, 1919.

BERT KEZAR, was one of five Wisconsin

brothers, who all saw military service. He enlisted on Dec. 20, 1917 at the age of 17. His two older brothers were already serving. He trained at Ft. Screven, GA and was assigned to Btry. F, 61st Regt., Coast Artillery.

He sailed for France on July 17, 1918 from Newport News. Despite submarines, the ship reached St. Nazaire unscathed. He served in France until January 1919. He was discharged at Ft. Screven on March 1, 1919. His unit never came under attack, but his brothers saw considerable action. He died in 1981.

LAWRENCE EARL KING, was born June

20, 1897 in Glasco, KS. He graduated from the Glasco High School class of 1916. He taught one year of grade school, 1916-17, a country school with 12 pupils from first through eighth grade.

He enlisted in the United Naval Reserve Force on July 10, 1918 at Denver, CO. He served aboard the *USS West Zula*, a cargo transport ship hauling nitrate. He was a Yeoman 1st Class, Captains Writer when he was released to inactive duty.

He enlisted in the U.S. Army Air Force during WWII, as a Captain. He was in active duty from July 19, 1942 until Aug. 29, 1945. He attained the rank of Lt. Col.

He has a 70-year continuous membership in the American Legion and was a Past Commander from 1929-30 at the Oceanside Post No. 146 in Oceanside, CA. He is a member of the Bakersfield Post No. 26 since 1930, VFW Post No. 6601 in Oildale, CA and a member of the Reserve Offices Association, Bakersfield Chapter.

He retired in June 1972 from 53 years in the lumber business. He owned and operated the King-Marshall Lumber Co. The name later changed to Civic Center Lumber Co. in June 1940 until his retirement. He has been a member of the Methodist Church since boyhood. He regularly attends Sunday services at First United Methodist Church in Bakersfield, CA. He has one son, three grandchildren and one great-grandchild. Most of his time is devoted to the affairs of the Veterans of WWI. He is currently the Commander, Dept. of California, Veterans of WWI, Commander, 4th Dist. Dept. of California and Commander, Barracks No. 432 of Bakersfield.

FRANK E. KIRLI, was born Jan. 20, 1895, in Detroit, MI. He joined the service on Sept. 9, 1915 and was furloughed to the reserves on March 19, 1920. His final discharged was June 4, 1920.

He served with the 36th Div., A.E.F., 3rd Div. and achieved the rank of Sgt. He was located in Ft. Bliss, TX, Camp Bowie, TX, Camp Travis, TX and Camp Pike, AK. He also served in France and Germany.

In the Mexican Border contingent, he served with future Generals Pershing, Patton and Eisenhower. He was one of six soldiers who were sent to Ft. Worth to establish Camp Bowie. He met his future wife there and returned after the war and married her. He received medals from the Mexican Border Campaign, Army of Occupation and a Bronze Victory Medal.

He married Katherine Runion in 1920. They had one daughter, June, three grand-daughters and two great-grandchildren. He died on Jan. 8, 1992. He had worked for T&P Railroad for 20 years and for F.W. Stockyards. He was on the Livestock Comm. Co. for 42 years. He was active in Veterans of WWI, American Legion, which he founded, VFW and a 65 year member of the Masonic Lodge. He was a member of the Methodist Church.

JOHN KIPPEN, was born Aug. 6, 1896 on his father's homestead in Omemee, ND. He enlisted on Sept. 9, 197 at the age of 21 in Glasgow, MT. He was discharged on Oct. 12, 1919. He was with the 304th Supplies and achieved the rank of Sgt.

He married Hazel Harrison at Malta, MT on Nov. 12, 1924. They returned to Omemee and lived on the family farm. He is retired. They are both in pretty good health.

JAMES E. KNIGHT, was born Nov. 23, 1900, in Jupiter, FL. He joined the service on Feb. 12, 1917 and was discharged Sept. 26, 1919 in Mobile, AL.

He was a member of the U.S. Navy and served on the *USS Maine* and the *USS Celebes*. He was an Electrician 1st Class. He was also stationed in Guantamo Bay, Cuba.

He is married with two sons, one daughter, seven grandchildren and nine great-grandchildren. He holds an amateur radio license and is now retired.

FRED KNOPFLEWAS, was born Jan. 29, 1892 at Ashley, ND. His parents were Adam Knopfle and Christina Ammon.

He served in the U.S. Army from April 2, 1918 to 1919. He married Lillian Peterson and she passed away with cancer. On Dec. 23, 1930 he married Orvetta Owens at Malta, MT. He farmed and worked mining for other farmers. They moved to Whitefish, MT in 1943. He worked at the Great Northern Railway Round House until 1957, when he retired.

They had two boys and two girls. One boy was killed in a car wreck in 1962. He was a member of the American Legion Post No. 108 and Barracks No. 362. He passed away on Jan. 22, 1979 at Columbia Falls Veterans Home, at the age of 87.

EVERETT KNOTTS, was inducted into the Army at Kingwood, WV on May 25, 1918. He arrived at Camp Lee, near Petersburg, VA at about noon the next day. At Camp Lee, he was assigned to the 34th Co. of the 9th Bn., 155th Dept. He remained at Camp Lee for his indoctrination training, until about July 11, 1918.

He sailed on a cattle boat down the James River from Richmond to Newport News, VA. They camped in Newport News and then boarded a ship and sailed to Brest, France. He sailed from Newport News, VA on July 18, 1918.

He served with the American Expeditionary Force in France from July 18, 1918 to April 27, 1919. During that period, he was in the Muesse Argonne Offensive. He earned the WWI Victory Medal for that service. He was gassed and shell-shocked from that offensive in the Muesse Argonne area of France. He was assigned to the 111th Inf., 29th Div., Co. C. During a short period, from Sept. 26, 1918 until Oct. 7, 1918, he was in the Theacourt Sector of France. He left for Lemans on March 14, 1919 and then left for a seaport and sailed to the United States.

He arrived at Camp Dix, NJ on April 28, 1919, and in a few days left for Pittsburgh, PA. From Pittsburgh, he went to Camp Sherman, OH. He was discharged there on May 13, 1919.

ALBERT KNUTSON, was born Oct. 8, 1893 in Kalispell, a son of Peter O. and Annetta Sands Knutson. He received his education in Kalispell, and in 1918, he entered the U.S. Army. He served as a wagoneer in Co. E until receiving his honorable discharge in 1919.

On Aug. 9, 1921, he was married to Marion Brocken in the Bethlehem Lutheran Church in Kalispell. On Aug. 3, 1943, he enlisted in the U.S. Navy at Helena and served as a Machinist Mate

2nd Class until his honorable discharge on May 17, 1944, at Santa Cruz, CA.

He then returned to the Flathead, where he engaged in the lumber industry, working as a sawmill worker and dozer operator. He also engaged in ranching. He worked for several sawmills in the area, including the Kila Mill.

He was a member of the Bethlehem Lutheran Church, the American Legion and the WWI Barracks. He had one son, one daughter, six grandchildren and one great-grandchild. He passed away on Dec. 7, 1979.

FRED KNUTSON, was born May 14, 1897 at Dayton, MT. His parents were Peter O. Knutson and Annetta Sands. He served in the U.S. Army from 1918 to 1919.

He was a member of the 1st French Motor Btry., 1st Div. He married Hattie Conrad on Nov. 15, 1923. He was a farmer and ran a threshing crew. He was also a sawyer in different saw mills. They had twin boys that served in WWII and also two girls. He belonged to Barracks No. 362 and was a Past Commander. He died on Dec. 23, 1990 at the age of 93.

JOSEPH JAMES KOCARNIK, was born in 1894 in Plasi, NE. He entered the U.S. Navy in September 1917.

He was a Radioman 2nd Class and served aboard the *USS Essex, Comodore, City of South Haven, George Washington* and Submarine No. 13. He was honorably discharged in June 1919 .

He moved from Nebraska to Scappose, OR, where he taught elementary school. He married Lillian Fischer in 1921 and they had three sons and two daughters. He owned and operated Kocarnik Grocery Store in Scappoose from 1926-63. He grew rhododendrons as a hobby. He took charge of the Memorial Day decoration of veteran's graves on local cemeteries until his death in 1977.

CLAVE V. KOOGLER, was born on May 22, 1894 in Las Vegas, NM. He joined the service on March 1, 1918 and was discharged on Aug. 10, 1919. He passed away on May 8, 1894.

He was a member of the 89th Div. located at the Evacuation Hospital No. 16. He was stationed in Ft. Riley, KS and Camp Mead, MD. He fought in the Meusse Argonne, Chateau Thierry and the Great Forest Offensive. He served in the Army of Occupation in Coblenz, Germany. He was awarded three bronze stars.

His parents were Washington Graham and Clara Rose Housel Koogler.

WILLIAM HOUSEL KOOGLER, was born Sept. 8, 1892 and died on Feb. 3, 1951. His parents were Washington Graham and Clara Rose Housel Koogler.

He was a member of the 89th Div., 342nd Machine Gun Co. at Falzal. He served in the Army of Occupation in Coblenz, Germany.

CLARENCE R. KROGSTAD, was born July 2, 1899 in Milwaukee, WI. He joined the service on July 5, 1918 and was discharged on Sept. 30, 1921.

He was a member of the U.S. Navy's 6th Battle Squadron of the Grand Fleet. He was a member of the 3rd Div. aboard the battleship, *USS Texas*. He achieved the rank of Seaman 1st Class, Storekeeper. He was stationed in Great Lakes, IL for Naval training for two weeks, to Ireland aboard the *USS Kenawa*, an oil tanker, briefly aboard the *USS New York* and the *USS Texas* until his discharge.

He remembers having to climb to the crows nest on the *USS Kenewa*, during a horrible storm to close a flapping trap door that came loose after his watch. He also remembers the surrender of the German fleet at the Firth of Forth and the number of German captains who either shot themselves, or went down with their ships rather than face disgrace. On Armistice Day, they met and joined the French and British sailors in life boats on the sea and exchanged wine and other drinks. They transported President Wilson to Brest, France.

He is a widower with two daughters, grandchildren and great-grandchildren.

PAUL W. KRUG, at age 26, enlisted in the U.S. Army at Gettysburg, PA, during the summer of 1918. He was a prime candidate for the cavalry from the horsemanship gained on his father's farm. He was attached to the M Troop, 6th Cavalry.

After only three months of basic training at Camp Lee, VA. The 6th Cavalry took their horses aboard ship and departed from Newport News, VA for France. Both troops and horses suffered seasickness. Part of the American Expeditionary Force, he served his tour of duty in Gierves, France. He received the Bronze Victory Button and the AEF Ribbon when he completed his service

on July 3, 1919. He was discharged at Camp Dix, NJ.

For five years following military service, his occupation was farming. He then passed the Civil Service exam and drove a rural mail route, first with a horse mail wagon, then a Model T, then a Model A, for 38 years until the mandatory retirement age of 70.

He marched on the local Hanover, PA Memorial Day Parade with the March With Pride Veterans of all wars, until age 92. He became a centenarian on March 22, 1992. He and his wife, Leah, age 94, will observe their 73rd wedding anniversary this year. Both reside at the Brethren Home, New Oxford, PA.

JOHN E. KUZARA, was born Jan. 22, 1900 in Chicago, IL. He joined the service on April 25, 1917 and was discharged on March 26, 1919.

He was a member of Co. M, 163rd U.S. Inf., 41st Div., and achieved the rank of Corporal. He served guard duty in Montana and was also located at Camp Gohicary in Lormont, France. He fought in the Alsace, Chateau Thierry and the Soissons.

He was second oldest of 12 children and now is the oldest of 350 descendants. He retired after 27 years.

ORAL J. LACOMBE, was born Feb. 19, 1896, in Negaunee, MI. He joined the service on May 25, 1917 and was discharged on Jan. 28, 1919.

He was a member of Co. C, 107th Engineers, 32nd Div., and achieved the rank of Sgt. He fought in the Alsace-Larraine, Chateau Thierry, Meusse Argonne and Soissons. He received the Purple Heart for his service in the Argonne Forest.

He married in 1921 and had four children. He married for the second time in 1954. In 1957, he retired from the Postal Service after 30 years of service.

WILLIAM MONROE LANCE, was born Sept. 24, 1896 in Wayne, OK. He joined the service on April 8, 1918 and was discharged on April 12, 1919.

He was a member of the 54th Ammunitions

Train, C.A.C., where he attained the rank of Pvt. He was stationed in Angouleme, France. His most memorable moment was on Nov. 11, 1918, his company was making preparations to go to the front. It was 8 p.m. before they got the news. In February 1919, they left camp to return home.

He had four brothers in France, three in comfort service and one in medics. He is a retired farmer living on a small farm with his wife of 57 years. He gets around with the help of a walker and is doing well.

MARION POTTER LANE SR., was born Feb. 24, 1898 in Nashville, TN and passed away on Dec. 20, 1960 in Dallas, TX. He joined the service on April 16, 1917 in Dallas, TX.

He was stationed at Great Lakes Training Station as a 3rd Class Seaman. He was then transferred to U.S. Receiving Ship, Pugit Sound, Washington. He was promoted to 2nd Class Seaman. In September 1917, he was sent to the Government Hospital, Bremerton, WA. He was discharged on Sept. 24, 1917 with a service connected disability.

He was employed by the U.S. Post Office in Dallas, TX. Because of a heart ailment he retired on May 31, 1955. He was very active with the D.A.V., and served as Commander of Buddies Chapter No. 11, in Dallas, TX. He married Lousie Pullen. He had one son by a previous marriage.

CHARLES MARTIN LANG, was born Sept. 16, 1892 in New Orleans, LA. He was in the reserves in 1917 and was discharged in 1918.

He was in the Army and stationed in France. He also served in WWII, where he achieved the rank of Capt. He fought in the trenches.

He married Marie Lang and they had one daughter, Dorothy. He had three grandchildren and three great-grandchildren. He lived to be 89 years old and died in an auto accident.

JAMES L. LATCH, served with the 375th Aero Sqdn. in England and France. He was married Sept. 22, 1923. Latch died in 1975.

JOHN R. LAUGHLIN, was born Jan. 20, 1893 in Zwingle, IA. He was a member of Co. A, 10th MG. Bn., 4th Div., and achieved the rank of Pvt. He was killed in action on Aug. 7, 1918.

LESLIE R. LAUGHLIN, was born on July 30, 1898 in Cape Charles, VA. He was in the service from July 1917 - 1918. He was a member of the France Inf.

He had a wife, Florence and no children.

NEAL LAVANWAY SR., was born May 2, 1896 in Coloma, MI. He joined the Navy on July 23, 1917 and was discharged on July 20, 1920.

He served on the *US Hancock*, of the Atlantic Fleet and achieved the rank of Boatswain Mate 2nd Class. He was stationed at Glen Burnie, Baltimore, MD and in Philadelphia, PA at a Navy base. He arrived in Brest, France in May 1918. During the return trip the *USS Lincoln*, was torpedoed. He left for Azores and he was promoted to Seaman 1st Class, Coxswain, BM. 2nd Class.

He married Selma N. Ertman on June 24, 1922 and they had one son and one daughter. The son served in WWII and he died of cancer at 61 years of age.

MAX LAYCOCK, was a big boy for his age. He ran away from home, lied about his age, and joined before he was 16. He had a brother already in the service that was stationed on the Mexican Border. He wanted to get to where his brother, Anders Laycock, was. He didn't make it to the border, because his father missed him and managed to get him stopped and returned home. That didn't stop him, he left again. He didn't make it to the border, but he did enlist.

He was in New York, and his outfit, The Dixie Division, set sail for overseas, but he was left behind in the hospital with that dreadful disease, influenza. He survived and later was aboard ship that was out of territorial waters when the Armistice was signed. They turned back to the states.

His brother, Anders Laycock, was the first Tuscaloosa County boy to be killed in WWI. He was barely 18, when he was discharged. Thirteen hundred from Tuscaloosa, served in that war.

He was active in the Veterans Affairs all of his life. He died at the age of 65 in 1966. There has never been a more dedicated worker than Max. His wife is still active in working for the good of veterans, but feels her greatest accomplishment was marrying Max.

MARTIN JOSEPH LEE, was born in St. Paul, MN on Feb. 12, 1895. He attended public schools, graduating from high school in 1912. He worked for a grocery store owner, driving a horse and wagon to deliver groceries. He was an avid baseball player. His team was sponsored by Minnesota Tent and Awning in 1910-11.

In March of 1918, he and his buddies decided to do the patriotic thing and join up. They joined the Navy, because they heard they would be sent to Pensicola, FL. Since it was winter in Minnesota, warm weather in Florida sounded mighty good. They never made it, but spent the first few days at the Raddison Hotel and then to the Great Lakes. He was shipped out on a converted banana boat.

He was stationed at the U.S. Naval Air Station, Parillac, France. He assembled bi-planes that were shipped overseas in sections and assembled in France. His job was to attach the top wing to the bottom wing.

While in France, he discovered there was no such thing as a French pastry. At wars end, the people from town walked to the base shouting, "Fini la guerre, fini la guerre." They then spent the rest of the night serenading the men at the base.

He was discharged in February 1919, and went back to Minnesota. There he worked days and went to school nights, graduating from St. Paul College of Law in 1922. He passed the Minnesota bar exam but never practiced law.

He married Lillian West in 1921. They moved to Los Angeles, CA in 1924, where he got a job with the Veterans Administration. His position called for a background in law. He retired from the Veterans Administration in 1962.

He belonged to the Veterans of WWI, VFW and the American Legion, of which he was the commander in the mid 1940s. He had one daughter, Virginia. He died on Jan. 26, 1992, just 17 days shy of his 97th birthday.

SAMUEL LEITNER, was born Sept. 25, 1894 in Trugler, Austria. He joined the service on July 5, 1918 and was discharged on Dec. 18, 1918 at Camp Funston, KS.

He was a Pvt. 1st Class, Ind. Co., Ind. Bn., 164th Depot Brigade, U.S. Army. He trained in Waco, TX and was very glad to get home. He came to the United States when he was 17 years old, he was very uneducated.

He had one daughter, Mary Ann Schummer, one grandson and two granddaughters. He had five half brothers and one half sister. Coming back from

service, he worked in the Homestake Mine, and purchased a farm 30 miles east of Sturgis. His daughter and her husband came to work there. He worked at Ft. Meade Veterans Adm. form 1946-56. He was a member of the American Legion for 35 years and a charter member of WWI. He passed away at the Ft. Meade Hospital on March 16, 1963, and is buried at the Black Hills National Cemetery.

CLARENCE LIEN, was drafted into the service in September 1918, then was sent to Camp Dix and

then from there overseas. He later served with the Army of Occupation in Germany. He came home in 1919.

CLARENCE ALFRED LIND, was born Feb. 1, 1895 in Harrisburg, SD. He joined the service on May 7, 1917 and was discharged on May 18, 1919.

He was a member of the 308th Inf., 77th Div., and achieved the rank of Pvt. He sailed on the English boat, the *Horaration*, and landed in Liverpool, England after 17 days. He then rode a train from Liverpool to Southhampton, England and then caught a channel boat to Le Harve, France. He was then put on a freight train for three days and arrived at St. George, France. His unit was broken up and sent as replacements to the 77th Div. He saw action in the Vesle Sector, Meusse Argonne and others.

As the war ended, he was sent to Base 80 Hospital to recuperate for about a month. He came home on a German ship, the *Vaterland*. He landed in New York and was then sent to Camp Dodge where he was discharged.

He passed away October 1991, at 96 years old. He worked for over 30 years as a Railroad Engineer for the Southern Pacific Railroad.

LEO JOSEPH LINBERGER, was born Aug. 20, 1893 and died on Dec. 20, 1991. He joined the service before the Mexican Campaign in 1916.

He was discharged in the spring of 1919. He was a member of the U.S. Army's National Guard and served as a Medical Corp., 135th Machine Gun Co., 37th Div. His trip overseas was on the troopship, *Leviathan*. Any awards were unknown.

His wife was Isabella, who is now deceased. They had two daughters, Ann Troyan and Mary Merz, and nine grandchildren.

GEORGE LEE LINN, of Grafton, Taylor County, WV, served at Camp Lee, VA from Sept. 4, 1918 until his discharge on Jan. 12, 1919.

While at Camp Lee, he was hospitalized and survived a near fatal attack of influenza.

He was experienced as a sawyer before his induction, he returned to that profession and worked for many years in the Grafton/Fairmont area as a carpenter and cabinet maker. In 1922, he married the former Viola Finch. They raised two sons and three daughters on their farm in Taylor County. Following their father's example of national service, his two sons later served in the Army and Air Force.

AARON WARD LIVINGSTON, was born June 30, 1896. At the time of enlistment his address was Deweese, NE.

He served in the U.S. Navy from Aug. 2, 1918 to Oct. 6, 1919. He served on stations in Yerba Buena, San Francisco, CA and Norfolk, VA and onboard the *USS New Mexico.* He attended signal school and served on the signal bridge on the *USS New Mexico.* While on the *New Mexico,* they traveled through the Panama Canal and up the West Coast, stopping at all the major cities.

ECHOL R. LIVINGSTON, was born Nov. 30, 1894 in Blackwater, VA. He joined the service on May 25, 1918 and was discharged on Aug. 2, 1919.

He was a member of Co. F, 47th Inf., 4th Div., where achieved the rank of Pvt. He served in France in the Vesle Sector, Cusine Warne, St. Mihiel and the Meusse Argonne. He was gassed and sent to the Argonne Hospital in Paris. He received the Purple Heart and the Expert Rifleman. He was married and had four daughters and one son. He also had 11 grandchildren and 18 great-grandchildren. He was a farmer.

LOYD OTIS LIVINGSTON, was born Sept. 6, 1893 and died on May 8, 1966. He served in the U.S. Army from Sept. 3, 1918 through Sept. 16, 1919 at Camp Funston, KS and Ft. Snelling.

He served in the Medical Corps overseas. His home address at the time of entering the Army was Deweese, NE.

JOHN O. LOHRE, was born Feb. 8, 1894, in Winthrop, MN as the son of John and Anna Winthrop. He received his education in Winthrop and moved to the Flathead Valley in 1923, where he had lived in the Smith Valley.

On April 25, 1936, he married Elinor Isch in Kalispell. The couple had farmed in the Deer Park area until 1943, when they purchased a farm in the Lower Valley. In 1971, they retired and moved to Kalispell.

He was a veteran of WWI and a member of B, 43rd Inf. He was also a member of the WWI Barracks of Kalispell. He passed away on Jan. 8, 1979.

WILLIAM H. LOWTHER, was born in Wildcat, WV on Oct. 1, 1888, son of the late Jacob and Sarah Lowther. He was born and raised on a farm and stayed there until he was called away to war.

He took his basic training at Ft. Lee, VA. During his tour of duty overseas, he served with Co. D, 320th Inf., 80th Div. He fought with the British and the French and then went to the Argonne Forest with the American A.E.F. He was a machine gunner with the infantry all the way through. He finished up on the front lines when the war ended, after having spent almost two years in that position. He can remember that he was sitting under a little pine tree and didn't believe it when he heard the war was over.

After returning to the United States and Wildcat, WV, he resumed his farming duties. He also did some black-smithing which he always said required only a strong back and a weak mind. He helped start the American Legion Post 4 in Weston, WV, and has been a continuous member. In March 1989, he was awarded a Certificate of Continuous Membership for 70 years.

In 1956, he was married to the former Madge Furr. Having waited so late in life to find the right girl, it was too late for him to have a family of his own. He sort of adopted his great nieces and nephews as his family, and has remained very close to them throughout his life. He and his wife owned and operated a grocery store in Ireland, WV, for several years. He sold the store in 1968, and semi-retired to gardening. He continued to raise a garden until 1989. His wife passed away in 1985 and since that time he has lived alone and maintained his home with some help from family members.

In July 1991, he was presented with an American Flag that had flown over the Nations Capital in Washington, DC, by Congressman Bob Wise. The ceremony was in honor of his upcoming 103rd birthday. He is proud to be an American and proud to have served his country during WWI.

STANLEY MERRITT LUKENS, was born Aug. 25, 1899 to Courtland Clayton Lukens and Ida Elizabeth Southoot in Philadelphia. He served from Sept. 16, 1916 to Aug. 20, 1920.

He was on the *USS Tacoma* in 1917 on patrol duty off the Mexican Coast in the Mexican Border War. When President Roosevelt declared war on Germany, the *USS Tacoma* returned to the east coast and made many trips convoying troop ships to Europe. In December, on their third trip, they heard and felt a big explosion. They put in for Halifax, Nova Scotia and found two munitions ships had collided in the harbor, killing more than 1600 people. They assisted in relief work for three days, assisting the devastated port community.

He was one of a party of 12 who took over a German cargo ship, the *Prechterland*, while on the Direchter Land. They made five voyages carrying Army supplies to Europe. She was returned to Herowners on July 12, 1919. He was then sent to the North Sea, and assigned to mine sweeper, *USS Thrush*. There 70,000 mines had been planted, covering an area of 60,000 sq. miles.

On Aug. 20, 1920, he was discharged in San Diego, from the *USS Mine sweeper Brant*, as a Chief Quartermaster, Mine sweeper Div. He came to Missoula, MT in September 1920 and graduated with a degree in Forestry. He became a U.S. Forest Ranger in 1925. He married Ann Sustak Lukens and they had a son, Russell, and a daughter, Anne Lukens Pedigo. He had been badly injured in the war and retired in 1951, because of his war injuries. He died on July 6, 1990 at the age of 89 years old.

THORWALD LUNDE, was born Nov. 19, 1895 in North Dakota. He enlisted on Sept. 22, 1917 and was discharged on Feb. 3, 1919.

He was a member of the 101st Regt., Bn. I, Co. A.E.F., where he achieved the rank of Pvt. He was stationed at Camp Pike, AK and in France. He fought in the Verdun and the Belleau Wood. He crossed the Atlantic on July 4, 1918 and he remembers a narrow escape from the hayloft of a barn. He was wounded on Oct. 25, 1918 and stayed in a hospital in France until his discharge.

He is the ninth of ten children. He had three children, 15 grandchildren and 20 great-grandchildren. He is now in a nursing home in Camas, WA.

EVERT LYNCH, was born Feb. 1, 1896 in Missouri. He enlisted on April 26, 1918 and was discharged on June 19, 1919.

He was a member of Co. E, 357th Inf., 90th Div., where he achieved the rank of Corporal. He fought in the St. Mihiel Offensive from Sept. 12-16. He was wounded on Sept. 16, 1918 in St. Marie France. He received the Purple Heart. He died on May 26, 1977 and left his wife Ozella Lynch.

HENRY MADARIZ, WWI Vet, drafted in 1918.

LAWRENCE MARSTON, and his twin brother, Clarence, were born April 10, 1893 in King City, CA. He enlisted on July 27, 1917, at Ft. McDonald, Angel Island, in San Francisco, CA. Twins were not asked to go into combat.

Cooks were needed as well as infantry divisions. He told of bad weather and conditions that made their job difficult and uncertain, but they still came up with a product that the French would trade almost anything for, a loaf of white bread.

At the end of the war, when they began to discharge members of his company, his commanding officers offered each man a sheet of paper and asked him to sign his name. Since he had the best handwriting, he was chosen to write the discharges. He was promoted to Quartermaster Corp on July 14, 1919, after a number of months of writing discharges for fellow members. He wrote his own.

He married Lynda Marston in June 1957, in Carson City, NV. Though he never said much about the war, he was very patriotic and was active in veteran's organizations, as well as community services. Soon after returning from the war, he met and married his first wife, Leah. They had three children, Edna Mae, Ruth and James, of whom he was very proud. Leah passed away and all the children were grown up. He had two grandchildren and six great-grandchildren. He passed away on Jan. 10, 1968.

JOHN MARTINELLI, was born Oct. 18, 1899 in Souk-el-Arba, Tunisia, then a French Protectorate. He was an outstanding athlete during his school and Army career days.

He left Schenectady, NY High School in 1917, volunteering for the Army at Ft. Slocum, NY. Ten days later, he was on board the transport, *Poshatan*, bound for France as a member of the 5th Field Arty, 1st Div. Upon arrival in France, he was transformed to combat engineers assigned to the 1st Combat Engineers, 1st Div., and participated in six major battles, Ansauville Montdidier, Noyon, Oise-Aisne, Aisne-Marne, Saizerais and St. Mihiel, where he was wounded.

The Meusse Argonne culminated with the 71 kilometer forced march on Sedan, followed by the march to the Rhine and duty in the Army of Occupation in Germany. He also participated in Victory Parades led by Gen. Pershing in New York and Washington. Upon graduation from the Coast Artillery School of Ft. Monroe, VA, he was assigned as the Master Gunner for the 52nd Coast Arty. Railway at Ft. Eustis, VA.

He is a distinguished alumnus and a 1925 graduate of Tri-state University in Tangola, IN with a Bachelor of Science Degree in Chemical, Civil and Mechanical Engineering. As a Captain, he served in the Civilian Conservation Corps in command of CCC Companies at Springfield, Summit, High Bridge, Branchville in New Jersey and Paradise Valley in Nevada. He was subdistrict commander of 10 CCC Companies in south Jersey.

He subsequently served in WWII and the Korean Conflict, respectively, as an artillery battalion and group commander at the Anti-aircraft Artillery Center at Ft. Bliss, TX. He retired at Ft. Bliss in 1955.

CLAUDE MATTHEWS, was born Aug. 6, 1893 in St. Francis, KS. He enlisted in May 1918 and was discharged in May 1920 at Camp Devon, MA.

He was a member of the 28th Div. in Boise, ID and achieved the rank of Pvt. 1st Class. He also served in the German Infantry.

His only family is a nephew in Boise. He worked as carpenter and miner. Today he lives at

the Idaho State Veterans Home and sometimes attends WWI meetings with Sawtooth Barrack No. 217.

HORACE WILLIAM MAY SR., was a WWI

veteran. He was born in Orosi, CA on Oct. 25, 1894. He grew up on a farm. There were three brothers and one sister. His brother, Howard E. May, is also a WWI Veteran. Their dad died while they were still young. They were poor and spoke of taking lard sandwiches to school.

He joined the Army on Nov. 1, 1917 in Visalia, CA. His boot camp was a Ft. Lewis, WA. He spoke of miserable D.I.'s. His first company was, Co. 26, 166th Div. from Nov. - Dec. 1917. He was transferred to Co. C, 316th Div. from Dec. 6, 1917 to Sept. 20, 1918. He left for France on July 7, 1918. His port of landing was Brest, France. He spoke of being seasick on the renovated cattle boats strung with hammocks. He spoke of big meals on holidays laced with laxatives and long latrine lines as a result. He also mentioned cleaning animal dung in the town and villages of France and the Frenchmen had gone to war and no one was there to do it. Animals were driven to the countryside daily to graze and brought back to the towns at night for safekeeping. The soldiers tired of gold fish, canned salmon.

He was in the Signal Corp. and carried messages across the front lines. He was in reserve in the St. Mihiel Offensive from Sept. 12, 1918 to Sept. 16, 1918. He became ill as a result of breathing mustard gas. He was transferred to Co. 341, from Sept. 28, 1918 to Jan. 24, 1919 to Camp Kearny, CA, where he was discharged honorably on Feb. 7, 1919. He received the Bronze Victory Button. His rank was Pvt. 1st Class.

He returned to Orosi to take care of his mother. He attended Redlands University and graduated from L.I.F.E. Bible College in Hollywood. He bicycled 200 miles twice from Orosi to Los Angeles. He took tennis lessons from Bill Acherman at U.C.L.A., who later became athletic director when he helped recruit Rafer Johnson from Kingsburg, CA to attend U.C.L.A. Rafer was one of the Olympic Decathlons.

He married Mae O. VanHorn in Weeping Water, NE on June 1, 1941. They established a home in Kingsburg, CA. A son, Horace W. May Jr. was born May 16, 1942. He worked in farming and fruit, and owned a fruit market in the 1950s until his death on Jan. 25, 1962. He had a heart attack while at a produce market in Fresno, CA. He was a self-made, proud, hard-working and Christian man, who was educated for the ministry. He preferred to work for himself. His main love and only vice in life was tennis. He ran two tennis tournaments yearly in Kingburg, CA in the 1950s until his death in the 1960s. He also coached tennis briefly in the 1940s at Kingsburg High School.

HOWARD EWIN MAY, was born Oct. 10,

1896 in Orosi, CA. While he was in high school his brother, Horace, joined the WWI and was sent to France to serve in the Signal Corp. Later he was sent with 64 young men from Visalia, CA to San Diego, CA for service. He was appointed as leader to see that they got there O.K.

At Los Angeles, CA, they had to change from Santa Fe to Southern Pacific trains, walking down the street with a little traffic. While at Ft. Rosecrans, Point Loma near the harbor, San Diego, many of them got the flu. Only the sickest was sent to the hospital, due to so many sick. In the National Guard, they were to guard the harbor until the Armistice was signed on Nov. 11, 1918.

After the war was over, the city of San Diego celebrated the end of the war by having 212 small planes in the air at one time over the harbor. When they were no longer needed, they were honorably discharged and sent home for Christmas. After being discharged from service at San Diego, CA, he went through the Bible College at Los Angeles, CA. He served in pastoral work, receiving his 50 year award in 1972. After his wife died, he served as a V.A. Hospital Volunteer Chaplain for 12 years at Loma Linda and Fresno, CA.

HAROLD L. MCCAMMAN,
was born on May 30, 1897 in Morrow Co., OH. His parents were Doty and Harriette McCamman. He enlisted in the U.S. Army on Aug. 26, 1918.

He served as Pvt. in 69th Field Arty. at Camp Zachary Taylor, KY and Camp Knox, Stithlon, KY. He was discharged on Dec. 4, 1918.

He worked at many things, but has been a salesman of monuments for the past 45 years. He has been an active member in the T.P. Johnston American Legion Post No. 329 in Mt. Gilead for 72 years. He was also a member of the Ohio State Highway Patrol Auxiliary from April 8, 1955 to June 1, 1975. He was honored for 27 years of service in the National Foundation of March of Dimes. He served several years as Director of Morrow County's Campaign. He is now serving as Chairman of the Morrow County Veterans Service Commission, having started in 1968 when it was called Soldiers and Sailors Relief Commission.

He was married to Dorothy E. Alexander in 1947. He has one daughter and three grandchildren. One grandchild is serving in Air Force at Patrick Air Force Base, FL. He also served in the Desert Shield Conflict in 1991.

FRED LEE MCDOWELL SR.,
was born March 25, 1894 in Killen, TX. He enlisted on May 11, 1917 and was discharged on Aug. 5, 1920.

He was on the Navy boat, the *USS Nero*, and served as Chief Storekeeper. The boat carried supplies from the British Isles to France. He received an award from Jimmy Carter, as a devoted and selfless consecration to the service of our country in the armed forces of the United States.

Ford Motor Co. presented him with two service emblems for 25 years and 35 years as Productive Manager with their company. He retired from Ford and traveled to both U.S. World Fairs. He died on June 30, 1979 of high blood pressure and results. He is buried in Grove Hill Cemetery in Dallas, TX. He was a good father, Boy Scout leader and golfer.

WARD MCMILLIAN,
married Una Jungberg Sept. 20, 1917. He died in 1966.

DR. RAYMOND M. MCMURDO,
was born July 13, 1890. He enlisted with the Medical Corps of the U.S. Army on June 13, 1917 in Worcester, MA.

He served first at Ft. Ethan Allen, VT and then transferred to Camp Devens, MA on July 3, 1918. He then sailed overseas and landed in Brest, France on the *Leviathan*. He arrived at Brest on July 11, 1918. He served as head of the Eye Clinic at the Base Hospital No. 7 until Nov. 11, 1918. They were relieved by another company and sent back to the United States. He arrived at Camp Devens in March 1919. He was discharged there.

He returned to Worcester, MA, resumed his practice, and got married. In the fall of 1919, he joined the American Legion and was elected Commander in 1932. He served two years with honor. While commander, he formed a boy's baseball team and a Fife and Drum Corps. He retired in 1960, in Massachusetts and moved to Florida and joined the Veterans of WWI. He became Adjutant and several years later became Quartermaster and then Commander of Ridgewood Groves Barracks No. 2533 of Seminole, FL. He is a regular attendant of Veterans of WWI Florida Dept. meetings.

He became dual member of the Florida Dept. of the Veterans of WWI and San Antonio's Davy Crockett Veterans of WWI, Barracks No. 1877 in 1986. He was elected Commander of Barracks No. 1877 in 1988. Recently, he was elected Chairman of the Registration Committee of the National Veterans of WWI, Inc. He attended the 1989 National Convention of the Veterans of WWI and Ladies Auxiliary held in Daytona Beach, FL. Each year in June, he attends the State Convention of the Veterans of WWI Dept. of Texas. He regularly visits the buddies of WWI at the VA Hospital, various nursing homes and shut-ins in San Antonio.

Fraternal activities in San Antonio; past Master of Masonic Lodge in Massachusetts; member of the Eastern Star in San Antonio and past worthy patron. He organized a branch of the Chamber of Commerce in Spencer, MA in 1932. Still active when he left in 1960. He is a Past President of the Massachusetts Society of Optometry and past President of the New England Council of Optometry. He is an active member of the First Congregational Church in Spencer, MA and was elected Deacon in that church.

MILO MEANS, was born March 4, 1895 in Dalles, OR. He enlisted in Eugene, OR on June 9, 1917 and was discharged on May 10, 1919 at Camp Lewis, WA.

He was a member of the 361st Amb. Co., 316th Sands, where he achieved the rank of Pvt. 1st Class. He was stationed in France and Belgium.

He was a teacher and a vocation rehabilitation counselor. He now lives at the Idaho State Veterans Home and used to attend meetings of the WWI Sawtooth Barracks No. 217.

DOMINICK MENCE, was born June 16, 1894 in Calabria, Italy. He joined the service on June 16, 1915 and was discharged on March 19, 1918.

He went to Europe on March 19, 1918 and participated in four battles and two skirmishes. He was wounded in the Meusse Argonne Battle on Oct. 14, 1918. He was in a base hospital in Europe from Oct. 15, 1918 through Jan. 3, 1919. He carried a piece of shrapnel above his ear until early 1960s, when he had it removed at a hospital in Houston.

After his retirement, he grew vegetables for his neighbors at his residence in South Beaumont on two acres of land until he had a prostate operation in March 1991. He slipped and fell in the bathroom at the hospital on May 1, 1991. He was totally paralyzed for more than six hours from a very bad bruise on his spinal cord. He had to completely relearn how to move arms and legs in the rehab hospital. He died on Dec. 13, 1991.

EDMUND E. MENDENHALL, served with the 114th Inf. in France. He married Bertha Safty on June 23, 1916. He died May 7, 1966.

OLIVER LEONARD MESSINGER, was born Jan. 5, 1890 in Coeur Aleine, ID and passed away on Jan. 23, 1977 in Freeland, WA.

He enlisted in the Navy in Spokane, WA and was sent overseas to France. He was a fireman on a ship. He moved to Seattle, WA in 1928 and then to Whidbey Island in 1974.

FRED METCALF, was born in Pleasantville, IA in 1893. He is the youngest of 11 children. He came with his family to the Flathead at the age of nine and went to school in the Half Moon and LaSalle area. He was employed in woods work and logging as a young man.

He was with the engineers, serving in France during WWI. He was also a survivor of the *Tuscania* troop ship, which was torpedoed off the coast of Ireland. After his discharge, he returned to the valley where he married Grace Graham in 1917, and worked in logging until 1920 when he was employed by the State Forestry Dept. and later by the U.S. Forest Service until his retirement in 1955.

He is active in veteran's organizations and Senior Citizens. His wife passed away in 1970 and he had been at the Veteran's Home at Columbia Falls until July 1980 when he entered Immanuel Home. He lost a son, Fred, in WWII and has a daughter, Helen Sonntag, in Kalispell. He has five grandchildren.

AUGUST MILLER, was born Feb. 1, 1890 at Omaha, NE, a son of Mr. and Mrs. John W. Miller. At an early age he moved to Minnesota, where on April 29, 1918, he entered the U.S. Army.

He served with Co. A, 358th Inf. and had been gassed at St. Mihiel, France on Oct. 3, 1918. He was honorably discharged on March 1, 1919 at Camp Dodge, IA. He had received the Purple Heart and the Silver Star.

On July 21, 1923, he married Ethel Jackson at Algona, IA. He had attended the machinist pattern making school at Minneapolis and was transferred to Duluth, MN. In 1926, he moved to Bigfork, where he lived until 1931, when he moved to Kalispell and has resided there since. He was a carpenter by trade until his retirement. He had three sons, two daughters, 12 grandchildren and five great-grandchildren. He died on May 13, 1972.

PERCY L. MILLER, was born Feb. 28, 1895. He served in the Medical Overseas Transport. He left the United States for France on June 14, 1917 and arrived about two weeks later.

He was stationed in St. Nezaire, France however he was not engaged in any battles. He was honorably discharged on Oct. 12, 1919 on his mother's birthday. He was assigned for duty on Havana of Ward Line for transport of combat units.

WALTER MITTELSTADT, was born Aug. 27, 1890 in Eau Claire, WS, a son of August and Mathilda Mittelstadt. He had received his education in Wisconsin and when he was about 20 years of age, he moved to Valley County in Eastern Montana, where he homesteaded. In 1917, he was married to Viella Scott in Glasgow and was preceded in death by her in 1957.

He was a veteran of WWI, having served in Co. C, 362nd Inf., Regt. 91, Div. U.S. Army. In about 1930, he moved to Kalispell and was employed in Glacier National Park for many years. He had also worked as a foreman for the Kilpatrick Brothers for a number of years prior to his retirement.

He was a member of the Eagles Lodge, Kalispell Senior Citizens and the WWI Barracks. In 1971, he was married to Violet Anderson in Kalispell and is now survived by her at the family home. He had two step-children and two grandchildren. He passed away on Sept. 1, 1975.

CHARLES MONROE, was born Jan. 17, 1894. He served in the military from 1917-18 as a member of the 367th Div. He was stationed in France.

His wife was Evelia, and they had five children, four boys and one girl. He is now in a VA Medical Center in Hampton, VA.

CLARENCE LLOYD MOONEY, enlisted for service in Kansas. He was born on July 17, 1894. He died on Sept. 23, 1983. He was the son of James David and Flora Wright Mooney.

FERRIS R. MOONEY, was born at Blue Mound, KS on Oct. 24, 1896 and died in the hospital at Ft. Scott, KS on Oct. 2, 1925. He died at the age of 28. He suddenly took ill with appendicitis and was urged to submit to an operation at once. He reluctantly yielded, but it was then too late, for he was not strong enough to overcome the effects of the operation.

He was married on April 7, 1918 to Miss Ruth Bingham. They had one daughter, Maxine Mooney. When WWI started, he was very anxious to enlist as a volunteer, but because of physical deficiency, he was not permitted to go. When the draft was made, he responded and was willing and ready to go in defense of his country. He was a fine young man, a good husband and father and a Christian citizen.

FRED MOONEY, was born Jan. 8, 1887 and lived with his parents until 17 years of age, when he began his teaching career. He taught several years about Blue Mound and won many friends while teaching.

He answered the call of his country on April 15, 1918, and caught a train for Camp Funston. After five weeks on the train, he embarked for France. He was wounded in the noted battle of September 12, and remained in the hospital for about a month for his recovery. Being anxious to be on duty again, he went back to his company and again went to the front, where he nobly gave up his life for his country.

He enlisted in Kansas and was a member of the 23rd Co., 87th Div. His younger brother remembers seeing him march by and waving farewell. He was the son of James David and Flora Wright Mooney.

BEVERLY BRYAN MOORE, was born March 10, 1901, in Washington, NC. He enlisted on Aug. 16, 1917 and was discharged on March 8, 1919.

He was a member of the Army's 30th Old Hickory Div., 113th Field Arty., Btry. B. He was stationed in France and Belgium. He fought in the Meusse Argonne, and the St. Mihiel.

He was a lanky 16 year old North Carolina boy, who was two years too young to legally join the Army. With the collusion of an uncle, he convinced an Army recruiter that he was 18. However, there still remained a barrier to his enlistment. For his height of 6 ft., he needed to weigh a minimum of 127 pounds and he weighed only 119. The recruiter suggested that he go downstairs to the grocery store, and eat enough bananas, he might make the weight limit.

With three dollars from his uncle, he stuffed himself with bananas, ginger snaps and soft drinks, as he periodically checked his progress on a scale in the store. He finally weighed 127 and returned to the recruiting office. The Army scale, however, put him at 128.

He had a dental laboratory and made teeth for almost 60 years in Houston. He passed away on

July 4, 1991 at the age of 90. His wife Jean is still living. He was a loving husband, a man who loved his Lord, and a loyal friend.

DAVID GILMORE MORRIS, was born Sept. 18, 1891 in Rockbridge Co., Collierstown, VA. He enlisted on July 15, 1918 and was discharged on July 17, 1919.

He was a member of Co. A, 72nd Engineers, where he achieved the rank of Pvt. He served in France from 1918-19. He left the United States in September 1918 and was back in the United States on July 17, 1919.

After he returned, he served as 4th Class Postmaster at Collierstown, VA for 23 years or until they closed the 4th Class office. He had a wife, Ruth, six children, Laurene, Iona, Irma, Jessie, Elias and Shirley. He died in January 1983 at 92 years of age.

ELMER CLIFFORD MORLEY, was born to Cephas and Ermina Holtzman Morley on Sept. 20, 1891 in Clayton County near Garber, IA. After finishing his schooling in 1907, he attended a one year teacher's college in Fayette, IA. In 1908, he began the first of 20 years teaching rural schools in various townships in Clayton County, IA.

He teaching years were interrupted when he entered the Armed Forces on Aug. 26, 1918. He served in the 305th Bn., Tank Corps, at Camp Greene in Charlotte, NC. His company was ready to be shipped to Europe, when word was received that the war was over. He returned to civilian life in January 1919.

On Aug. 26, 1919, he was united in marriage to Grace Blanche Hansel in Garber, IA. Five children were born to this union. After teaching, he served as Postmaster at Garber. He then served as rural mail carrier there until his retirement. He was a mason for many years and was an active member of St. John's Church in Garber. He was a faithful participant in the WWI Barracks from 1960-77. During that time he only missed one meeting. He died on Jan. 6, 1978 at the age of 86.

OWEN M. MORRIS, served with the U.S. Infantry. He died on Sept. 28, 1918 in Ft. Lee, VA. He was not married.

CHARLES B. MULLENNEX, was born Jan. 3, 1894 in Whitmer, WV. He was inducted on July 23, 1918 and was discharged on July 11, 1919.

He was stationed at the 19th Hospital and a member of the Veterinary Corps of the U.S. Army. He achieved the rank of Pvt. 1st Class. He was stationed in France.

He married Opal A. Mallow on Aug. 20, 1922 and they had two daughters and one son. He was the son of Martin Sr. and Rachel Teter Mullennex. He was a farmer. He died on Aug. 31, 1956.

WILLIAM HENRY MULLNER, was born Oct. 23, 1891 in Crete, NE. He enlisted on July 18, 1917 and was discharged on July 17, 1920.

He was a soldier in the Navy. He joined in Bellingham, WA and was discharged in Bremerton, WA. He was under a Capt. Henryhan and served as a cook. After the war, he made several trips across the Atlantic on the *Leviathin*, as a cook to bring troops home.

He married Bernice L. Carlson Mullner. He passed away in May 1971 at the age of 81. In civilian life, he was a musician and for many years was a lumber grader from which he retired at age 65.

EMERY MULVANEY, was born Nov. 29, 1894 in Eureka, CA. He enlisted in San Francisco, CA on Feb. 26, 1917 and was discharged on June 4, 1920 in McAllen, TX. He was in the Army and achieved the rank of Corporal. He had no overseas assignments.

He had two step-daughters. He worked as an electrician. He now lives at the Idaho State Veterans Home and is active in the WWI Sawtooth Barracks No. 217.

EARL MACKLIN MURPHY, was born in his parents home on a farm in Delaware County, OH on Aug. 8, 1897. His parents were Grant E. and Hallie Dell Murphy, both natives of Ohio.

He enlisted in the U.S. Navy in Detroit. His rate was Lands man for Electrician. He had basic training at Brooklyn Navy Yard. He attended the U.S.N. Electrical School, Pratt Institute for studying electrical engineering. He also attended the U.S.N. Submarine School at New London, CT. He was ordered to duty on the U. S. Sub, the *USS Narwhal*. He served aboard submarines, D-1, H-5, S-18 and S-38.

He was awarded the WWI Victory Medal with Submarine clasp and one bronze star. In November 1919 he was made Chief Electrician.

On Feb. 13, 1920, he married Florence Grace Brookings in Boston, a native of Inverness, Scotland. They had a good marriage until her death in Santa Rosa, CA. They had one son, Bruce Macklin Murphy. Bruce was a paratrooper in WWII, and served in France and Germany. He has four grandchildren, 15 great-grandchildren and 8 great-great grandchildren. Two years after his first wife died, he married Ina Belle Cowden. They were married for 14 years before she died in Santa Rosa.

MARK A. MURPHY, enlisted on Nov. 17, 1917 in Rock Island, IL. He was a member of the 4th Am. Trans, 4th Div., of the Army. He achieved the rank of Sgt.

His military job specialty was company clerk. He served in France, Germany and the United States. He was awarded the Victory Medal for the battle at Chateau Thierry, Aisne Marne, Verdun, St. Mihiel and the Meusse Argonne. He was discharged on Sept. 18, 1919 in Rockford, IL. He had been gassed and shell shocked.

JOHN J. MURRAY, was born May 16, 1888 at Sinclair, WV. He was a son of Andrew J. and Sarah A. Sidwell Murray, one of 13 children.

He was inducted in the U.S. Army on July 25, 1918 at Kingwood, WV, and received his training at Camp Lee, VA with the 1st Co., 1st Bn., 155th Depot Brigade. He received his honorable discharge on March 27, 1919.

He returned to his home at Sinclair, WV to help his family on the farm as his father's health was failing. His father passed away on Oct. 21, 1920. He married Mary E. Colebank on March 14, 1931. They had nine children, five girls and four boys. He worked in the coal mines and farmed all his life.

He passed away at his home at the age of 92 on Feb. 17, 1980. He is buried at Mt. Zion Cemetery near Marquess, WV.

LESLIE MUSSEN, was born March 26, 1895 in Lodi, WI. He enlisted on July 16, 1917 and was discharged in September 1919.

He was a member of Co. A, 1st Inf., of the National Guard. He achieved the rank of Corporal. He went overseas on Feb. 18, 1918 to Brest, France. He participated in the Aisne-Marne, St. Mihiel and the Meusse Argonne Defensive Sector. His most memorable experience was on May 10, when Gen. Pershing announced his name with a few others to report to Beorges, France for a special assignment. He received the Bronze Star.

He is the oldest and only son of Frank and Elizabeth Mussen. He had three sisters and only one is surviving now. He is still living on his homestead alone. He has help with housekeeping and meals.

ROWE B. MYERS, was inducted into service March 29, 1918 at Frankfort, IN. He trained at Camp Taylor, KY. He was then sent to Camp Upton, NY for transfer overseas. They had one time on the firing range, one hike, and some lectures. At Camp Upton they were scattered amongst various companies of the 112th Inf., 28th Div. of the Pennsylvania National Guard. This division had been in training at Camp Hancock, Augusta, GA for six months.

They sailed for Liverpool, England aboard the HMSS *Acquitania* on May 7. They arrived in England May 14. Their platoon was assigned to the "Glory Hole," the compartment above the ship's propellers. There was a constant roar. Most of the time, some played cards, slept when tired, and had fire drills. All soldiers were ordered below out of sight so that there would be no evidence of troops aboard.

Once arrived, he saw action in the following

locations, Trimbly, an area on the Marne River near Chateau Thierry. At Chateau Thierry and Belleau Woods, the fighting was fierce. Many gas and artillery attacks. He also participated in other campaigns.

He received the Purple Heart for being gassed and received an award from Col. George C. Richards, 112th Inf., 28th Div. for exceptionally meritorious and conspicuous service.

WILLARD J. NEAMY, was born Sept. 14, 1898, in Lead, SD, to Finnish immigrant parents who came to America. His father was a timber man in Homestake Gold Mine. He also worked for the gold mine, driving ore wagons.

When WWI broke out, he and his best friend enlisted. His father was displeased, because he was only 19 years old and he thought the boys should have waited to be drafted. He enlisted on May 17, 1918, and crowds of Lead citizens saw the boys leaving on the train.

He received his training at Lakehurst Proving Grounds. He was commissioned corporal on June 10, 1918. During one gas drill practice, his sergeant lost his face mask. He pulled him to safety and put his own mask on him. His sergeant applied for his recommendation for bravery, but the sergeant died before the papers were completed.

Small pox immunizations were given before going overseas. He was immune, so he had no scar. This disqualified him from going overseas. His dear friend went, and didn't return. He was put on detail to survey and map New Jersey Swamps. He was honorably discharged from the U.S. Army on Nov. 15, 1918.

On his return, he lived with relatives in Wisconsin. He got married and they had two children and several grandchildren. He worked for a bakery company and was their part time salesman in three states. Later, he worked for Minnesota Car License Bureau. He died in February 1988.

ALBERT WALLACE NEWHALL, was born Dec. 6, 1885, in Worcester, MA. He joined the Army and was discharged early in 1918.

He was a member of the 612th Aero-Squadron that was stationed at Camp Kelly, TX on March 11, 1918. His unit was ready to go overseas when the war ended. He achieved the rank of Lt.

He married Edna Torreno on June 13, 1914 and they had three children. He also had three grandchildren, 10 great-grandchildren and five great-great-grandchildren. He passed away on Sept. 26, 1948 in Los Angeles, CA.

EDGAR LEVI NEWTON, was born Feb. 3, 1895, to Bing and Mollie Newton of Iredell, TX. He registered for the draft and was inducted into the Army on Sept. 19, 1917.

He was assigned to Camp Travis, Utilities Q.M.C., San Antonio, TX. He handled clerical duties for the electrical section. He was discharged as Sgt. 1st Class, on May 13, 1919. He was appointed to same position as a civilian the day after his discharge. He worked for the war dept. for two years and the Veterans Adm. for 37 years. He retired as a supply officer.

He married Jewell Binney on June 5, 1921. He had three children, seven grandchildren and eight great-grandchildren. His wife and one daughter are now deceased. His son lives in Seattle, WA and daughter in Canyon Lake, TX. He is retired and lives alone in Canyon Lake, TX. He has a part-time housekeeper/chauffeur, who looks after his daily needs. He enjoys reading large print books, listening to radio, playing old-time records, and watching the news and sports on television.

EDWARD JOHN NIEDERMAIER SR.,

was born July 5, 1895, in Eudora, Douglas Co., KS. He joined the service on Feb. 23, 1918 in Thurman, IA. He was discharged on July 11, 1919.

He was stationed at Camp Dodge, IA, Camp Custer, MI and Camp Montierchaume, France. He achieved the rank of Corporal. He was mustered in at Camp Dodge, IA on Feb. 22, 1918. After a month he was transferred to Co. A, 55th Construction Engineers. The 1st Bn., 55th Engineers, sailed on June 30, 1918 on the *SS Siboney*. Upon arrival at Brest, France, Co. A, 55th Engineers, was attached to Service of Supplies at Camp Montierchaume, France which was being constructed. Warehouses were badly needed. He was assigned to oversee a group of laborers hired from the Italian or Chinese government. German prisoners were also used. American service men were seldom used. The Italian laborers were trustees from Italian prisons.

There were three work crews building the warehouses. The first work crew dug holes and set the poles. The second work crew framed the roofs and sides. He was given about 35 laborers to put the sheet iron roofs and sides on. He continued that until June 1919.

In the meantime, he was given opportunities to visit Paris, Rheims in the war zone and Grenoble in the vacation area after the Armistice. He sailed from St. Nazaire on the *Santa Ceselia*. He arrived in New York on July 4, 1919 and was discharged at Camp Dodge, IA.

He married Louise, and they have two daughters and a son. He is Commander of Dept. of Texas Veterans of WWI. He is also Dallas County Barracks No. 765 Commander. He does volunteer service for the vets of WWI.

JOHN COLIN O'BRIAN,

was born Jan. 9, 1893, in the Indian Territory of Oklahoma. He entered the U.S. Army on June 13, 1917 at Ft. Mead, SD.

His infantry was stationed at Ft. Meade. He was then transferred to Camp Greene, NC, Camp Mills, Long Island, NY and Camp Merrit, NJ. He left the United States on Jan. 11, 1918 and arrived in England on Jan. 17, 1918 at Liverpool. He left South Hampton, England and arrived in LeHarve, France in January 1918. He left St. Nazaire, France in May 1919, and arrived in Hoboken NJ on May 11, 1919.

After serving June- September in Ft. Meade, SD, he was sent to Camp Green, NC, and the company was changed over from the Infantry to a machine gun company. They trained as a machine gun outfit until about the first of March 1918. Then there were about 55 men from the company who were transferred to the 1st Div., Inf. as replacements to replace men lost in the first American engagement. He joined the 18th Inf., 1st Div., Co. L, at the front, not far from Nancy on the Toul Sector. He there received his first baptism of fire. They were not in this sector long until they were pulled out and sent to the Chateau Thierry front, where they were thrown into the battle to stop the Germans on their famous drive on Paris in March-June.

On May 28, 1918, the American 18th and 28th Inf. Regt., went into what was to be the first American offensive battle, when on the morning of May 28, they attacked and took the town of Cantigney and held it against nine counter attacks in three days, before being relieved. The town of Cantigney was taken from the Germans twice before, once each by the British and the French. It was lost back to the Germans both times by counter attacks. At this time, the 1st Div., was working with and under orders of the 10th French Army Corps., which entitled him to the French Commemorative Medal, which he later received. He also received the Chateau Thierry Medal.

After leaving the Cantigney Sector, they relieved the French on another sector, where they stayed until July 12, 1918, when they were pulled out in a hurry and rode in trucks for two nights and then marched for three days and two nights until they went into trenches on the western front. On July 18, 1918, they went over the top. This battle is now known as the Second Battle of the Marne. He fought with them for five days, when he was taken back to a first aid station and sent back to a hospital. He was carried back to the first aid station by two

German prisoners who were being taken back along with many others. It was in this battle, that he received wounds from shell fragments and was wounded in three places with a bayonet. He was also gassed. It was also in this engagement, that he received the Silver Star and the Purple Heart. However, he did not actually receive the medals until 18 years later.

In 1936, he wrote to the War Dept., asking for the Victory Medal, which all WWI soldiers were entitled to. In looking up my service record, they found where I was entitled to the Purple Heart and had been recommended for the Silver Star. Neither of these had been delivered to me, therefore, they sent them to me.

After going through the hospital in France, he was sent to a camp and put to work driving a truck until May 1919, at which time he was sent home and discharged at Camp Dodge, IA.

EINAR OFFERDAHL, was born Jan. 31, 1895 in Ofredal, Norway, a son of Ola and Severina Offerdal. He received his education in Norway and when he was 17, came to America to join his three brothers homesteading near Conrad. He took a job preparing railway bed from Vaughn Junction to Choteau. He was a cowboy for Sen. Tom Larson, and for three years broke horses used on the ranch and sold to homesteaders. In 1916, he filed on his own homestead east of Conrad.

In 1918, he joined the U.S. Army at Ft. Benton, and served in the infantry until receiving his honorable discharged in 1919 at Camp Lewis, WA. He returned to the Larson ranch for a time, before becoming a bus driver for Whitworth College in Spokane.

On Dec. 28, 1921, he married Ida Rosvold in Spokane. They moved to Great Falls, where he worked for the smelter and later drove a cab. He drove for Jack Dempsey, on his way to the famous fight in Shelby in 1923.

In 1924, they moved to their homestead at Conrad and farmed there until 1960. He was preceded in death by his wife, Ida, on April 26, 1978. He had one son and four grandchildren. He passed away on Jan. 24, 1985.

HARRY OLSON, was born Oct. 13, 1894 in Rame, ND, to Mr. and Mrs. Jenesene Olson. He lived in Belle Fouche, SD, for a while and enlisted in Ft. Meade, SD in May 1917.

He served in battles in the Center Sector, Alsace, Aisne-Marne, Aise-Aisne and the Meusse Argonne. He was a Corporal in the 120th Machine Gun Bn. of the U.S. Army's 32nd Div. He sailed from the United States on Jan. 11, 1919. He was in the Army of Occupation in Germany after the war, until his demobilization.

He married Grace Ballou in Wagner, SD in 1922. They had two girls and a boy. Grace died in

1963 and he remarried Violet Hudspeth in November 1966. They lived in Sundance, WY and Sturgis, SD. He ranched on Indian Creek, north of Belle Fourche until the 40s. He was Deputy Sheriff in Belle Fourche, SD from then until 56, when he moved to Sundance. He then retired. He passed away at Ft. Meade on July 14, 1980.

AMOS ORR, was born near Sturgis in February 1894, to John and Sarra Orr. His father had homesteaded near Sturgis, and there he grew to manhood.

He enlisted in the Army and went to Ft. Dodge, IA. From there, he went on to France. He was ready to be shipped to the front, when he came down with the mumps. The war ended and he was shipped home.

He homesteaded across from his parents and married Charlotte Lehman on Sept. 14, 1926. To this union two girls were born. He farmed there and raised some cattle. He also worked in Sturgis, 10 miles away. In 1945, he went to work at Ft. Meade VA Hospital, and retired from there due to medical reasons. He lived in Sturgis until his death on Dec. 5, 1971. He is buried in the Bear Butte Cemetery in Sturgis, SD.

JASON CURRY OUTLER, was born Aug. 18, 1898 in Jeffersonville, GA. He enlisted on Jan. 12, 1918 and was honorably discharged on Jan. 12, 1922.

He was a member of the U.S. Marine Corps Reserve, where he achieved the rank of Corporal. He was stationed at Paris Island, SC. He helped build Paris Island. He received the Expert Rifleman and the VOC Medal of Honor. He was knighted by King Haakon VI of Norway by order of St. Olaf, for service as Vice Consul.

He married Helen Rebecca Hart and they had two children, six grandchildren and four great-grandchildren.

MAXWELL OSWALD PARRY, was born on May 27, 1886 in Indianapolis, IN. He was the eldest son of David Parry, one of the captains of industry. He grew up on his parents' estate at Golden Hill, Indianapolis. He graduated from Yale and became a playwright. His play, *The Lie Beautiful*, was produced on Broadway, where it received favorable reviews.

He enlisted in August 1917. He became an aviator, and was among the first to reach the line of battle. He shot down his first plane, on July 4, 1918. He scored several more kills during the next few days.

On July 8, his patrol sighted 13 German planes. After giving chase, the patrol turned back, all but Maxwell parry. He single-handedly attacked and was shot down and killed in a dogfight. He was posthumously awarded the Croix de Guerre and the Distinguished Flying Cross. He is buried in France.

GEORGE SILVEY PARTRIDGE, was inducted on Oct. 3, 1917 into Co. A, 325th Inf. Regt., 82nd Div. at Camp Gordon, Atlanta, GA. At the end of October, he was assigned to Co. C, 122 Inf. Regt., 31st Div. at Camp Wheelers, Macon, GA.

In June 1918, he was assigned to Co. 2, June Automatic Replacement Draft to Hoboken, NJ. He shipped out on the *HMS Euripides* to Liverpool, then South Hampton, England. On July 5, he was assigned to Co. D, 163rd Inf. Regt., 41st Div. in Gondrecourt, France. On July 10 he was assigned to Co. F, 38th Inf. Regt., 3rd Div. in the Marne and then on July 18-20 he served with Co. F, 38th Inf. at the front on the Marne River, east of Chateau-Thierry.

He fought with Co. F, 38th Inf. in the Aisne-Marne (Chateau Thierry and Vesle Sectors); St. Mihiel Sector; and the Meuse Argonne (Montfaucon Sector). He marched 250 miles from Nov. 17-Dec. 17, 1918 in the March to the Rhine from Hannonville, France to Obermendig, Germany. On March 15, 1919, he was assigned to the 38th Inf. Supply Co., where he remained until his return from Brest, France on Aug. 10, 1919 on the *USS Agamemnon*. He was discharged on Aug. 26, 1919 at Camp Gordon, GA.

WILLIAM M. PATTERSON, was born Sept. 2, 1896, in Savannah, GA. His parents were the former Irene Hodges and John J. Patterson. In 1918, he married Kathryn Ostertag and raised two sons, William M. Jr. and John J.

He served in the Mexican Campaign. In WWI, he served as a Ensign in the U.S.N. He was torpedoed by a German U-boat and taken prisoner and later set free at sea in a life boat. In WWII, he served as a engineer in the Merchant Marine. He was an inspector for the Navy, winning the coveted Navy E. He was an inspector for the Maritime Commission and was in charge of inspections of the liner *United States*.

He retired in 1958, and moved to Tavares, FL. His wife died in 1972. In 1976, he married Eve Webster and moved to Waycross, GA. He belongs to Veterans of WWI and the Masonic Order.

GLENN PEARCY, was born July 7, 1891, in New Milton, WV. He enlisted on Sept. 21, 1917 and was discharged on April 2, 1919.

He was a member of the U.S. Army and achieved the rank of Pvt. 1st Class. He was stationed in Battle Creek, MI. He was in active duty for two years at Hagrs. He was transferred to a non-recoverable hospital unit during the influenza epidemic of 1918. An orderly came in and shaved him. He began to improve at once and survived and lived 68 years longer to age 95.

He was married once and had no children. His parents were Thomas and Julia Pearcy. He was a 50 year member of the American Legion Post No. 5, D.A.V. and WWI Barracks No. 17 in Tampa.

DON R. PEARS, was born Sept. 18, 1899, in Buchanan, MI. He enlisted on Sept. 20, 1917 and was discharged on June 19, 1919. He enlisted for WWII on Jan. 18, 1942 and was discharged on July 1, 1945.

He was a member of the American Legion Post 51, VFW, Amvets, Retreads and Elks Lodge of St. Joseph. At age 89, he was elected a National Commander of the Veterans of WWI Org.

He taught school in Big Bay, MI and Elkhart, IN. On Feb. 18, 1931, he married the former Gladys Seidlitz in Elkhart, IN. They had two daughters and five grandchildren. He passed away on July 17, 1992.

ARCHIE L. PEARSON, was born at Springfield, IA on Jan. 6, 1893. When he was 10 years old, he moved with his parents to Montana and lived in the Deer Park area, south of Columbia Falls, where he also attended school.

He later moved to Kalispell, where he worked for Sykes Grocery for more than 30 years and also owned and operated the grocery for a number of years.

He was a member of Co. D, 44th Inf. from Aug. 27, 1918 until Feb. 4, 1919. He was a life member of the American Legion, Post No. 7 of Kalispell. He married Clara Helen Shouse on Nov. 25, 1919 in Columbia Falls and was preceded in death by her in November 1963. He had three sons and one daughter, 11 grandchildren and one great-grandson. He passed away on April 17, 1976.

OSCAR W. PERNER, was born Feb. 17, 1892 in Blanco Co., TX. He was a member of the U.S. Army's Co. C, 3rd Supply Train. He served overseas and participated in the Meuse Argonne, Champagne and Verdun, France from Oct. 30-Nov. 11, 1918.

He was discharged on June 17, 1919 at Camp Bowie, TX. He passed away on Jan. 18, 1974 in San Antonio, TX, at the age of 81.

WILLIAM C. PETERSON, was born May 30, 1894 in St. Thomas, ND. He enlisted on March 29, 1918 and was discharged on May 14, 1919 at Camp Dodge, IA.

He was a member of Co. A, 137th Inf. and Co. F, 163rd Depot Brigade in France. He fought in the Meuse Argonne Defensive Sector, Alsace and the Larraine. He remembers trading a horse he was riding, with a man who became President of the United States, Truman. He also remembers reading letters from home in the trenches with others.

He married Evelyn Nard in January 1917, and they had two daughters. He later remarried and had one son. He passed away on Jan. 8, 1970.

GEORGE E. PHELPS SR., was born June 25, 1896, on a farm in North Dakota. He enlisted on April 21, 1918 and was discharged on March 12, 1919.

He was a member of the Coast Arty. Corps., where he achieved the rank of Pvt. He was stationed at Ft. Coswell, off the coast of North Carolina.

He married his childhood sweetheart on June 20, 1920. He is retired and enjoys visiting his children, grand-children and great-grand-children.

CARL F. PHILLIPS, was a Pvt. in the 354th Aero Observation Squadron from its birth in San Antonio in 1917, until its death in 1919. Before going to France in August 1918, they trained young cadets to fly at San Antonio, Hicks, Texas, Waco and Ft. Worth.

He sailed from Mitchel Field, Long Island for Brest, France in August 1918. After going through a siege of flu, they went through Colombey La Belle, France Air Depot. From there they went to Saizerais, where they immediately took an active part in the war and where they were equipped with the Liberty Airplanes. They were given qualified air pilots and artillery officers, who were to operate the gun on their airplanes.

He was classed as an Airplane Technician, which meant to be qualified to make any repair to the airplane engines as well as to be able to rig the plane at the proper angle so that the plane would be balanced in the air. From Colombey, they went to Saizerais, France, where they were completely equipped with Liberty Airplanes, photographic equipment, air pilots and artillery officers. This is where they immediately took an active part in the war by directing artillery fire, taking pictures, and spying on the Germans.

Their planes took part in the Verdun Offensive. As far as he knows, the 354th Aero Squadron lost no planes in combat, however they lost several planes and officers in accidents primarily because flying was a new industry and the pilots liked to experiment and take chances. They got one German airplane that a U.S. Army doughboy in the trenches shot down with his rifle. His bullet pierced the gasoline line with a lone bullet and the German plane lost its gasoline.

Shortly after the Armistice, the 354th, was moved to Toule, France, where they had better quarters and where the airplane that he kept in repair, carried mail to and from Chaumont, Pershing's headquarters. From Toule, they went to Sinzig, Germany and took part in the Army of Occupation. Before leaving Germany, the 354th broke up in a group to fit the steamship on which they were to return to the United States. After arriving in the United States, they were sent to Mitchell Field on Long Island, to assist in the landing of the British Dirigible, that they had obtained as reparations from Germany. They were there for a week or more until after the Dirigible left. The British Dirigible was known as the R-34.

CLARENCE LEE PIERCE, was born May 12, 1892 in Ubley, MI, a son of William and Florence Pierce. As a child he moved with his family to Kalispell, where he received his education.

On April 16, 1917, he entered the U.S. Army and served in France during WWI. He received his honorable discharge in 1919.

He moved to Spokane, WA, where he was employed with the SP&S Railroad until his retirement in 1958. He then returned to the Flathead Valley, where he lived since. He was a member of the First Baptist Church, Kalispell Senior Citizens and WWI Barracks, where he was Quartermaster for 10 years.

He had a wife, Eva, three daughters, nine grandchildren and five great-grandchildren. He passed away on Jan. 18, 1983.

JAMES E. PIERCE, was born July 30, 1896. He was an Auburn, NY native. He was in the 46th Regt. Coast Arty. Corps. in the A.E.F. to France in 1918. He was also the national bugler for the Veterans of WWI organization.

He was a member of the Smithfield Union Lodge 18, the Kiwanis Club, Carrollton Chapter 1881 American Association of Retired Persons, George F. Dashiell American Legion Post 49 and Pagan River Barracks 1409 Veterans of WWI. He had two daughters, nine grandchildren and 13 great-grandchildren.

RICHARD JULIUS PIERCE, was born July 3, 1895 at Hiawatha, KS. He enlisted on July 22, 1918 at Rosebud, SD.

He served at Camp Dodge, IA. He was discharged by Pes. N.D. Tel. Washington on Dec. 1, 1919

He passed away on May 19, 1989 and left his wife Viola E. Pierce.

MICHAEL J. PLONY, was in the Navy and made 11 round trips across the Atlantic carrying troops. He was in the Medical Corp. and served on the *Martha Washington* and the *Mercury*.

He received a certificate "In the name of Disabled American Veterans, awarding sincere appreciation for valuable and devoted membership of over one-half century."

LUKAS C. PORTENTO, was born Oct. 16, 1893, in Skapy Loka, Austria, a son of Peter and Antonio Prento. As a young man, he moved to the United States, where he was involved in mining most of his adult life.

He served in the U.S. Army from Oct. 24, 1916 until June 24, 1919. On Aug. 8, 1966, he married Winnie Johnson. He had one stepdaughter and two stepsons. He passed away on Oct. 26, 1981.

ELMER E. POTTS, was born May 23, 1895 in Philadelphia, PA. He enlisted on May 22, 1918 and was discharged on Jan. 27, 1920.

He was a member of the 435th Inf. He was stationed at Ft. Dix and in France. He saw no action. At the time of the Armistice, he was convoying Y.M.C.A. goods up to the front. He left France about Christmas time.

He and his wife were together 65 years before her death on Dec. 1, 1991. She was memorialized at the 1992 convention in Louisville, KY.

EMMETT POWELL, was born March 7, 1899, in Grand Forks, ND. He married Stella J. Ratchford in Kalispell, on Aug. 26, 1925.

He worked as a yard foreman and brakeman for Great Northern Railroad, retiring in 1971. He was a member of the Columbia Falls Masonic Lodge for more than 50 years. He had one daughter, one grandchild and one great-grandchild.

He served in WWI from June 1918 until Feb. 12, 1919. He was an engineer. He passed away on July 21, 1987.

RODOLPH M. PRICE, was a member of the Army's 29th Div., 104th Engineers. He enlisted in the Virginia National Guard with the sinking of the *Lusitania*. He trained in Norfolk and went to Anniston, AL.

From that, the 29th Div. was created and installed in Camp McClellan. He was a private. They then transferred him to the 104th Engineers train and made him a mule skinner. He was wounded by mustard gas.

He is retired from the Norfolk Fire Dept. and the Norfolk Navy Base, where he was a security officer. He is a member of the VFW Post 3160 and the 29th Div. Association.

ALBERT J. PYLE, was a member of the U.S. Navy. At the recruiting station, the Chief Petty Officer asked if he had any skills. He said he played the flute and piccolo and had experience in orchestras and bands. He promptly gave him the rating of 2nd Class Musician.

At the Portsmouth, VA Navy Yard, he entered the band school directly and thereby avoided boot camp. After finding that he could play fairly well, the bandmaster sent him to the Admiral's band in the Portsmouth Navy Yard. That winter was one of the coldest on record. Some of the boys in the tents froze to death, but those in the band barracks had heat and were very comfortable. When out marching, the cold froze their instruments so some of the parades had to do without them.

He feels that Uncle Sam treated him exceedingly well. He had the advantage of band school, electrician school and O.M. School. Later he was given a bonus for war service. He passed away in 1989.

DANA J. PYLE, was born Aug. 21, 1897, in Wilmington, DE. He enlisted on Aug. 21, 1918 and was discharged on Jan. 31, 1919.

He was a member of the Coast Arty. and achieved the rank of Pvt. 1st Class. He was stationed at Ft. DuPont, DE. He remembers keeping an eye open for German submarines along the Atlantic Ocean coast of Delaware. He achieved an award from the state of Delaware.

He was elected Commander, Dept. of Delaware for Veterans of WWI in 1980, National Commander from 1986-87 and National Quartermaster from 1991-93. He also played the violin in Coast Orchestra and the cymbals. He was invited to France in 1987 in celebration of 70 years after the American troops landed in France. He was knighted by the Hon. Andre Giraud, Minister of France.

He retired in 1965 after 50 years in the family lumber business that was started by his father in Wilmington, DE. He was President of Pyle Lumber Co. from 1948-65. He also volunteers at the Veterans Hospital in Wilmington, DE and has served 10 years and 700 hours. He is also a violinist for the Wilmington Symphony Orchestra for 40 years.

MERRILL A. RAPER, was born on a cold winter day in Canby, IA, on Dec. 27, 1887. As it was told to him, ice and snow covered the ground so that a horse and sleigh had to be sent 10 miles away to Adair, IA, to retrieve a doctor and bring him back. Adair is about 80 miles west of Des Moines, IA. Merrill was the first of four children born to John and Rosetta Bell Stilwell Raper. He had a brother, Wesley, and two sisters, Grace and Mable. All are deceased at this time.

In 1900-01, John W. Raper, his father, became interested in a new city being planned by a man in Chicago. This man was John Alexander Dowle, who is listed in the encyclopedias as the founder of the city of northeast Illinois, called Zion. On or about 1902, the John W. Raper family moved to Zion City, located between Chicago and Milwaukee. Merrill was 15 years old at the time.

Zion City was founded on the principles of a city under which God would reign. As a Utopian Community, Merrill's family believed this to be the best place on earth to live. The rules of Zion

City were, to believe the word of God from Genesis to the Revelations and to allow no negatives to enter the city. Divine healing was practiced as well as all laws regarding the Old and the New Testaments, including the Leviticus.

Merrill, to this day, proclaims these principles as the reason for him being able to reach 103 years of age on Dec. 27, 1990. He was married to Mable Young Raper in 1920. Together they raised three children, John, Lois and Paul. These three children have given him 17 grand, 29 great-grand and eight great-great-grandchildren and heaven only knows how many more to come before he leaves this earth. Mable, his wife, passed on to be with the Lord on February 2, 1977.

Merrill spent most of his life raising bees, selling honey, raising chickens, and selling fryers and eggs. He also enjoyed fruit trees: plums, apples, peaches, pears and red and yellow cherries. His son remembers having to help him spray the fruit trees and work in the vegetable garden. His wife always had cows, so they had fresh milk. Merrill loved to work outside at his own pace.

He did work at various paying jobs during his life time but didn't like to be confined to factory or other repetitive types of limited jobs. He was also an election judge most of his adult life.

He now lives at the James A. Haley Veterans Nursing Care Center in Tampa, FL. He is of sound mind. Reading with the help of a magnifying glass, he maintains an active interest in religion, politics and current events all around him. He smiles and laughs a lot, but when things go wrong, he calls God from heaven to guide him and handle his problems.

He served at Camp Grant, IL, from 1918-19. His discharge indicates he was a telephone inspector.

JOE REDDER, WWI Vet, drafted in 1918.

DANIEL REED, was born Jan. 30, 1889 in Floyd Co., VA. He enlisted in the Regular Army at Ft. Snelling, MN on Aug. 27, 1913.

He served in the Philippine Islands and later on the Mexican Border. He left the United States on March 18, 1918 and arrived in France on March 30, 1918. He was in the 3rd Div., 3rd Sanitary Train, Ambulance Co. 27 and served as a mess Sgt. He was in the Aisne Champagne Marne, Aisne-Marne, St. Mihiel and the Meuse Argonne. He also served in the Army of Occupation on Dec. 1, 1918. He left France on Aug. 13, 1919 and arrived in the United States on Aug. 22, 1919. He was discharged on June 4, 1920. His service was described as honest and faithful.

He married on April 4, 1920 to C. Elizabeth Mangus. He went to Akron, OH to work in the rubber mills. In 1922, he moved to Warren, OH to work in steel mills. He was a charter member of Barracks 468 in Warren, OH, Veterans of WWI of the U.S.A., Inc. He died on Feb. 26, 1979 at the age of 90. He was survived by his wife, C. Elizabeth Reed and his son Eugene.

EVERETT OMAR REED, was born July 25, 1898 in Handley, TX. He enlisted at Ft. Worth, TX on April 4, 1917.

He was a member of the Army's 36th Inf. Div. He fought on two fronts, the Champagne and the Meuse Argonne. He was wounded in his left foot while facing cross machine gun fire in the Meuse Argonne. He received the Purple Heart. He was discharged on March 9, 1929. He had achieved the rank of Captain. He died on Feb. 16, 1985 at the Audie Murphy Hospital in San Antonio, TX.

RALPH H. REED, was born in Reynoldsville, PA. As a child, he moved with his family to Roundup. After finishing school, he worked as a boiler man in Roundup-area mines for a time.

In 1917, he entered the U.S. Navy, and served until 1919. He served on the *USS Pennsylvania.* After his discharge, he was employed for 30 years by the Yellowstone Park Service, working with maintenance crews and as a powerhouse operator until his retirement.

He married Christine Knittel at Hosmer, SD, on Sept. 26, 1933. In 1959, he moved to Bigfork, where he resided until his death. He was survived by his wife, three daughters, one son, 16 grandchildren, seven great-grandchildren and two great-great-grandchildren. He died on Sept. 30, 1983.

JOSEPH REESE, was born Oct. 1, 1893, in Haven, SD, a son of Albert and Anna Reese. He served in the 33rd Div., 129th Inf., Co. A, U.S. Army during WWI.

In 1934, he came to Glasgow from Minnesota and worked as a contractor there for many years. In 1942, he moved to Kalispell and operated a saw mill at Essex. He also did clearing for the Hungry Horse Dam.

He was a member of the Church of God. He served as Commander of WWI Barracks 362 and

was past commander of the American Legion Post 7, of which he was a member for more than 50 years. On Oct. 31, 1920, he married Serena Jensen in Minot, ND, and is now survived by her at the family home in Kalispell. He was also survived by two daughters and numerous grandchildren. He passed away on Oct. 26, 1985.

HANS H. REINKE, was born Dec. 5, 1893, in Woodstock, IL, a son of Herman and Margaret Reinke. In 1905, he moved with his family to Lisbon, ND. On Oct. 14, 1925, he was married to Anna Johnson in Lisbon. The couple lived at Nome, ND, until 1956 when they moved to Kalispell.

He had engaged in farming in North Dakota and had been custodian at the Nome schools. Since coming to Kalispell, he was employed in the maintenance department of Kalispell General Hospital for a number of years. He had also been custodian at the Immanuel Lutheran Home and Bethlehem Lutheran Church.

He was a veteran of WWI, having served in the U.S. Army during that time. He was a member of the Bethlehem Lutheran Church and the WWI Barracks. He was preceded in death by his wife, Anna, on Nov. 7, 1978, and is now survived by two daughters, six grandchildren and 12 great-grandchildren. He passed away on Dec. 27, 1991.

DR. CHARLES BENJAMIN REITZ, was born Jan. 4, 1890 in Cherryville, PA. He was the first honor graduate from Hahnemann Medical School in Philadelphia.

He joined the service in Aug. 29, 1916 and was discharged in December 1918 at Ft. Riley. He was a member of the 37th Div., Medical Corp. of the U.S. Army. He achieved the rank of 1st Lt. He fought at the Mexican Border in Ft. McAllen in August 1916. He was located in Texas for minor surgery then went to Rochefeller Institute in New York City for post graduate courses supplied by the Army. He was also stationed at Ft. Benjamin Harrison, IN, Ft. Sheridan and Ft. Riley, KS in which he was the head doctor in control.

He was honorably discharged from Ft. Riley, KS in 1919. He joined the Army Medical Corp. Reserves for 25 years. He served as a Pathologist in Allentown State Hospital, Allentown, PA. In 1919, he left and started a private medical practice in Palmerton, PA. His wife Minnie served as his assistant.

In 1946, he moved from Palmerton to his family homestead in Walnut Post, PA. He died on Oct. 28, 1972 in Tapton Home, PA. He was a member of the 32nd Degree F & A. M., Tall Cedar, Noble of Mystic Shrine, School Board, American Legion, Fellow Am. College of Pathologists, American Board of Pathology and American Society of Clinical Pathologists.

He was the son of Rev. Dr. James J. and Ada Fallweiler Reitz. His father graduated from Hahnemann College in 1903.

KARL DUSTIN REYER, was born Aug. 22, 1899 in West Lafayette, IN. He enlisted on Dec. 13, 1917 and was discharged on May 10, 1919.

He was a member of Btry. C, 150th FA, 42nd Div., where he achieved the rank of Pvt. He served in Camp La Courtine, Guer, France and the Army of Occupation in Badenheim, Germany. He went to France on the *Hell-rolling Mallory* and remembers marshaling train yards at Rennes, Red Cross and Knights of Columbus doughnuts, sweetened condensed milk and cheese ate out of the can, camp built by Napoleon in 1812, weekend pass to Paris and an older lady invited him in, they sent Christmas cards for years and Easter dinner on the *Leviathan*, coming back.

He also served in active duty in WWII from Sept. 23, 1940 to Dec. 28, 1945. He received two campaign stars from that service.

Today he is busy distributing life-long collections, books, pictures, papers and correspondence. He attends local chapter meetings of Reserve Officers Association and American Legion. He also attends the Methodist Church, takes guests out to eat, writes letters, watches L.S.U. athletic events on t.v. and participates in activities and outings in the retirement center.

MERLIN REYNOLDS, was born Nov. 16, 1893, in Bangor, MI, to Nelson G. and Ida Reynolds. He was raised and educated in Bemidji, MN.

He served in the Army from 1917-19. He was a member of Co. B, Hospital Dept. He married Alice Nunn on Aug. 20, 1926, in Bemidji, MN. They moved to the Flathead Valley in 1936.

He worked as a cook in Glacier National Park for 10 years, he helped build the snow sheds for the Great Northern Railroad, and later he worked as a cook at the high school in Forest Grove, OR. He was assistant superintendent at Montana Veterans Home for several years. He was commander of Montana Veterans Home from April 1, 1962 to March 31, 1964.

He was preceded in death by a brother, a sister and three grandchildren. He was survived by his wife, seven sons, three daughters, 38 grandchildren and numerous great-grandchildren and great-great-grandchildren. He passed away on Dec. 15, 1985.

JOHN LATHRUP RHODEN, was drafted on June 24, 1918 from Sturgis, SD. He went overseas on Aug. 16, 1918, arrived in England six weeks later.

He went to Camp Stoney Castle, England. Four or five days later, he went to Southhampton, then crossed the Channel and landed in Cherbourg, France. He had some training in Posillinay and received more at Champley.

Soon after arriving in Champley, he came down with the flu. There were no hospitals in that area, so they were quartered in a leaky barn and it rained a lot then. He said many mornings when he awoke, many men had died during the night and there were bodies right next to him. In October, the convalescents were sent to better conditions in a camp south of there.

He rejoined his company near Fullern. The 88th Div. was in conflicts near villages of Ammerzwiller and Englingen. On October 24, the Fullern sector of the 88th Div. was put into supporting position at Manspack. On October 31, the division participated in four raids when the Germans attacked the 351st Inf. on the Schonholz salient. They also ran into some activity in the Alsace area. The 88th crossed No Man's Lands at will as there was no opposition from the Germans.

When the 88th Div., was sent to France in the summer of 1918, they were in a quiet sector, but without proper equipment. They gave a splendid account of themselves in the Haute Alsace Sector. From there, he was detailed to Leffo LeGrand to convey supply trains to Coblenz, Germany. In February, he contracted the mumps and was hospitalized in Bozoilles.

After the Armistice, Co. E and others came home. He was discharged in good health, but soon had a 10 percent disability and pension of $19.00 a month. He received a bonus of $172.00 in 1929.

He farmed on his homestead, before and after marriage. His wife was a school teacher, Helena Bulgreen. They had four children. She died in 1930. He then married Helen Westall in 1939. The family stayed on the homestead, until because of health, moved to Sturgis to be near his doctor. He died in 1967 and is buried at Red Owl Cemetery in South Dakota.

CHARLES A. RICE, was born Nov. 5, 1895, at Montrose, Randolph Co., WV. The son of Joseph R. Rice and Mollie Wilmoth Rice.

He served in the U.S. Army from May 29, 1917 to July 26, 1919, as 1st Class Pvt. He was stationed at Hospital 1, Ft. Sam Houston, TX from June 2, 1917 to Dec. 8, 1917, Hdg. Field Hospital sec. 15, from Dec. 8, 1917 to Dec. 14, 1917, the Ambulance Co. 39 from Dec. 14, 1917 to June 10, 1919, the Post Hospital Romagne from June 10, 1919 to June 30, 1919, the Brest Casual Co. 2718 from June 30, 1919 to his date of discharge on July 26, 1919. His service in France was from August 1918 to July 26, 1919 at Mitchel Field, L.I.N.Y.

In 1923, he married Anne Williams and moved to Sharon, PA, where he worked for the Westinghouse Electrical Co. Later he retired and returned back to West Virginia, where he owned a small farm and lived there the remainder of his life. His only child, a son, was born Aug. 8, 1924 and died on May 26, 1930.

He was authorized to wear a Good Conduct Ribbon, WWI Ribbon and one Gold Service Chevron. He belonged to Veterans of WWI, Barracks 1060 of West Virginia, American Legion Post 29 of Elkins, WV and the United Methodist Church. He died on Feb. 13, 1976 at the age of 81.

EUGENE W. RICHARDS, was born Dec. 25, 1895 in Meade Co. He was discharged from the military in 1919.

He had achieved the rank of Sgt. He served in the Verdun and the Argonne. He has passed away but is survived by his wife, Mrs. E.W. Richards.

JAMES D. RILEY, was born Sept. 30, 1889, in North Dakota. On June 30, 1919, he married Sina Lovisa Alme at Havre. The couple had homesteaded south of Gildford until 1924, when they moved to Oilmont.

He had engaged in oil refinery work until 1941, when the couple moved to Kalispell and had resided there since. He was a member of Bethlehem Lutheran Church, WWI Barracks of Kalispell and the VFW.

He served with the Btry. B, Field Artillery in France from May 29, 1918 to Sept. 30, 1921. He was preceded in death by his wife and is survived by one daughter. He passed away in November 1972.

JOE RITZMAN, was born Dec. 16, 1897, at Coaltown Township, PA. He moved to the Flathead Valley area when he was a boy. He was a veteran of WWI, and he married Violet Moerke on Oct. 22, 1923, at Libby.

He was a member of Co. F that was stationed in France from 1917-19. He was a truck driver for J. Neils Lumber Co., from 1926 until his retirement in 1962.

He was survived by his wife, two daughters, 12 grandchildren and eight great-grandchildren. He passed away on Jan. 4, 1977.

ELMER R. "JIM" ROLLIN, was born in Port Townsend, WA, on Sept. 25, 1896. He grew up on his grandfather's farm, planting oyster beds at Quilcene, WA, where he attended high school. After his father died, he worked at a cafe, baking 12 pies before breakfast, taking meals to inmates of the jail, and then working in logging camps on the Peninsula.

He enlisted in the Naval Reserve in Seattle, WA. The 12th Seaman Co., trained at the University of Washington. As he was very strong, he was the stroke when they divided into rowing crews and raced in Lake Washington. The men slept in two-men pup tents and when many of them contracted influenza, he seemed to have a natural immunity and became a male nurse. The 12th Co., was sent to Philadelphia, PA to be called into service. He received a marksmanship medal.

When the Armistice came, a bus took the 12th Co. to New York City to watch the Victory Parade. He was discharged on Aug. 9, 1919.

After being a successful business man, he retired to Whidbey Island, where he grew a large vegetable garden. He died on Dec. 24, 1986, in Freeland, WA at the age of 90.

AL ROSS, was born Oct. 11, 1901 in Brooklyn, NY. He was discharged from the Navy in March 1917.

He achieved the rank of Seaman 2nd Class. He was stationed on the *USS Richmond* out of Norfolk, VA. When he enlisted, he was not quite 16 years of age. He doesn't remember anything exciting happening.

He now handles public relations for the *Palm Beach Life* and the *Palm Beach Daily News*.

LEWIS GEORGE ROSS, was born on a farm in Indiana near Denham. At age 12, he moved to

Medaryville, IN, and graduated from high school at Winamac, IN. After turning down an offer of a contract to pitch for the Chicago Cubs, he moved to Chicago and entered a training program at Read Murdoch Wholesale Grocers.

He completed three years of training before enlisting in the Navy in June 1917, in Indianapolis, IN. His basic training was in Newport, RI. He served for two years, and was discharged in June 1919, as a Yeoman 2nd Class.

He returned to his grocery training job, but soon fell ill with tuberculosis and spent six months in a t.b. sanitarium. After that, the grocery company would not give back his job. He tried selling hardware, but later got back into the food business with the A&P stores in Chicago. He was selected to manage the A&P's first self-service market in the late 20s.

His family moved to LaCrosse, WI in 1931, where he opened his own grocery store, only to loose it during the Great Depression in 1933. He ended his career as a supervisor of I.G.A. Grocery Stores in a three state area, Iowa, Wisconsin and Minnesota. He and his wife, Frances, moved to Phoenix, AZ, in 1956 to be near their two daughters, Jeanne and Nancy. In retirement, he was a school bus driver and a crossing guard for the Scottsdale Public School District until age 71. After being married for over 60 years, he was widowed nine years ago in 1984.

His patriotism has never wavered, nor has his love for his country and her flag.

He married in 1920 and had two sons and one daughter. His wife died in 1969 and one son in 1970. He now resides at Highland Convalescent Hospital.

JAMES ROWE, was born in Ft. Benton, a son of Charles and Annie Rowe. His father was a Montana pioneer and former Mayor of Ft. Benton.

The family moved to Great Falls in 1902, and after a stint with the Navy during WWII, he learned his trade, a cook at Great Falls' Rainbow Hotel. During WWI, he served on a U.S. Navy destroyer. In 1923, he moved to Butte, where he first was a chef for the Olde Butte Grill, then operated the Main Grill with Annie Powers.

The business partners were married in Libby in 1939, then moved to Kalispell. After retirement, they lived in California and Arizona, before returning to Montana and settling in Billings in 1969. He passed away on March 22, 1983 and was survived by his wife, a daughter and three grandsons.

RAYMOND M. ROSSBOROUGH SR., was
born July 23, 1902 in Groveville, ME. He enlisted on July 18, 1918 and was discharged on Aug. 15, 1919.

He served with the U.S. Army's 323rd Mobile Laundry Unit, where he achieved the rank of Pvt. 1st Class. He was stationed in Glascow, Scotland and he traveled through England to France and then to Coblenz, Germany. He remembers losing laundry equipment in Glascow, Scotland and found it when they reached Coblenz, Germany in the spring of 1919.

He was discharged at Camp Devens, MA and had to take a taxi to Portland, ME because of a railroad strike. He married on Jan. 16, 1921 and raised five children. Today he is retired and living with his youngest son.

CHARLES H. ROTH, enlisted at Chicago, IL
on Aug. 31, 1918. He was discharged on March 22, 1919 at Camp Grant, IL.

During WWI, he made poison and mustard gas at Edgewood Arsenal in Edgewood, MD. He was in good physical condition at the time of his discharge.

MORRIS B. "MOE" RUBIN, enlisted in the U.S. Army on April 24, 1917 in Boston, MA. He was then sent to Ft. Slocum, NY and then to Ft. H.G. Wright, NY, where he was assigned to the Coast Artillery Corps.

In June 1917, he departed from Hoboken, NJ on the Army transport, the *Kilpatrick*, for the Panama Canal zone. After seven days, they landed. He was then assigned to 9th Co., C.A.C. at Ft. Grast. In June 1918, he was transferred and was made Sgt. Major. He went to school at Ft. Monroe, VA. In December 1918, he was put in charge of a special unit at Camp Devers, MA.

On December 12, he was discharged from the Army at Camp Devers, MA. He was born in Boston, MA on Aug. 7, 1901. He was a life member of Veterans of WWI, American Legion and the Davy Crockett Barracks 1877.

HARVEY RUDELL, was born Oct. 21, 1894 in Butler, MO. He enlisted on July 18, 1918 and was discharged on Jan. 19, 1919.

He entered in Missouri and was discharged in Kansas. He achieved the rank of Pvt. while in the Army. He stayed stateside with the 10th Div.

After the war, he was a mechanic in California. He now lives at the Idaho State Veterans Home.

SEBASTIANO (SAM) SALERN, on Aug. 5, 1918, in Omaha, NE, volunteered to join the U.S. Army Infantry, provided that he would be stationed in California. He was stationed in Palo Alto, CA, and was accepted in the military band under Capt. O.J. Stevens, 8th Div., where he achieved the rank of Pvt. 1st Class.

On Saturday and Sunday afternoons, the band played from two to four at Golden Gate Park in San Francisco. One Sunday, instead of returning to the base at 5 p.m., he temporarily went AWOL. He returned to the base at 10 p.m., finding his name on the bulletin board. He was assigned and reported to, kitchen duty the next morning. That afternoon he went to headquarters to ask for other duty. They questioned if he knew how to drive a motorcycle and since he did, he was assigned duty to deliver mail at headquarters and around the base. On the third week of this duty, he was ordered to go to France.

On board ship, the Captain of the company assigned him as a scout on the lookout for enemy German submarines. They arrived in Liverpool, England and then crossed the English Channel to Brest, France. While in training there, he was called out to be a member of the Honor Guard to accompany President Wilson at the signing of the Armistice in Paris. As a member of the 8th Div., he was sent to the front line at San Genice, France.

He was then assigned to the Occupation Army, crossed the neutral territory and served under Gen. Pershing in Germany, to replenish his diminishing Army, in the 1st Div. On Aug. 28, 1919, he was given orders to return home via Paris, where he was assigned to pick up six wounded soldiers and accompany them on their voyage back to New York and the Army hospital on September 1. On September 2, 1919, the company division paraded in New York City and then left on September 5 for Des Moines, IA. He went to the Army hospital for a checkup to see if he had any health problems.

There he was discharged on Nov. 15, 1919, and was awarded the Victory Medal from France. He arrived home in Omaha, NE, on Nov. 18, 1919.

He was born in Carlentine, Italy on March 22, 1897. He has resided in Vallejo, CA, for 60 years, where he worked as a sheet metal worker at the Mare Island Naval Shipyard. He retired in 1962. He has four children, 11 grandchildren and 16 great-grandchildren.

FRED SANDERS, was born June 14, 1891, in Nassau, MN, the oldest of 10 children of John and Christina Sanders. He attended schools at Sissiton, SD.

He served in the U.S. Navy during WWI. He homesteaded at Big Sandy, and worked in South American oil fields. On Nov. 28, 1930, he married Anna Osterman at Big Sandy, and the couple moved to Lewistown where they established a sheep ranch. They moved to Kalispell in 1946 and continued to ranch until he retired in 1954.

He was a member of Bethlehem Lutheran Church and the VFW. He passed away on July 29, 1985. He was survived by his wife, a son, two daughters and six grandchildren. He was preceded in death by a daughter and her three children.

LEONARD SCHRYVERS, was inducted into the Army on June 24, 1918 from Todd Co., SD. He was a Corporal in Co. C, 312th Inf., 78th Div., A.E.F.

After training in the United States, he was sent to Europe. He was ill when arriving in England and was hospitalized with pneumonia. He was on guard duty in Liverpool, England when the Armistice was signed. He was sent to France for a short time and then back to the United States, where on June 3, 1919, he was discharged at Camp Dodge, IA.

He returned to South Dakota and continued his work as a builder and contractor in Todd Co. In the early 1930s, he moved to the Black Hills, where he worked on constructing camps for the Civilian Conservation Corps. and settled in Sturgis, SD.

In a short time at Ft. Meade, adjacent to Sturgis, a Civil Service position as supervisor of maintenance and repair came open. He applied, got the job, and worked there until retiring in the early 60s.

In January 1966, he had massive brain hemorrhages and died on January 23, a week before his 72nd birthday. He was buried in the Black Hills National Cemetery near Sturgis. He left his wife, three daughters and four grandchildren.

WALTER L. SEIFFERTT, was born Oct. 28, 1895 in Okawville, IL. He enlisted on Feb. 26, 1918 and was discharged on April 14, 1919.

He was a member of the Army's 5th Co., 161st Btry., 119th Inf., 30th Div., where he achieved the rank of Pvt. He was stationed in France, Belgium and England. He was in the hospital in France because of influenza, which probably saved his life, when the Armistice was signed. It was preceded by intensive fighting in which most of his buddies were killed.

His parents were Anna Barbara Herrmann Seiffertt and Nicholas August Seiffertt. He married Ella Harpin on July 30, 1922 in Belleville, IL. They had one daughter, Shirley A. Seiffertt Gump. He was a stove mounter until his retirement in 1960. He died at the age of 83 in Belleville, IL in April 1979. He is buried at Valhalla Cemetery in Belleville, IL.

LOUIS SELLA, was born July 1, 1894 in Laghi, Italy. He enlisted on Dec. 1, 1917 and was discharged on March 25, 1919.

He was a Pvt. 1st Class in the Air Force. He was stationed at Baron Field, Baron, TX and Ft. Worth, TX.

He came to the United States in 1909. He married Emma Frasine and they had five children,

24 grandchildren and 42 great-grandchildren. He owned and operated a grocery store and restaurant for 50 years. He served as Mayor of Nashwauk in 1952. He was a member of the Nashwauk School Board, Board of Director for 1st National Bank, Board of Directors for Western Messabi Oil Co., Fire Chief in Nashwauk and Vice President for Columbus celebration of Statue of Columbus in St. Paul. He was also Commander of the American Legion.

LUCIOUS DAVID SHAW, was born March 13, 1896 in Gordon Co., GA. He joined the service on July 25, 1918 and was discharged on Aug. 27, 1919.

He was a member of the Army's 3rd Div. Regt., 38th Inf., where he held the rank of Pvt. 1st Class. He was stationed in France and Germany. He fought in the Meuse Argonne Offensive. He remembers hiking around a mountain in Germany and the horse pulling the water cart would not go. They were told to get behind the cart and push. The horse started backing up and ran the cart over a ledge and fell several feet. The horse survived. His character at discharge was excellent.

His wife is now deceased. They had two sons, who both served in the Navy during the Korean War. They also had one daughter. Today he is in good health.

DAVE SHEPPARD, was born Sept. 13, 1898, at Acton, ND, a son of Edward and Elizabeth Sheppard. He later moved to Minnesota, where he had attended school at Greenbush.

On Dec. 15, 1916, he entered the U.S. Army at Vancouver Barracks, WA, and served as a corporal in the Motor Transport Corps. until receiving his honorable discharge on June 4, 1920 at Manila, Philippine Islands.

About 1923, he moved to the Flathead Valley and has lived at Kalispell since. He was a mechanic until his retirement. He was a member of the WWI Barracks. On May 16, 1925, he married Eloise Williams in Kalispell and is now survived by her at the family home. He also had two sons, three daughters, 15 grandchildren and three great-grandchildren. He passed away on April 2, 1972.

DEANE SHIPPLEY, was born March 19, 1896 in Missouri. He enlisted on Feb. 14, 1917 and was discharged on May 13, 1919.

He was in the Army and received the Purple Heart when he saved the life of a comrade. He was also hit with shrapnel in the right leg.

He was a potato-onion broker. He was the oldest of 12 children of which eight are still living. He now lives at the Idaho State Veterans Home. He is an active member of the Sawtooth Barracks 217. He is a very knowledgeable and keen minded fellow. His wife lives in Idaho and visits often. He loved to elk hunt and got his elk 22 out of 23 years.

GEORGE SHORT, was born March 10, 1897 in Lansing, MI. He enlisted in the Army on Sept. 3, 1918 and was discharged on March 10, 1919.

He was in the infantry, where he achieved the rank of corporal. He was stationed at Ft. Lewis, WA and Camp Grant, IL. He arrived at the port of embarkation when the Armistice was signed. He taught soldiers how to use a rifle.

He worked in construction. He likes to hunt. He is now a resident at the Idaho State Veteran's Home.

JOHN SIEGMANN, was born Feb. 27, 1896 in Plum Hill, IL. He enlisted on June 24, 1918 and was discharged on July 18, 1919.

He was a member of the Co. I, 22 Engineers. He achieved the rank of Pvt. He was stationed at Camp Zachary Taylor and also served in France. He met his half brother, Henry Glauert, overseas.

He married Mary Weibler and they had seven children, Frances Novak, Reta Klein, Linda Ringering, John Siegmann, Virgil, Siegmann, Betty Zapp and Robert Siegmann. His parents were Henry and Henrietta Siegmann. He passed away on May 7, 1955.

EARL N. SKAGGS, was born May 4, 1897, a descendant of one of the early settlers from England in the early 1700s. His name can be found registered at Elis Island.

He enlisted in the Marine Corps. at the post office in Holloway, OH. He was sent to a recruiting station in Cincinnati, OH, where he was accepted and sent to Paris Island, SC for boot training.

After boot training was completed, he was sent to Quantico, VA for advance training where he earned the Sharp Shooter Medal. He was placed in the 13th Regt., U.S. Marine Corps. He was under Gen. Smedley Butter. After completing advanced training, he was elevated to Pvt. 1st Class and sent to France on the ship, *Von Steuben*, formerly the German ship, *Crown Prince Wilhelm*, that was captured in New York Harbor with its machinery destroyed. It was sent to Boston for new machinery and returned for service.

He then loaded with the 13th Regt. Marines. They were on their way to France accompanied by 12 other ships and three destroyers looking for submarines. About half way across, the *Henderson*, caught fire. It was loaded with the 15th Regt. Marines. The *Von Steuben*, stopped and took all the troops on board.

They arrived in Brest, France and unloaded. He became a butcher while in France. Instead of being discharged at the war's end, he was sent to St. Nazaire, a seaport, to administer to veterans who had saw active service on their way home. After this they landed at a Naval Base in Hampton Roads, VA. He was discharged there.

RALPH W. SLEATOR, was born Sept. 29, 1900, in Vicksburg, MS, the son of James and

Mary Higgins Sleator. He received his elementary education in Vicksburg and Jackson, MS.

He entered the service at 16 and served in France and Germany. After his return, he served with the Immigration Service in Montana until 1941, when he returned to active duty. He was a lieutenant colonel, retired from 30 years service in the Army and U.S. Immigration Service Border Patrol. He served in Ft. Hood, TX, until 1945. He returned to France and served there until 1949. He then returned to the Border Patrol and retired in 1951.

He was commander of Kalispell's Reserve Unit for several years. During his retirement, he completed 24 years as Flathead County and Kalispell Civil Defense Director. He was a member of Galata Lodge 106 A.F. & A.M., and active in several Masonic organizations, including the York Rite Bodies, Scottish Rite and Algeria Shrine.

He held offices in the VFW and Veterans of WWI in state and local positions. He was a member of A Co., 4th Inf., 3rd Div. from April 15, 1918 to Aug., 23, 1919.

He had two daughters, one son, 14 grandchildren and nine great-grandchildren. He passed away on Feb. 15, 1980.

CARL W. SLOCOMBE, was born Feb. 5, 1896, in Worthing, SD, to John and Nellie Slocombe. He received his education in South Dakota and in 1911, moved with his family to the Flathead Valley.

On Sept. 20, 1916, he entered the U.S. Army at Kalispell and served in the 34th Spruce Squadron. He received his honorable discharge on Dec. 23, 1918 at Vancouver Barracks, WS.

He returned to Kalispell and was employed with a creamery for a time and later by Beatrice Foods. He had worked in Billings and Great Falls, and was superintendent of the Beatrice Foods Plant there from the early 1930s to 1964.

He married Florence Forhan in 1935 in Polson. He was a member of the Bethlehem Lutheran Church. On April 16, 1964, he married Deva Parr, in Coeur d'Alene and is survived by her. He also had one son, one daughter, two step-daughters, eight grandchildren and three step-great-great-grandchildren.

CLARENCE SMALL SR., was inducted into the Army on May 1, 1918, at Terrell, TX. He was sent to Camp Travis at San Antonio, TX, for a short time and then to Camp Meade to be shipped out. The crossing was uneventful and they landed in Liverpool, England, then on to Brest, France and from there to the front lines.

He saw action in the St. Mihiel Offense, Toul Sector and the Meuse Argonne Offense. He remembers there was a tent set up in the woods, hid from the Germans, where they could get coffee. Every morning, some of the men would go for coffee and they had to go through a clearing. One morning the ones who went for coffee were on their way back, when they heard the Germans. They started running and spilled the coffee. They really got eat out when they got back without the coffee.

One time he was in the trench, and two other soldiers and he, decided to get out of the trench because it was so muddy. They got out and got under a tree. A shell came over and went through the tree and liked to have tore the tree up. He jumped in the trench and hit his side on the trench, but was not hurt. They other two men under the tree were killed.

When the war was over they were sent back to New York. While in New York, he asked for a leave to go to a ball game. He got the leave and went to see his first ball game between the Giants and the Yankees. He was sent to Camp Bowie, TX, and was discharged on April 21, 1919, and was given $85.00 discharge pay.

He went back to Kaufman, TX and bought a farm at Ola, a community just out of Kaufman. He married the girl he left behind, Ruby Bailey, on May 17, 1919. They had four children, two boys and two girls. He lived on the farm until 1942, and went to work in defense work during WWII. He then worked at the U.S. Government Hospital in Ft. Worth, TX until he retired at age 70.

After he retired, he and his wife traveled a good bit for the next 20 years. Failing eye sight caused him to have to quit driving at age 90. His wife of 69 years passed away in 1989 at the age of 92. He was 97. Since then, he has made his home with a daughter at Ola, Kaufman Co., TX on the old farm place. His eye sight is failing, he is hard of hearing and has heart problems. He has been confined to a wheel chair since April 1991, when he fell and broke a hip. He still likes to go out to his favorite places to eat and he loves to have company. He has four children, 12 grandchildren, 24 great-grandchildren and three great-great-grandchildren.

GEORGE EARL SMITH, was born Sept. 23, 1899 in Macon, MO. He enlisted in the U.S. Army on Sept. 6, 1917 and was assigned to Co. F, 117th Engineers, 42nd Rainbow Div. This division was composed of 27,000 selected men from National Guard units from 27 states. They were under the command of Gen. Douglas MacArthur.

This division left the United States on Oct. 12, 1917 and landed at St. Nazaire, France on Nov. 1, 1917, and was ordered to the Luneville combat area on Feb. 14, 1918. A quote from historical records says that between Feb. 23, 1918 and Nov. 11, 1919, the Armistice date, the Rainbow 42nd Div. "fought in the face of the enemy for 164 days and nights." From the original 27,000 men, 14,683 were killed or wounded in action. They had over 50% casualties. The division started at Luneville, France then moved to Baccarat, the Champagne Front, the Aisne-Marne, St. Mihiel Salient, Argonne Front and the Ardennes Front.

He was gassed by German artillery shells and had burn scars on his lungs. He and hundreds of others, never left the battle front to turn in for medical care. After serving for five more months in the Army of Occupation, he was honorably discharged on May 14, 1919.

In 1920, he married Iva Gertrude Shallenberger. In 1921, tuberculosis attacked the gas scars in his lungs and he was forced to move to Arizona for his health. He and his wife obtained a homestead near Williams in 1923. This became their lifetime legacy. He later obtained a farm near Phoenix, AZ in 1932.

They had 13 children and 134 grand and great-grandchildren. Both he and his wife were very active in the VFW, Veterans of WWI, Veterans of the Rainbow Division and the auxiliaries thereto, on local, state and national levels.

Throughout his life, he was in VAMC hospitals in Phoenix, AZ, Prescott, AZ and Tucson, AZ for many months. He was presented the French Medal of Appreciation, 72 years after he was discharged. He passed away at VAMC in Phoenix, AZ on Aug. 7, 1990 at age 90. His wife passed away on Dec. 1, 1991 at age 93.

PEARL G. SMITH, was born Sept. 22, 1891 in Macon, MO. He enlisted on March 6, 1918 at Macon, MO.

He was a member of the Hdqrs. Co., 45th Artillery, C.A.C. He achieved the rank of Musician 3rd Class. He served with the A.E.F. in France. He was discharged on Feb. 18, 1919 at Camp Grant, IL.

He married Clella Johnston in Macon, MO on Nov. 1, 1919. He had one daughter, Anna. He returned to farming after his discharge and then became a barber. He worked at Camp Carson Co. until his death in 1958.

ALOYSIUS SMYTHE SR., was born May 19, 1893 and died on Oct. 15, 1991. He joined the service at Carnegie Tech.

He was discharged on June 5, 1919. He was a member of the U.S. Army's Co. C, then Co. F, 25th Engineers. They fought at the Argonne, Belleau Wood, Chatteau Thiery and the Marne. As a private, he had full control of 125 men. He was headed to officers training school when the Armistice was signed and his training was canceled. He did the work of a Leit, all through the war.

He had a wife, Mary Eveln, who lives in Valencia. They had two daughters, Mary Lou and Susan Hart, one son, Al Smythe Jr., and seven grandchildren.

ALFRED SORENSEN, was born Jan. 13, 1892 on the family farm between Alzada, MT and Camp Crook, MT. Belle Fourche, SD is considered his hometown.

He is uncertain as to the date he joined the service. He served with the 6th Training Btn., Signal Corps. for a three year period. He was a sergeant at the time of his discharge. He served in England and France. He recalls being injured in France. There were 12 soldiers hiding in a shell hole when a bomb struck. He was the only survivor and required 12 months hospitalization following the incident.

They only honor he recalls receiving is a commendation from the French Legion for his service in France. His wife, Ellen, died young. The couple had no children, but he has numerous nieces and nephews in South Dakota's Black Hills area. He is no in a VA nursing home.

MATTHEW HANS SORENSON, was born in Whitewood, SD on Oct. 1, 1893. He helped his parents on their farm before entering the Army on June 23, 1918. He enlisted at Belle Fourche, SD.

He was assigned to Co. M, 2nd Bn., Chemical Warfare service and was stationed in Maryland. He achieved the rank of Pvt. 1st Class. He was discharged on Jan. 11, 1919 at Camp Funston, KS. He was awarded the Victory Medal.

After leaving the service, he returned home to farm, which he did until he retired in 1971. From June 1930 to February 1931, he was also employed at the Monarch Mine in South Dakota. The Belle Fourche Sugar Beet Co. was also a source of part-time employment starting in 1930 until 1969.

On June 27, 1923, he married Dora E. Gutsche. He was very active on the Butte County Fair Board for over 25 years. He served on the ASC Board for 10 years. He was a charter member of the American Legion in Nisland, SD and also a member of the WWI Association in Sturgis, SD, starting in 1971. He died on April 8, 1980, in Sturgis, SD.

JOHN B. SOUSA, enlisted at the age of 17 in the Air Corp. Being a stenographer-typist, just out of business college, they pushed him into the Quartermaster Corps. and kept him there too long to help organize the division at Camp Fremont, CA.

He was discharged as Sgt. 1st Class in 1919

and was offered an appointment as Army field clerk, now known as warrant officers, and he stayed in the Army until 1921, serving in many important capacities. While in Hawaii, he was at the headquarters, Ft. Shafter, part-time in Gen. Charles P. Summerall's office and the Hawaii Headquarters of the Army.

He was discharged in 1921, on account of reduction of the Army. The Army dropped to 200,000 men, quite a change from the total during the high point in WWI of 4,700,000 men. He has headed several Veterans Day celebrations which made records in attendance. His last promotion was promoting a veteran's flagpole over the new $3,000,000 Y.M.C.A., honoring their member Tom Popl, Alhambra's only veteran to earn the Congressional Medal of Honor. A year ago, they made arrangements for their Barracks 736 membership and history to be in the Alhambra Museum. He served as Commander of Barracks 736.

FRANK SPARANO, was born Nov. 1, 1890 in Altmonta, Italy, a son of Joseph and Catherine Sparano. He received his education in Italy and in 1910, he moved to the United States and went to work in the steel mills in Gary, IN.

During WWI, he served with the U.S. Army. He served with the medical dept. After the war, he moved to Whitefish, where he worked for the Great Northern Railroad as a section foreman, retiring in 1952. He was a member of the American Legion of Whitefish and a 50-year member of the Moose Lodge No. 642 of Whitefish. He was also a member of St. Charles Catholic Church.

He married Grace Strong, on Sept. 19, 1921 in Kalispell. He had two sons, two daughters, eight grandchildren and nine great-grandchildren. He passed away on Feb. 17, 1979.

BERNARD SPIRO, was born March 18, 1898 in New York, NY. He enlisted in California on June 25, 1918 and was discharged in Illinois on Sept. 30, 1921.

He was a Navy Yeoman 1st Class. He served in the Panama Canal Zone. He is now a retired

salesman who loves to dance and play the violin. He lives at the Idaho State Veterans Home and attends WWI meetings at the Sawtooth Barracks 217.

WILLIAM W. ST. JOHN, enlisted on May 3, 1917 at Jamestown, NY. His grade was a wagoner. He was discharged on Aug. 6, 1925 in Mayville, NY.

He fought in the Aisne-Marne Offensive from Aug. 2-6, 1918, the Vesle Sector from Aug. 7-17, 1918, the St. Mihiel from Sept. 12-14, 1918 and the Meuse Argonne Offensive from Sept. 26- Nov. 11, 1918. He left the United States on May 19, 1918 and arrived back in the United States on July 29, 1919. He served in the Army of Occupation from Nov. 21 to July 10, 1919.

BENJAMIN F. STOVALL, was born on Dec. 17, 1886 in Lavonia, GA. He died on June 12, 1957 in Atlanta.

He was commissioned at Ft. McPherson, GA on Aug. 14, 1917. He was a member of the Co. I, 122nd Inf., attached to the 163rd, 47th and 359th. He achieved the rank of 2nd Lt. He was honorably discharged on July 2, 1919.

He graduated from the University of Georgia in 1912, pre-med. He enlisted and went directly to France for the duration. He fought in the Chateau Thierry. He was then sent into Germany to advance and secure billeting for his men during the occupation.

After he returned he opened a Lettershop, a direct mail service, in Atlanta and he wrote for local papers. In 1931, he married Evelyn Linch, a schoolteacher from Flovilla, GA. They had three daughters. He died from cancer in 1957, at his home.

THEODORE J. STREENZ, was a 21 year old carpenter when he was inducted into the Army as a private in Btry. E, 3rd Field Artillery, A.E.F.

He served in France in the trenches in the battle of Argonne. He was discharged on June 27, 1919 with a notation that his character was excellent.

He married Myra Rozell. After her death, he married Emma Palmer. Following discharge, he worked as a rural mail carrier. He made friends with everyone on his route. Children often waited for him at the mailboxes and were rewarded with a candy treat.

He was responsible for teaching children patriotism by placing a copy of the Bill of Rights surrounded by President's pictures and framed in each school. He had other copies made and framed for other children also. He served as president of Veterans of WWI. At the same time Emma, served as president of the Auxiliary to WWI.

When he died on Sept. 13, 1977, he was given military rites at the cemetery. He has a military marker. On Memorial Day, a flag flies over his grave.

GUSTAVE STREETER, entered the service in 1918, underwent training and shipped out overseas. After dodging submarines, he arrived at Brest, France and was in the battle zone by September 12.

They kept advancing for the next month and

a half through territory the Germans had held for the last four years. They continually moved forward through heavy shelling. He remembers that on the morning of Nov. 11, 1918, the barrel of his rifle was hot enough to fry an egg.

After November 11, he was billeted in several German cities in the Army of Occupation for six months until honorably discharged at Rockford, IL. His Division received both football and baseball championships.

FREDERICK EARL STREETS, enlisted
on Dec. 12, 1917 at Parkersburg, WV. He achieved the rank of Fireman 5th Class and Tireman 2nd Class.

He was born in Phillipi, WV on Dec. 9, 1896. He sailed on the *USS Prinz Friedrich Wilhelm*. He was discharged on Nov. 25, 1919 at New York, NY. He was also a veteran of WWII in which he was wounded. He received the Purple Heart because his ship was sank in Lahar when it was struck by a mine. He passed away on May 11, 1986 and is buried at Wooddale Cemetery in Grafton, WV.

HOWARD EARL STREMBEL, was born
Oct. 8, 1899 in Kansas. He joined the service Oct. 6, 1917 and was discharged with the rank of sergeant in February 1919. He served with the 10th Inf. Co.

His legs were inured during the war and he has been unable to work. He has a son, daughter, and three great-grandsons.

WILLIAM H. STURM, was born Feb. 2, 1897
and died on Dec. 18, 1978. He enlisted in the Navy after two years of college in Michigan.

He was stationed in the Great Lakes and Bremerton, WA, where he studied French with a flashlight under the blankets. He wanted to be an officer, if he had to be in WWI. His sister died and left four children, so he was transferred to Pigeon, MI. The war then ended.

While he was still in uniform, he was asked to teach school in a country school, which he did for a couple of years. Then he entered the University of Michigan and worked as a waiter in a fraternity

house and as a hospital attendant in the men's ward. He was a top student and graduated from dentistry in 1923.

He practiced in Detroit and retired in July 1955, because the state of Michigan had bought his building. He was then divorced with two daughters in Florida. He studied philosophy in San Francisco, where the dental convention was held and he always drew portraits and painted portraits. He earned his minimum social security at age 78 as a portrait painter.

He married Edna Young Sturm, his third wife, on Dec. 31, 1955 in San Francisco. They traveled the world on cruise ships and 747's. He became ill in 1977 and had surgery three times. He lost his life to cancer on Dec. 18, 1978.

ROY SWEENEY, served with the 19th Military
Police, U.S. Camp Dodge. He married Meale Johnston July 6, 1921. He died April 16, 1974.

JOSEPH SZCZUREK, was born on Nov. 1,
1889 in Austria. After coming to the United States, he worked as a machinist and enlisted on May 25, 1917.

He was a member of the 6th Reserve Regt. This was Michigan's only volunteer regiment and was organized to be a rail construction unit. In the summer of 1917, the unit was renamed the 16th Engineer Regiment (Railway), while training at the Michigan State Fairgrounds in Detroit, MI.

He arrived in France in late August 1917, and proceeded to build the infrastructure for the A.E.F., as a machinist and barber. He served with the British during the Lys Defensive operation in April 1918 and with the A.E.F. during the Meuse Argonne Offensive from October-November 1918.

He was discharged on May 8, 1919 from Co. F as a Pvt. 1st Class. He married Mary Rozozinske and worked as a machinist in Detroit, MI. He died in 1969.

VALENTINE SZMANIA, was born Feb. 1,
1897 in Poland. He enlisted on May 27, 1916 and was discharged on May 24, 1919.

He was a member of the Army's 32nd Div.,

107th Ammunition Train. He fought in the Alsace, the Aisne-Marne, Oise-Aisne, the Meuse Argonne and served with the Army of Occupation. He was gassed in Broucourt Woods, France on Sept. 26, 1918.

He married in 1920 and had six children. He also had 18 grandchildren and 15 great-grandchildren. He is retired from textile engineering and pattern designing.

HERVEY F. TERRILL, was born Nov. 6, 1898 and died on March 13, 1980. He enlisted in the Navy on April 26, 1917 and was discharged on Aug. 25, 1918.

He was stationed in South Dakota and his serial number was 1907824. After his Navy service, he lived in Michigan. He belonged to WWI Barracks 17.

BENJAMIN THOMAS, was born Dec. 22, 1895 at Avoca in Jefferson Co., KY. He was called into service in September 1917.

He trained at Camp Taylor, KY and Ft. Benning, GA, before being sent overseas in September 1918. He was struck with shrapnel and severely wounded the first day he was in active combat. The next few months were spent in the hospital, then he was sent back to Camp Taylor and was discharged on April 2, 1919.

He married Annie Elizabeth Gaunt on Aug. 24, 1931. His family consisted of one son, one foster son, eight grandchildren and a number of great-grandchildren.

He was awarded the Purple Heart on Nov. 25, 1987. He died Feb. 17, 1990 and was buried in Middletown Cemetery, Middletown, KY.

THEODORE THOMAS, "BILL", was born April 3, 1899 in Silverlake, KS. He enlisted on Aug. 5, 1917 and was discharged on May 10, 1919.

He was stationed in France and spent 102 days in combat. He was a member of the Btry. A, 130th Regt., which started in Kansas as a National Guard unit on Jan. 7, 1917. It was a horse detachment and they had 60 horses. He served as a chief mechanic. If something was broke he fixed it. He

got a load of gas one time and it felt more like a scald.

He received three Gold Stars for rescuing wounded men. He graduated from a French Artillery School. Today he lives at the Idaho State Veterans Home.

WILBURN RONALD THOMAS, was born March 19, 1900 in Waco, McLennan Co., TX. He enlisted on May 11, 1916 and was discharged on Jan. 6, 1919.

He was a member of Co. G, 2nd Inf. in Texas, Co. K, 141st Inf. and the Panther Div. and 36th Div. He achieved the rank of Sgt. He served in Mexico under Gen. Pershing. He was to go overseas but collapsed getting on the train to leave. He had typhoid fever and was hospitalized and nearly died. He recuperated in Orange, NJ.

He was the son of William Radford and Minnie May Beauchamp Thomas. He was the youngest child of seven. He married Rachel Elizabeth Meier in 1921 and they were the parents of Ruth, Martha, W. Radford, Henry and Cynthia Thomas. He was a fireman in Waco, TX and fire chief when he retired in 1943. He owned a wholesale drug sundry business and retired in 1963.

ROBERT L. TOMBAUGH, enlisted on July 22, 1918, at Sturgis, SD. He was a private in the Veterinary Corps.

In September 1918, he developed influenza and spent the next three months in the Veterans Hospital at Camp Lee, VA. As a result of this illness, he was discharged in January 1919.

In November 1920, he married Anna Wurnig at Sturgis, SD and spent his entire life farming in Meade County of South Dakota. He died in March of 1971 at the age of 76.

GEORGE A. TRACY, enlisted on May 30, 1918. He joined with two Oregon troop trains of first enlisted period at Oregon City, OR railroad station. He then went to Percedio in San Francisco, CA, where three days were spent in the city.

The government issued uniforms to all. All enlistees were assigned to Co. L, 63rd Inf. Again by train he was sent to Salt Lake City, UT, where they were taken to the salt lake and removed their clothing and took their baths regardless of the people viewing them from the bank..

Again traveling by train, they arrived in Camp Meade, MA. Here they became quarantined due to some of the soldiers having a contagious ailment. He was able to drill every day with those able to do so, until the war ended. After the war ended, Co. L, 63rd Inf. served as body guards to aid the police in New York City streets. They cared for the returning veterans from overseas during the huge celebrations. He was discharged in Camp Lewis, WN on May 15, 1919.

He was born Nov. 4, 1894 in Logan, OR to Charles and Olive Tracy. He married Daisy A. Bouck on June 30, 1926. He and his spouse are both living in a retirement home. He walks several times a day and Daisy still drives their car. He is the quartermaster of John McLaughlin Barracks in Oregon City, OR. He is the only living member of the organization.

JOSEPH R. TUCKER, was born near Russellville, AK on Oct. 9, 1891. As a child, the family moved to Breckenridge, TX and then moved to Rogers Co., near Alluwe, OK in 1909.

He went into the service in 1917 and was discharged late in the year of 1918. He was sent to Camp Travis, TX and three weeks later he was sent to a camp near Indianapolis, IN. He was

transferred into an engineering unit and the men were from all the states. His unit was the 21st Engineers, Co. K.

He was in three battles, but since the discharge is not available the only one they can remember was the Meuse Argonne. His group was able to take Von Hindenburg's camp, where they had plenty of kraut and a piano. At once place, he was a corporal, but when he was placed in the engineering unit he went back to a private. He was awarded three ribbons.

His wife Lois Pittsenbargar, lives in Dallas, TX with their daughter, Emmalo Tucker Coody. A son, W. Jor R. Tucker lives in Crosby Tucker. He is now deceased and is buried in the City Cemetery in Nowata, OK.

JOHN HENRY TURLEY, was born in 1893, in Masonville, IA. He enlisted on May 26, 1918 and was discharged on Nov. 21, 1918.

He was a member of the 2nd Inf., where he achieved the rank of Pvt. He was stationed at Camp Dodge, IA. He was awarded one Bronze Victory Button.

He was a blacksmith and never married.

ALOYS URBANCZYK, WWI Vet, was drafted in 1917. He died as a result of the war.

CARL E. VAIL SR., was born Aug. 12, 1895. He served with Co. H, 305th Inf., 77th Div. He went to Camp Upton in 1917 for training. They shipped out for France with a convoy. As they were coming into Liverpool, German V-boats attacked. They began to drop depth charges as he was trying to get to the main deck.

He survived several German artillery barrages and mustard gas attacks.

He was discharged from Camp Upton. After the war, he opened an auto business.

The 77th Div. was the first national draft army to see action and it was reported that they gained more enemy territory than any other division in the AEF.

ROBERT VANCE, was born Jan. 29, 1894 in

Akron, CO. He enlisted in the service on Aug. 14, 1918 and was discharged on Dec. 11, 1918.

He served in the Army and stayed stateside. He was stationed at Ft. Collins, CO. He achieved the rank of Pvt. He was a hatchery man with five brothers and two sisters, all of whom are deceased. He lives at the Idaho State Veterans Home and attends meetings of the WWI Sawtooth Barracks 217.

GEORGE D. VANDERHOFF, enlisted in the 116th Engineers, Co. M on April 9, 1918. He was one of eight volunteers from Homedale, ID.

Bootcamp was in Ft. Douglas, UT and then transferred to Washington, DC. He sailed from Washington on May 28, 1918 aboard the *Baltic* and landed in Liverpool, England on June 7, 1918. Later, the *Baltic*, was lost in the Bay of Biscay, after being hit by German torpedoes.

He was stationed in Slowbucks, England with the 166th Engineers. He was one of the honor guard called to Manchester, England for the signing of the Ultimatum on Nov. 10, 1918. President Woodrow Wilson, Gen. of the A.E.F., John J. Pershing, Winston Churchill, Gen. Fouch and Mussolini were present. The end of WWI was announced the next day.

Later they were sent to Bath, England and on to Brest, France for one day. Following that, they were sent back to New York. He has resided on the same farm he bought in 1926 for 65 years.

MARINUS VAN ESTENBRIDGE, better known in his younger days as "red", was born Feb. 28, 1901 in Paterson, NJ. He joined the National Guard for enlistment in federal service.

He joined the guard unit the 5th Inf., Co. E out of Paterson, NJ on April 25, 1917. He was discharged on Oct. 3, 1919. His unit was the 29th Inf. Div., 57th Inf. Brig., 114th Inf. Regt., 114th Machine Gun Co. His unit sailed from the United States on May 24, 1918 on the *USS Wilhelmina*, arriving in Brest, France on June 27, 1918.

He achieved the rank of Pvt. He received a Purple Heart for wounds received on Oct. 27, 1918, when gassed during the Meuse Argonne Offensive. He also received the WWI Victory Medal with two clasps.

He is now 91 years old and lives in a beautiful nursing home in New Jersey.

JOHN VAN ZINDEREN, was born June 27, 1893 in the Netherlands. He enlisted in June 1918 and was discharged in July 1919.

He was a member of the 3rd Pioneer Inf. He fought in the St. Mihiel and the Argonne Forest. He saw many casualties but was able to survive and keep out of the hospital..

All of his immediate family has passed on. He is the only one left and walks with a cane after a fall in 1983. He has been retired since 1955.

MARSHALL H. VERRAN, who passed away last year was a WWI Veteran and most recently the Quartermaster for the Glendale Barracks 646. He is survived by two granddaughter's, Heather Lynn Verran and Sheri Verran Determan.

He was born in Tombstone, AZ, on Dec. 25, 1894. He left school after the eighth grade to go to work full-time and help support his family. On Feb. 6, 1913, he became a member of the Amalgamated Meat Cutters and Butcher Workmen of NA. union, and left on May 30, 1917. He joined the U.S. Army, and after his service, he became a title contractor in the Los Angeles area.

He enlisted on Oct. 2, 1917 at Douglas, AZ. He left Douglas on October 3, and arrived at Camp Funston, KS on October 5, with the 38th Co., 164th Depot Brigade. He left Camp Funston on October 26 and arrived at Camp Kerney, CA on Nov. 1, 1917.

He left Camp Mill, NY on Aug. 10, 1918 and went to Jersey City, NY, which he left on August 11. He arrived in La Havre, France and from there traveled to Garigny, France on August 27. He left Garigny on Oct. 4, 1918 and arrived in Orgarin on October 9. He also traveled through Nerondes, Cheles, Lageny, Paris and attended school at Moisiel.

He saw the President in Paris on Dec. 14, 1918 and remembers an inspection by Gen. Pershing in which he had to wait for two hours in the mud. He was discharged on March 14, 1919.

EDWARD J. WAGNER, was born Dec. 17, 1894 in Ft. Madison, IA. He enlisted on April 17, 1917 and was discharged in June 1918.

He was a member of Co. K, 132nd Inf., 66th Brigade, 33rd Div. He fought in the Verdun, Albert, Somme, Forges, Homel Consonvoye. He received the Purples Heart and Silver Star awards.

He has been married to Mildren Schilling for 53 years. He is now retired and paints oil paintings.

LUTHER E. WALDRIP, was born March 20, 1892, at Crawfordsville, IN. He enlisted in the First Army, 23rd Regt., Engineers on Dec. 7, 1917 in Seattle, WA. He was discharged on July 9, 1919, at Ft. D.A. Russell, WY.

He was first sent to Camp Lawton, WA and then on Dec. 23, 1917 he traveled by Milwaukee Railroad to Camp Meade, MA, where he joined the First Wagon Co. 5. He was in the hospital and was unable to go to France with his Regt., but later landed in Bordeaux, France on July 14, 1918 to rejoin them.

The 1st Wagon Co. 5 was called the "Road Builders of the A.E.F.", as they were building new bridges and highways or repairing them. The engineer battalions traveled behind the infantry and the troops and supplies were behind the engineers. He was gassed somewhere along the line of the Argonne and St. Mihiel Forces, that resulted in stomach ulcers that bothered him all of his life.

He also had a knee injury, but instead of returning home then, he stayed there to help with kitchen guard and duties. Once, he said he was commandeered to serve as Gen. Pershing's driver for a night trip without any lights. He came home on May 31, 1919 aboard the ship, *Cape Phinister.*

He felt too weak to climb the ladder to board ship, so buddies helped him and he hid until he was found the next morning. He was put in the hospital and told he had spinal meningitis. There were 22 other patients there also, but only three arrived back to Hoboken, NJ on June 15, 1919. He was hospitalized at the Embarkment Hospital in Hoboken, NJ. He later was transported to Laurel Hospital at Camp Funston near Kansas City, KS.

He received a Verdun Medal from Gen. Foch of France, and other medals but not the Purple Heart. On July 1, 1919, he went to Ft. D.A. Russell in Wyoming, where he was given his discharge papers and was sent home to Havre, MT with $60.00 on July 9, 1919.

EMMONS H. WARD, was born Dec. 1, 1889 at Beverly, Randolph Co., WV, son of John W. and Margaret Rosencrance Ward. He served in the U.S. Army from March 8, 1918 to July 22, 1919, when discharged at Camp Sherman, OH.

He served as 1st Class Pvt. at Post Hospital, Fort Oglethrope, GA. He left Elkins with the first draft from Randolph Co., WV.

After coming home from the Army, he took an agriculture course at the West Virginia University.

He then went into dairy and poultry farming. In 1936, he married Mittie Rice. They continued farming until 1973. There were no children.

He was authorized to wear a Good Conduct Ribbon and Victory Medal. He belonged to the Veterans of WWI, Barracks 1060 of West Virginia and the American Legion Post 29 of Elkins, WV. He was also a member of the Presbyterian Church. He passed away on April 27, 1982 at age 92.

MILES WASSON, a native Iowan and an adopted Texan, spent more than 70 years of his 97 1/2 years assisting veterans and their families as both a vocation and avocation.

Wasson was born Sept. 10, 1893, on the family homestead near Lineville, Iowa, the only son and oldest of six children of Hardy and Elizabeth Wasson. He died Jan. 31, 1991, in his home in San Antonio, TX. In between was a rich life filled with family, friends, church, patriotism, veterans organizations and veterans work.

Leaving Lineville in 1915 to work for city director publishers, he was traveling the country when World War I broke out. He enlisted in the Army on May 8, 1918, in Princeton, MO, and entered training at Camp MacArthur, Waco, TX. Three days later he was promoted to Private First Class and assigned to Signal Platoon, Headquarters Co., 34th Infantry, 7th Division. (He turned down a chance to go to Officers Training School to have time to go home and say "goodbye" to his parents.)

In August the division was sent to France where he served on the St. Mihiel Front lines for 33 days. He remained in Army Communications in France until he returned stateside and was honorably discharged at Camp Zachary Taylor, Louisville, KY, June 28, 1919.

He was married to Eula D. Cunningham on July 12, 1919, in Des Moines, Iowa, and the next year they moved to Houston, TX, where his veterans work — begun in Corydon, IA — gained rapid momentum.

In Houston, he served as commander of American Legion Post 77; Veterans of Foreign Wars Post 5619 and was Chef de Gare of the Forty and Eight. He helped organize and was commander of Houston's Space City Barracks 1877, Veterans of World War I, later serving as District and Department of Texas commander, WWI. He was appointed to several national VWWI committees and was Assistant National Chief of Staff. He also was commander of American Legion Post 89 in Texas City.

In 1937, Wasson was recruited to work for the Veterans State Service Officer (now the Texas Veterans Commission) and in 1944 was recruited by the Veterans Administration. He was chief of the Contact Division of the Houston Region VA Office for 17 years until retirement in 1963. He continued voluntary work with veterans.

The Wassons moved to San Antonio in 1975 to be near their only child, Mildred Wasson Whiteaker, and her family. Mrs. Wasson died in 1979.

He became active in Davy Crockett Barracks 1877, VWWI, serving as commander and continuing to recruit members almost until the day he died. His world was so synonomous with veterans that he was the subject of numerous newspaper articles and television interviews. In 1989, he was honored on Veterans Day at a banquet for more than 500 military guests given by the San Antonio Chamber of Commerce.

Besides his daughters, he is survived by two sisters, one grandson, one granddaughter and seven great-grandchildren. The last two bear his name, Miles Wasson Whiteaker and Catherine Miles Jenkins.

EDWIN WATERSTREET, was a member of the 339th Inf. and served in the area out of Archan-

gel, Russia, near the Arctic Circle. He fought in trying weather conditions, sometimes 40 inches or snow or more. Their war did not end on November 11.

ERNEST WEBER, was born Dec. 2, 1896 in Colonia, MI. He joined the service in 1918 and was discharged as Seaman 2nd in 1919. He served with the Navy at Great Lakes and Hampton Roads. He remembers Armistice Day 1918.

He has one daughter. His wife has passed away. He is 95 years old retired.

ROBERT TALLY WEED, was born Nov. 1, 1896 in Columbia, SC. He enlisted on Aug. 28, 1918 and was discharged on April 2, 1919.

He served with the Army's Co. H, 107th Inf., where he achieved the rank of Pvt. 1st Class. He

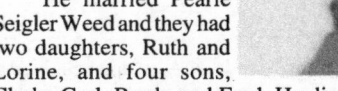

was stationed at Camp Jackson, SC and fought in the Meuse Argonne in France on Nov. 9, 1918. He was on the Hindenburg Line at the end of the war.

He married Pearle Seigler Weed and they had two daughters, Ruth and Lorine, and four sons, Clyde, Carl, Brady and Fred. He died in 1969.

ARTHUR RAY WHEELER, was born on Dec. 27, 1895 in Western Salina Co., NE. He enlisted on April 26, 1917 and was discharged on Dec. 26, 1918.

He served with the U.S. Army Air Corp., where he achieved the rank of Pvt.. He served in Canada, Kansas, Oklahoma and England. His most memorable experience was the signing of the Armistice.

He has a wife, Pearl. He worked in road construction and sold tires. He was a jack of all trades. Today he lives in Boise, ID and has been active in the WWI Barracks 217 for many years.

HY WHITE, was born on Oct. 31, 1895 in St. Joseph, MO. He enlisted on March 28, 1918, at Camp Funston, KS. He was discharged on Oct. 23, 1918.

He was a member of the 5th Co., 164th Depot Brigade, where he achieved the rank of Corporal. He was stationed at Camp Funston, KS, where he was assigned to entertain.

He received no awards but did receive disability discharge. He married on the same day he joined the Army and they were married for 65 years. He was a reporter for the newspaper, *The Palm Beach Daily News*, and a correspondent for the *Jewish Post and Opinion*.

JULIAN WILLIAM WHITE, was born Feb. 5, 1898 in Newberry, SC. He enlisted in April 1917 and was discharged in June 1919.

He was a member of the 54th U.S. Inf., Supply Co., where he achieved the rank of Sgt.. He was stationed in France and fought in the Voyges Mountains and the Meuse Argonne. He got influenza in a French hospital. He remembers getting lost in a French truck train move, however he found his regiment that night.

He received campaign medals for two battles. He has a wife, three sons, 15 grandchildren and 17 great-grandchildren. He is now retired from being an insurance executive.

LLOYD EDWARD WHITMAN, was born June 21, 1892 in White Cloud, MI. He enlisted on Dec. 14, 1917 and was discharged on April 22, 1919.

He was a member of Co. C, 142nd Inf., where he achieved the rank of Sgt. He fought in the Champagne on Oct. 5, 1918, where he received a gunshot wound in the upper jaw. He worked in the Red Cross Hospital No. 1 in Paris, in the amputation division. He received an award for marksmanship.

He married Edith Newell Whitman on June 21, 1963. He died on Oct. 1, 1981. He owned and operated a dental laboratory for 56 years.

HENRY KARL WILDBERGER, was born Aug. 30, 1895 in Canistota, SD. When he enlisted, he was 23 years old and was by occupation a farmer. He fought in France.

He had a wife, Laura, and four daughters. He passed away on July 21, 1988.

CHARLES M. WILLIAMS, was born Dec. 17, 1901 in Chicago, IL. He enlisted at the age of 18 in Chicago, IL on July 24, 1917. He entered into active service on Aug. 3, 1917.

He left the United States on May 27, 1918 and returned on May 24, 1919. He was a member of the Btry. E, 122nd F.A., 33rd Div., in which he achieved the rank of Cpl. He received the Silver Star, WWI Victory Medal with three battle clasps for St. Mihiel, Meuse Argonne and the Defensive Sector.

Today he is a widower. He is taking it easy.

FRANK EDGAR WILLIS, was born in Viola, WI on Sept. 23, 1889 to American born parents, William and Minnie Willis. He grew up in Soldiers Grove, WI. He was the eldest of 10 children. Upon high school graduation, he attended business school at LaCrosse, WI. His family moved to a farm homestead called The Badger Home Farm at Rhame, ND, in 1907.

He was inducted into the Army on June 23, 1918 at Bowman, Bowman Co., ND. After induction, he was sent to Camp Dodge, IA and served in Co. K, 349th Inf., 163rd Depot Brigade, until his discharge as a Pvt. on June 11, 1919. He served overseas from Aug. 9, 1918 to May 30, 1919. His engagement overseas was Defensive Sector Center in Alsace, France.

After his discharge, he returned to North Dakota, where he spent the remainder of his life

raising his family and working on his own farm. He married Ethel Chadwick, formerly from Little Falls, MN on Dec. 29, 1919. Ethel was teaching school in the rural Rhame community when they met. They had three daughters, Elaine, Gene and Mae Ione. The Willis's home was affectionately known as "The house by the side of the road", where everyone was welcome. He was an active life member of the American Legion. He passed away at the age of 90 in November 1979.

EDMUND E. WILLMAN, was born on Oct. 28, 1895 in Harshaville, OH. He enlisted on June 4, 1917 and was discharged on April 19, 1919.

He was with the Machine Gun Co., where he achieved the rank of Pvt. 1st Class. He fought in the Alsace Loraine, Meuse Argonne, St. Mihiel and the Ypres-Lys.

He never married and had no children. He is now living in a nursing home after retiring from carpentry.

LUTHER HARMON WILMOTH, was born May 30, 1900 in Omaha, NE. He registered for the draft on June 1, 1918. He enlisted in the U.S. Army's Student Army Training Corps. at Wesleyan University in Lincoln, NE, on Oct. 3, 1918..

He was made Corporal on Oct. 17, 1918. He received his honorable discharge on Dec. 3, 1918.

CHARLES WOOLEY, was born March 22, 1896 in Dixon, MO. He was discharged in 1919.

He was a member of the Det. Ser. B.E.F., 110th Engineers, where he achieved the rank of Sgt. 1st Class. He fought in the St. Mihiel, Meuse Argonne and the Verdun. He remembers the trip to Paris from Lenorrville on the railroad. He received a medal of honor from the United States and a medal of honor from the St. Mihiel in France.

He had a wife, three children, 20 grandchildren and 36 great-grandchildren.

ROSCOE WILSON, was born Sept. 24, 1892, in Emporia, KS, a son of Robert and Frances Wilson. He had received his education in Kansas, and in

1914, he came to the Flathead Valley and had lived at Echo Lake.

On Dec. 14, 1917, he entered the U.S. Army at Ft. George Wright, WA and had served in France. He received his honorable discharge on June 10, 1919, at Ft. D.A. Russell, WY. He then returned to Flathead and lived in Kalispell much of the time.

He had been employed with the Kalispell Lumber Co. until his retirement. He was a member of the Odd Fellows Lodge, American Legion and the Saw Mill Workers Union Local No. 2405.

On March 26, 1926, he married Gertrude Rawling n Poison. He passed away on April 3, 1988.

DAVID WISHART,

DAVID WISHART, was born July 8, 1895 in Pawnee City, NE, to David and Jennie Blaine Wishart. He later moved to Kansas with his family. In 1910, the family moved to Montana, where they lived south of Big Arm.

He served in the U.S. Army at Vancouver, WA in 1918. On June 6, 1929, he married Rose Burkhardt in Kalispell. They then bought a ranch in the LaSalle area. He continued ranching until 1959, when he sold the ranch and moved to Evergreen. He also did Christmas tree work for 35 years before his retirement.

He was a member of the LaSalle Grange and served as Master in 1951. He belonged to the WWI Barracks, serving as commander and also as quartermaster for 20 years. He also belonged to the American Legion Post No. 7, serving as historian.

He had a wife, two daughters, Louse Mitchell and Rose Marie Spring, six grandchildren and a great-grandchild. He passed away on June 3, 1983.

WILLIAM WORLEY, was born Nov. 22, 1898 in Ashville, NC. He enlisted in October 1917 and was discharged in May 1920.

He was a member of the Army's Medical Dept., where he achieved the rank of Pvt. 1st Class. He was stationed in Vancouver, WA. His most memorable experience was hauling the bodies of the soldiers who had died in the flu epidemic. He did not enjoy this, but someone had to do it.

He has been married and his wife taught him to cook, which he did most of his life. He now lives at the Idaho State Veterans home. He attends a few meetings with the Sawtooth Barracks 217.

JAMES WRIGHT, was born Nov. 28, 1891 in Glouchester, VA. He enlisted in 1917. He worked in a Yorktown Factory making shells.

He has a wife, Bertha, and no children. He lives in the VA Medical Center in Hampton, VA. He is now over 101 years old.

GEORGE PHILLP YOUNG, was born at Canby, OR on Feb. 2, 1896. He enlisted in the Regular Army at Freewater, OR.

He was then sent to Ft. Wright in Spokane, WA. He was sworn in on June 10, 1917 and assigned to the regular Army, 14th Inf., Co. H, at Vancouver Barracks. He was discharged on Dec. 14, 1918 from the 87th Inf. He received travel pay to Freewater, OR from Camp Dodge, IA.

CARL J. ZINN, was born July 19, 1894 in Taylor Co., WV. He was the son of John W. Zinn and Mary Corrothers Zinn. He attended school near the Monongalia Taylor County line, between Morgantown and Grafton. He became very knowledgeable in history of the Civil War.

He entered the Army in 1918 and was sent to Camp Meade, MD, where he served with the 71st Inf. After the war ended, he returned to his home in Taylor Co. A short time later, he was married to Josie Layman, whose home was in Fairmont. They became parents to two children, Marvin and June.

He spent the rest of his life farming near his original home. He died on Aug. 10, 1974, and is buried in the Hallick Cemetery in Monongalia County.

BENJAMIN DEXTER

Publisher's note: All members of the World War One Veterans Association were invited to write and submit biographies for inclusion in this publication. The preceding are from those who chose to participate. The biographies were printed as received, with only minor editing. The publisher regrets it cannot accept responsibility for omissions or inaccuracies.

Printed in the USA
CPSIA information can be obtained
at www.ICGtesting.com
JSHW022337140824
68134JS00019B/1540